THE JOB EVALUATION HANDBOOK

Michael Armstrong and Angela Baron

RBR:
COURSE: HORA
LECTURER: J. HAWER

INSTITUTE OF PERSONNEL AND DEVELOPMENT

Design by Paperweight
Typeset by The Comp-Room Aylesbury
Printed in Great Britain by
The Cromwell Press, Wiltshire

British Library Cataloguing-in-Publication Data
A catalogue record for this book is available from the
British Library

ISBN 0-85292-581-6

i))

**INSTITUTE OF PERSONNEL
AND DEVELOPMENT**

IPD House, Camp Road, London SW19 4UX
Tel: 0181 971 9000   Fax: 0181 263 3333
Registered office as above. Registered Charity No. 1038333
A company limited by guarantee. Registered in England No. 2931892

CONTENTS

ACKNOWLEDGEMENTS

The authors and the Institute of Personnel and Development are deeply grateful to the many people who have contributed to the research project upon which this book has been based. In particular, thanks are due to all those who spared the time to see the authors and who provided the information on best practice without which this book could not have been written. These people include:

Peter Akister
Jackie Anderson
Andrew Barker
Carol Barton
Harvey Bentall
Steve Bloomfield
Duncan Brown
Andy Chalmers
David Clifford
Ann Cummins
Fiona Goddard
George Harris
Paul Harrison
Mike Hayes
Sara Henry
Paul Hornsby
Ken Hutchinson
Ian Jenkins
Fiona Johnson
Eric Mead
Ralph McKee
Jo Morris
Helen Murlis

Daniel O'Donoghue
Mike Oram
Derek Pritchard
Dougie Pullen
Simon Ralphs
Jorg Rehmert
Heidi Roberts
Terry Rowland
Anne-Marie Southall
Peter Stemp
Roger Stones
Jacquie Thompson
John Thompson
David Uppington
Ian Watson
Louise Williams
Willie Wood
Clive Wright
Mandy Wright

The authors are especially grateful to Peter Wickens for his support, to Alistair Evans and Toni McAlinden for commenting on the typescript and to Sue Hastings for her help, advice and the useful comments on the typescript.

PREFACE

There is a catch-phrase in the radio programme *'I'm Sorry, I Haven't a Clue'* when chairman Humphrey Lyttleton says, 'And what do points mean? Points mean prizes!' For many years job evaluation has been something like that: jobs have been analysed in immense detail, descriptions written, factors determined, points awarded, weightings given and adjusted – and then the process of grievances began, until in the end we arrived at something that the vast majority of people felt was fair.

I often asked myself how much value this process added to the organisation's product or service, and the answer was often, 'Not very much.' In many of our organisations we had reached the point where the tail was wagging the dog ie the tail of job evaluation was wagging the dog of the need to respond rapidly to change, whether it be in methods of working, individual performance, or in the market. For many years I have been in the vanguard of those who argue that rigid job evaluation has little place in organisations that need to respond to new demands, and that it inhibits rather than facilitates change.

We cannot, however, abandon job evaluation overnight. What we can do is learn what is available to us and make informed judgements on its relative strengths and weaknesses. Having done that we can then decide whether we want to continue down this road or try another.

Why then a new book on job evaluation? This text fills the great need for a contemporary work rooted in modern methods of people management. We have come to realise that it is *people*, not *jobs*, who create value; that multiskilled, multifunctional work teams are a key to success; that during the course of a year an individual can play many roles; and that we must seek the continuous development and growth of all people as we genuinely devolve responsibility in our flatter, leaner organisations.

Michael Armstrong and Angela Baron have provided the answers to most of these issues. They have managed to combine a comprehensive description of what is available with a balanced critique of the claimed merits of the various approaches. But, most importantly, they fully discuss all the controversial issues surrounding the subject, distilling the key points clearly and succinctly and presenting their conclusions in a manner that flows logically from their presentation.

Job evaluation, when used, must support the values of the organisation; it must be a dynamic and evolutionary process; and above all it must facilitate change, not inhibit it. In pulling out these points the authors have provided a great service to the thinking practitioner.

Peter D Wickens OBE
Chairman, Organisation Development International and
President, Centre for Achievement in Manufacturing
and Management, University of Sunderland

INTRODUCTION

What this book is about

This book is about how organisations determine pay levels and structures. In a sense, every person who makes decisions on how much people should be paid for the work they do, the degree of skill and competence required to do that work, and the contribution they make in their roles to achieving organisational purposes is a job evaluation practitioner. Conventionally, however, the term 'job evaluation' refers to the formal procedures used to determine the relative value or worth of a job or role within an organisation.

The incidence of job evaluation

All organisations practise some form of evaluation, although it is often highly informal. The research conducted by the Institute of Personnel and Development in 1994–1995 that this book draws upon established that 55 per cent of the organisations which took part in the survey used formal evaluation procedures. Figures from other, earlier surveys reveal differences in the proportions of organisations that use job evaluation schemes. For example:

☐ ACAS (1988) – 40 per cent of manufacturing establishments and 35 per cent of service sector establishments have some form of evaluation of at least some of their employees.

☐ Wyatt and IPM (1989) – 61 per cent of a sample of 376 had a formal evaluation scheme in operation, and 11 per cent were about to introduce a scheme.

☐ Workplace Industrial Relations Survey (Millward *et al.* 1992) – about 26 per cent of workplaces had job evaluation schemes.

☐ IRS (1993) – 75 per cent of the 164 organisations participating in their survey practised job evaluation.

The variations in these figures could be attributed to differences in the samples.

Both the ACAS and the Wyatt/IPM surveys showed that the use of job evaluation was increasing, especially in the public sector. The Wyatt/IPM survey and the IPD survey revealed that job evaluation was more common in larger organisations. Formal job evaluation methods are less likely to be used in manufacturing organisations, especially where wage rates are negotiated.

The job evaluation scene

Job evaluation is often described as being concerned solely with the techniques used to establish the comparative worth of jobs within an organisation, and much of this book certainly concentrates on this aspect of the subject. But job evaluation is ultimately about making decisions on what people should be paid for the work they do (not how well they do it). It can therefore be said also to involve the systematic collection of data on market rates to provide a basis for pricing jobs, attaching pay brackets or scales to job grades and fixing individual rates of pay. Indeed, some businesses rely mainly on such external comparisons as a guide to rates of pay *and* internal relativities, and this process of 'market pricing' can be regarded as a type of job evaluation.

As noted above, many organisations do not have formal systems of job evaluation. They depend solely on managerial judgement, which is likely to be strongly influenced by market rates – what the business has to pay to attract and retain the type of people it wants. Other jobs are fitted around these datum points. If any thought is given at all to comparative worth within the organisation, it is simply accessed by the existing hierarchy who reckon to have a 'feel' for how jobs and people should be fitted into it. Such an approach is frequently adopted by small, growing, or autocratically managed businesses. It may suit their purposes, structures and cultures, and it can appear to function well because it is flexible when reacting to new demands or pressures. It may respond too quickly in one direction but it can quickly re-adjust itself. But it can lead to incoherent, illogical and inequitable pay structures which are difficult to manage and control and, more importantly, which demotivate employees and reduce organisational effectiveness.

The purpose of job evaluation

Job evaluation can help to overcome difficulties in managing internal relativities and maintaining an equitable and competitive pay structure. It can address grading issues logically and systematically, and it can reduce the subjectivity of value judgements that many people make about job worth. But it is not scientific, not fully objective, and certainly not a panacea.

Job evaluation is, however, based on systematic analysis and can provide a framework within which judgements can be made. It can help to produce order out of the chaos that exists in organisations which have allowed pay decisions to be made in an entirely *ad hoc* and subjective manner. A basic contention of this book is that such *ad hoc* approaches are inappropriate in any organisation which cares about creating and maintaining equitable, logical and coherent pay policies and structures that will enable it to attract, retain and motivate the people it needs, and provide equal pay for work of equal value.

Job evaluation under attack

A number of people we met during the course of our research felt that the inherent rigidity of traditional job evaluation procedures was completely at odds with the reality of work in many of today's organisations in which the emphasis is on flexibility with regard to structure, process and roles. They were struggling to reconcile the need to describe, value and position jobs in the organisational structure with the business imperative of removing barriers to organisational flexibility. We shall be addressing this question later in the book. Suffice it to say in this Introduction that there is a wide range of evaluation methods available and some of them can be used as flexibly as the organisation requires. Job evaluation need not impose inflexibility – although it can reinforce it, if it is allowed to.

The criticisms summarised below often refer to conventional job evaluation practices. We shall be examining their validity in the light of an analysis of approaches which many people believe are more fitted to the new organisations of the 1990s and beyond. However, although we believe that existing notions of job evaluation should be challenged, we still consider that some formal method of deciding on the relative value of jobs, even if it is not called job evaluation, is essential. Our research showed that in many organisations a conventional approach, albeit used flexibly, may still be necessary, and a number of people we spoke to had no doubts that such approaches *had* worked well and added value. Others are finding that traditional approaches are no longer appropriate and are paying more attention to competence-based methods, the use of generic role definitions rather than job descriptions and broad-banding. These are seen as a means of enhancing flexibility in line with new process-based cultures in which teamwork, quality and rapid response to customer needs are all-important. They are also perceived as essential to any 'learning organisation' in which the focus is on continuous development.

These organisations recognise that the old dogma of 'evaluate the job not the person' is no longer relevant today. They are adopting a people-oriented and more flexible approach in which the emphasis is on assessing the value added by individuals in flexible roles rather than on measuring the size of closely defined jobs in a rigid hierarchy.

It can indeed be argued that some traditional job evaluation schemes can fail to produce a return in terms of increased organisational effectiveness, competitive advantage and higher levels of shareholder value which justifies the considerable investment in time and money that a full and formal job evaluation process demands. Flexible, logical and equitable pay structures can, it is said, be produced by much simpler means as part of a coherent approach to managing people.

And to imply – as some people do – that job evaluation is justified because the role analyses carried out in a job evaluation exercise contribute to other key HR processes, such as organisation and employee development, is to miss the point. Such analyses can and should take place irrespective of the existence of job evaluation. For example, a number of organisations we visited during our survey had undertaken a massive change programme, often following a business procedure re-engineering exercise. These included Bass Taverns, The Benefits Agency, The National & Provincial Building Society and Triplex Safety Glass. In each of these organisations much thought was given to how people should be rewarded when new structures were being introduced, often de-layered and with an emphasis on horizontal processes, teamwork and flexibility. The existing job evaluation scheme or grade structure was being replaced in many of these organisations by a radical new approach which recognised the importance of flexibility, quality, teamwork, project and process management, and continuous development. But these innovations followed organisational and cultural changes: they did not initiate them, although it was recognised that they provided a valuable means of reinforcing the change process.

Formal approaches to job evaluation, especially the most popular variety (analytical point-factor schemes as described in detail in Chapter 4), have come under attack in recent years for being rigid, mechanical and bureaucratic. Claims that job evaluation is inherently rational have been refuted by a number of commentators who echo the remark made by Roethlisberger and Dickson (1939) of Hawthorne Studies' fame that: 'One of the most time-consuming passions of the human mind is to rationalise sentiments and disguise them as logic.' Moreover, some job evaluation schemes can be inherently inflexible when – as can happen – through the factors they use they impose values that are irrelevant to the real values of the organisation as they develop and change over time. If, for example, the core values of the organisation are flexibility, quality and teamwork, how can any evaluation or, indeed, any performance management process, have any relevance if it does not specifically refer to these values? Clearly, what has to be done is to ensure that the factors used in job evaluation are specifically oriented to the organisation's core values. In competence-based schemes as described in Chapter 6, the competences used for valuing roles should be derived directly from the core competence framework of the business.

An Incomes Data Services report (1991) summarised the arguments against traditional job evaluation schemes as follows:

The most damning charge against job evaluation for employers and employees alike, is that it simply measures the wrong things. The idea that the focus should be measuring the job, not the jobholder, runs counter to the way work is increasingly organised. More and more functions and businesses are subject to rapid change and depend on the ability of groups of employees to apply their skills in a flexible way. The established systems fail to measure what is important in the contribution of these 'knowledge workers'.

Ed Lawler (1986) thought that 'point-factor job evaluation seems to have outlived its usefulness'. In an ACAS report David Grayson (1987) suggested that, to survive, job evaluation 'will need to adapt to the organisational, technical and legislative changes which it now faces'. Quaid (1993) dismisses job evaluation as 'an institutional, rationalised myth', and contends that it 'beams back to employees and workers that the current structure of inequality is right and just'.

Emerson (1991) asserts that job evaluation schemes can all too easily 'value rigidity, insulation and ignorance'. She believes that: 'The systems used to value human resources can no longer be subjective ordinal rankings of factors that are indiscriminately subjected to inappropriate calculations.' She also contends that: 'The job evaluation system must identify and reward people for customer service, adaptability, profitability and market-related behaviour.' The search for fair and effective job evaluation continues and is driven by organisational need. This book is intended to help practitioners in that search whilst also exploring some of the more innovative techniques currently available.

The research base of this book

This book draws extensively on the information we obtained from our survey of the job evaluation practices of 316 organisations conducted under the auspices of the Institute of Personnel and Development in 1994 to 1995. It was supplemented by visits to 34 organisations, together with a number of discussions with management consultants, trade union officials, and other interested agencies. This book, therefore has a strong research base and aims to give a comprehensive picture of what is happening in the world of job evaluation in the UK today, and the direction in which it is going.

It was interesting to observe that a remarkable number of the organisations we visited were in the course of completely revising their approach to valuing jobs and/or the design of their pay structures. This was mainly the outcome of massive organisational and cultural change programmes these organisations had completed or were undertaking. In many cases they involved replacing the previous arrangements with a completely new approach that was more congruent with the changing values and processes of the organisation.

We have based many of our observations and analyses on the research findings, and these will be referred to at appropriate points throughout the book. We have, however, summarised the outcome of the research in Chapter 16, and in Chapter 17 we provide further examples of job evaluation in practice and of the development programmes some of the organisations we visited are currently carrying out.

We wish to express our gratitude to all those who completed questionnaires and spared the time to help us with this project by providing invaluable information on what they were doing or thinking about job evaluation.

Our approach

We have tried to avoid adopting a prescriptive approach. We shall indeed suggest criteria for choice between the various evaluation processes, but we shall emphasise that in making such choices it is essential to understand the true nature of job evaluation – its limitations as well as its benefits. Only by doing this can organisations avoid saddling themselves with complex, bureaucratic and, eventually, corrupt schemes, as many do. Because formal analytical methods of evaluation are still favoured by many organisations we shall be devoting much of this book to examining the choices to be made in developing such schemes and the programmes of work required.

Another important aspect of the subject we shall be addressing in this book is the process of developing and maintaining job evaluation. Too often the textbook approach has been to describe the different types of schemes and then to prescribe methods of introducing them through the use of job evaluation panels, etc. What has been neglected is the fact that making job evaluation work is not only a matter of selecting or designing the 'right' non-discriminatory scheme, but also one of managing the processes involved in applying the scheme fairly and equitably within the organisation's environment and culture – ensuring that they are properly integrated with other aspects of its corporate and personnel strategies. One of the points we shall be stressing in this book is that job evaluation should not be treated as a separate entity. It should be considered rather as an integral part of a total and coherent approach to human resource management in which each of the personnel processes used in the organisation interacts within the context of the business strategy.

Our research has established that, although selecting and designing a new job evaluation scheme is never easy, the real people problems begin when it is being introduced and peak when the implications of the exercise have been explored and the implementation process starts.

The purpose of this book is to provide a guide to job evaluation best practice, covering the choice of approach and its implementation. This guidance is given against the background of a conceptual review of the process of job evaluation. It is enhanced by the analysis of the results of our survey of job evaluation practices and illustrated by a number of case-studies.

The book is intended to present job evaluation on a 'warts-and-all' basis, addressing the fundamental problems associated with it so that the means of overcoming them can be devised. It is aimed at those practitioners who against this background want to install a relatively straightforward job evaluation scheme as a means of resolving a chaotic pay situation. It is also for those who are exploring new ideas about how to tackle the process of valuing jobs and people in rapidly changing organisations.

Plan of the book

To achieve this purpose, the book is divided into the following parts:

Part 1: The process of job evaluation. This part sets out the conceptual framework for the rest of the book. The purpose and meaning of job evaluation is considered, and the processes used in job evaluation are described in terms of the basic methodology and the different types of schemes. The case for and against job evaluation is also discussed.

Part 2: Job evaluation methodology. This part describes the different types of job evaluation schemes in more detail, and examines the processes of market pricing (which can be regarded as a type of job evaluation) and grading jobs. The use of computerised systems is also covered, and detailed consideration is given to the key issue of ensuring that jobs of equal value are paid equally within the framework of equal pay legislation.

Part 3: Developing, implementing and maintaining job evaluation. In this part practical guidance is given on how to introduce job evaluation or replace or improve an existing scheme, with and without the help of management consultants. The steps required to introduce and maintain job evaluation are also considered.

Part 4: Job evaluation today. This part describes the outcome of our research into current job evaluation practices. It includes a number of case-studies describing how organisations have developed and applied job evaluation.

In conclusion, we summarise our findings and review the future of job evaluation.

PART 1

THE PROCESS OF
JOB EVALUATION

1

JOB EVALUATION: DEFINITION, PURPOSE AND MEANING

The aim of this chapter is to provide a conceptual framework for the process of job evaluation that covers the following topics:

- □ definition
- □ purpose
- □ the meaning of value
- □ the meaning of comparative worth
- □ the measuring of job evaluation
- □ jobs and roles
- □ jobs and people.

Against this background, the next chapter will deal with the basic methodology of job evaluation, types of schemes, methods of assessing validity and reliability, and the case for and against job evaluation.

Job evaluation defined

Formal job evaluation is a systematic process for defining the relative worth of jobs within an organisation. The key words in this definition are:

- □ *Systematic* – The Oxford English Dictionary defines *systematic* as 'methodical; according to a plan; not casual or unintentional; classificatory'. This sums up precisely what job evaluation is supposed to be about.
- □ *Process* – Although job evaluation uses systematic methods for collecting and analysing data, it is not a 'system' in the sense of a series of routines applied rigorously to guarantee the delivery of valid results. It is much more of a process that facilitates rather than governs judgements,

albeit within a structured framework.

- □ *Relative* – Job evaluation essentially provides a means of *comparing* jobs with other jobs, or with some sort of scale that is defined in job-related terms. It does not determine their intrinsic worth.

- □ *Worth* – This is defined by the Oxford English Dictionary as 'of value equivalent to; deserving; bringing compensation for'. Alternative words used in job evaluation are *size* (but mainly in schemes which score jobs on a numerical scale), *importance* and *contribution*. We avoid using the word *importance* because it implies a value-judgement which categorises some jobs and, therefore, the people in them, as unimportant. All jobs are important in some way to an organisation (never mind to jobholders), and it is invidious to label them in this manner. *Contribution* is better because it is possible to make some assessment through performance management processes of how much individuals in their roles contribute to achieving organisational objectives. But note that we are referring to *individuals* in *roles*. Within the organisational context, it is the person carrying out the role who makes the contribution, not the job. We therefore believe that it would be inappropriate to include *contribution* in a definition of job evaluation, although it is clearly a factor when deciding on what individuals should be paid.

- □ *Job* – One of the dogmas of the traditional approach to job evaluation is that the process is one of 'evaluating jobs, not people'. This is correct in so far as job evaluation should not take account of the performance of the person in the job. But it is misleading if it implies that roles in organisations cannot be shaped to a considerable degree by the capacities and competences of the people who play them. And, inevitably, it leads to a focus on jobs not people. The limitations of this approach as well as the importance of distinguishing between jobs and roles are discussed later in this chapter.

- □ *Within an organisation* – Job evaluation is generally regarded as concerned solely with comparing jobs within an organisation in order to place them in a hierarchy, most often defined in the form of a grade structure. As Fowler (1992) notes, 'It does not of itself determine the "right" pay level for any job.' Murlis and Fitt (1991), for example, have contended that 'Job evaluation only ever sets out to assess the size or importance of one job against another. It does not purport to take account of market forces.' And Plachy (1987b) wrote that 'Job evaluation achieves only one thing – setting the value of a job compared with other jobs in an organisation. Job evaluation has nothing to do with money or markets.'

Internal and external relativities

As noted above, the generally accepted definitions of job evaluation emphasise that it is concerned solely with <u>internal equity</u> – the relative worth of jobs inside the organisation. Conventional job evaluation philosophy says that it is about getting internal relativities right so that jobs are equitably placed at appropriate points in the organisation's job hierarchy. The process of 'pricing' the jobs or attaching pay scales to job grades is completely separate. To produce a pay structure or to decide on the 'rate for the job', the procedure is first to evaluate the jobs to define internal relativities and then to establish external relativities, through surveys of market rates.

It can be argued, however, that a job is worth what the market says it is worth – or, as expressed by Livy (1975), 'The price of a job is much like the price of anything else: a subjective evaluation of what a willing buyer is prepared to pay and a willing seller accept.' In an analysis of the most popular type of job evaluation – the point-factor method, as described in full in Chapter 4 – Supel (1990) took the view that 'At the conceptual level the point-factor job evaluation system is quite dependent on market forces and, consequently, those who search for job and market correlations should not be surprised when such correlations are, in fact, very high.'

It is certainly the case that decisions on the internal relative value of jobs are only made in order ultimately to express them in terms of rates or levels of pay. And these decisions normally take account of market comparisons to ensure that the pay levels of the organisation are externally competitive even when the first consideration is internal equity or comparable worth. In fact, many organisations rely entirely on market pricing to determine both rates of pay *and* internal relativities. We are therefore treating this as a type of job evaluation in the widest sense of the term – ie attaching a value to a job or person in the form of a rate of pay. We recognise, however, that this approach may be deeply flawed as a basis for a fully equitable pay structure, not to speak of the problems it can produce when dealing with issues of equal pay for work of equal value.

The purpose of job evaluation

The purpose of job evaluation is

- [ ] to provide a rational basis for the design and maintenance of an equitable and defensible pay structure
- [ ] to help in the management of the relativities existing between jobs within the organisation
- [ ] to enable consistent decisions to be made on grading and rates of pay
- [ ] to establish the extent to which there is comparable worth between jobs so that equal pay can be provided for work of equal value.

Job evaluation enables a framework to be designed which underpins pay decisions. It can help with internal comparisons and, to a degree, external comparisons by providing a common language for use in discussing the relative worth of jobs and people.

Our research confirmed that the primary reason given by organisations for introducing job evaluation is to ensure a more equitable pay structure. Belief in job evaluation is based, in Quaid's (1993) words, on 'The greater power and validity of the "quantitative" [over the qualitative], of the "formal" [over the informal], and of the "objective" [over the subjective].'

Organisations commonly introduce job evaluation because they want to replace chaos with order, inconsistency with consistency, and political judgement with rational judgement. As Plachy (1987a) notes, 'Managers learn that it is easier to work in an identified structure produced by job evaluation than it is to work in chaos.'

Some people nonetheless think, naively, that job evaluation is a scientific and objective 'system' which, after it has been 'installed', will at a stroke remove all the problems they have experienced in managing internal relativities, fixing rates of pay, and controlling the pay structure. This is of course asking far too much of job evaluation which, as Pritchard and Murlis (1992) suggest, should be regarded as a process rather than a system. And we certainly believe that it is a process which, although it can be systematic and can reduce subjectivity, will always be more art than science and, because it relies on human judgements, will never be fully objective.

The meaning of value

If one of the main purposes of job evaluation is to establish relative values, it is necessary to understand just what the word *value* means in this context. Three concepts must be examined: those of intrinsic value, relative value, and market value.

Intrinsic value

The concept of intrinsic value is based on the belief that what jobs and jobholders are worth is related inherently to what they are and what they do, respectively. The factors taken into account may include all or any of the following:

- □ contribution – the level of the contribution or the impact made by the person who carries out the job on the achievement of business goals
- □ responsibility – the level of the particular obligations that have to be assumed by the person who carries out the job or role
- □ expertise – the level of knowledge and skills required to do the work
- □ competence – the level of competence required to carry out the job effectively
- □ physical and mental demands – the physical demands made by the job in terms of effort, working conditions and hazards, and the mental demands made in terms of pressure and stress.

Note that all these factors refer to the person in the job as well as the job itself. This casts doubt on the validity of the iron law of job evaluation, which states that it 'evaluates jobs, not people' (International Labour Office, 1986).

Job evaluation schemes which purport to measure the size of jobs by attaching point scores to them are, in a sense, using points as a means of indicating intrinsic value. They appear to state that a job is 'worth' so many points. But the points have no real meaning in themselves. They are simply *ordinal numbers* – ie they define the position of a job or a factor in a series: they do not represent any unit of measurement such as output, sales, pay or hours.

The problem with intrinsic worth as a concept is that there is no way in which it can be measured in absolute terms for evaluation purposes. It is all about perception – and value, like beauty, lies in the eye of the beholder.

Relative value

It can be argued that the value of anything is always relative to the value of something else. Internally, such an assessment is based on perceptions about relativities between jobs. Externally, it is related to data on relativities between market and internal rates of pay. It is this concept that governs the comparative nature of job evaluation.

Market value

The price of anything is related to the perceived value of the article or service to the buyer and the seller, but it is ultimately governed by the laws of supply and demand. As Hicks (1935) stated: 'Wages are the price of labour and thus, in the absence of all control, they are determined, like all prices, by supply and demand.' The way in which these laws operate, however, is affected by the degree to which transactions are carried out in what economists call perfect or imperfect markets. (An imperfect market is one that is affected by the relative power of suppliers or purchasers, restrictions on trade, limitations on entry, etc.)

A rate of pay for a job or a person is a price like any other price, and it is affected by the same supply-and-demand considerations operating in what are likely to be imperfect markets. The internal rates for jobs are thus affected by what is perceived to be the market rate, although – as will be explained in Chapter 7 – the concept of market rate is an imprecise one. Similarly, the rates of pay for individuals can be affected by their own 'market worth' – what other organisations are prepared to pay for their services and the value individuals attach to themselves.

Strictly, job evaluation is concerned only with intrinsic or relative internal value. But in most organisations, market value significantly influences rates of pay, subject to supply-and-demand considerations, to the effect of pay negotiations, to where the organisation wants to position itself in relation to market rates (its market stance) and, importantly, to how much it can afford to pay. As Plachy (1987b) emphasises, 'A pay structure is determined by the dynamic interplay of two forces, market prices and job evaluation . . . Pay structures attempt to resolve the often differing demands of these two forces.'

The meaning of comparable worth

In a sense, job evaluation is always about comparing the worth of one job with another. But the concept of comparable work focuses attention on achieving equal pay for work of equal value, thus eliminating gender discrimination. Job evaluation should be very much concerned, therefore, with establishing comparable worth within organisations and, as far as possible, ensuring that men and women doing work of equal value are graded and paid the same within the pay structure. Job evaluation can reveal inequities and show where market-rate considerations have led to higher rates of pay than those indicated by the internal evaluation.

The meaning of job evaluation

It has been suggested by Phelps Brown (1962) that 'Job evaluation is only a painstaking application of the way in which people do continually think and argue about relative pay.' And there is much truth in this statement. Job evaluation is certainly painstaking – which can be one of its merits – but it can also do no more than provide a rationalisation for the

assumptions people have already made about internal relativities.

To understand the meaning of job evaluation it is also necessary to study the misconceptions that surround it. These can be
described as the illusion of science, the mirage of objectivity,
and the myth of measurement. Having disposed of these, consideration can then be given to the key features of job evaluation
as a comparative, judgemental, analytical and structured
process. Finally it is necessary to consider the role of job evaluation as a process that fits an organisation's culture but can also
influence it, and that can serve as an integrating force – part of
a coherent approach to human resource management.

The illusion of science

According to the Oxford English Dictionary, a *science* is a
branch of study concerned either with a connected body of
demonstrated truths or with observed facts systematically
classified and brought under general laws.

Job evaluation does require the observation and systematic
classification of facts, but it does not consist of a connected
body of demonstrated truths that have been brought under
general rules. It is based on assumptions and propositions that
are subjective, not scientific. It involves value-judgements and
interpretations, not the application of laws or rules. It is not a
science. As Plachy (1987c) comments, 'Job evaluation is not a
scientific system; it is a human system. Human beings make
mistakes. They lose their objectivity and consistency, no
matter how hard they try, no matter how great their integrity.'

The mirage of objectivity

Job evaluators may have a vision of objectivity – but it
becomes unreal as soon as they get too close to it. Every step
in the evaluation process leads to value-judgements based on
the interpretation of data presented in the form of words. And
as Plachy (1987b) notes, 'People give words the meaning they
wish, sometimes intellectually, most of the time emotion-
ally.' Job descriptions can be partial (in both senses of the
word) representations of reality. The words used to convey
meaning in factor-level definitions are always subject to
interpretation.

The best that can be said of job evaluation is that it helps to make value-judgements explicit and requires evaluators to assess them within a framework. Although this may reduce subjectivity, it does not make the process objective. Madigan and Hills (1988) have explained that 'Evaluation procedures merely provide a means for structuring judgements about internal pay arrangements. Whether a particular pay structure is valid is a matter of judgement.'

The myth of measurement

The assumption made by most job evaluation schemes, especially point-factor schemes, is that it is possible to measure job value. But as noted earlier, points schemes simply use rank-ordered numbers – ordinal numbers – which have no meaning in themselves and do not, because they cannot, represent any unit of measurement such as the number of widgets produced. As Emerson (1991) noted, 'Ordinal structure without any ties to an empirical measuring system conveys the image of precision without providing any real, substantive measuring tool.'

The value attached to jobs is more a matter of perception than measurement. Points give an impression of accuracy, but are misleading. The numerical scores refer to value-judgements and cannot imply mathematical certainty. Moreover, these judgements vary according to when they are made and who makes them. Attaching scores to jobs may produce a rank order, but the scores have no validity in themselves. They do not measure intrinsic value.

The key features of job evaluation

To summarise, job evaluation may be regarded as

☐ a comparative process – It deals with relationships, not absolutes.

☐ a judgemental process – It requires the exercise of judgement in interpreting data on jobs and roles (job and role definitions or completed job analysis questionnaires), comparing one job with another, comparing jobs against factor-level definitions and scales, and developing a grade structure from a rank order of jobs produced by job evaluation.

☐ an analytical process – Job evaluation may be judgemental
but it is based on informed judgements which in an analytical scheme are founded on a process of gathering facts
about jobs, sorting these facts out systematically in order
to break them down into various elements, and re-assem-
bling them into whatever standard format is being used.

☐ a structured process – job evaluation is structured in the
sense that a framework is provided which aims to help
evaluators make consistent and reasoned judgements. This
framework consists of language and criteria used by all
evaluators, although, because the criteria are always subject to interpretation, they do not guarantee that judgements will be either consistent or rational.

Job evaluation and organisation culture

Job evaluation is a cultural artefact – it is a tangible process
that people can see in operation, hear about, and be affected
by. The factors used in analytical job evaluation schemes to
assist in making judgements about relative worth express the
beliefs of the organisation about what is felt to be important
when valuing jobs and people. They deliver two messages to
employees: this is how we value your contribution; this is
what we are paying for. Traditional values may emphasise
such factors as experience, qualifications and responsibility in
terms of the number of people or the size of the budget controlled.

Nowadays, organisations are increasingly tending to base
their judgements about job worth or the value of individual
contributions on such factors as skill and competence, adaptive behaviour, 'working smarter' with smaller numbers of
staff and leaner budgets, working effectively as a team
member, interpersonal relationships, including caring for
people, and relationships with customers and clients. They
also focus on values like creativity, flexibility and quality.
Above all, attention is concentrated on delivered performance: the contribution of jobholders and the impact they
make on results.

Tailor-made job evaluation schemes generally adopt, and
therefore reinforce, values which are already held to be important. They can thus underpin the culture of the organisation,

and this is desirable – as long as it is the most appropriate culture. They can also be used as levers for cultural change, as was happening in a number of the organisations we visited, including Pilkington Optronics, The National & Provincial Building Society and Thames Valley University.

Job evaluation does this by emphasising new values or by focusing on existing values to which more attention needs to be given. And this process is much more effective if it is not imposed by management but provides for employees to be involved in defining the value system in which they work.

But job evaluation may do no more than reinforce existing hierarchies and judgements about relativities. It can, if improperly used, simply confirm existing judgements about comparable worth and ignore the changes that are taking place in relativities or fail to indicate areas where pay levels are inequitable between men and women.

The job evaluation packages that can be purchased from management consultants are also value-based. But these packages rely on the consultants' values, and in selecting one of them it is essential to ensure that it is what the organisation wants and needs. It is worth bearing in mind that many of these schemes were designed in the 1950s and 1960s. The organisational values at the time they were designed are not necessarily appropriate today. It is vital to ensure that any outdated assumptions built into such schemes are corrected. But most consultants who offer these schemes are fully aware of the need to be flexible.

Job evaluation and human resource management (HRM)

It has been suggested by Armstrong and Long (1994) that three of the most important characteristics of the HRM model are that

- it involves the adoption of a comprehensive and coherent approach to the provision of mutually supporting and integrated personnel policies and practices
- the performance and delivery of HRM is a line-management responsibility
- it emphasises 'mutuality' – the common interests of all members of the organisation.

Job evaluation can play an important part in each of these aspects of HRM.

First, it can act as a powerful integrating force. The foundation of job evaluation is role analysis. This leads to definitions of role requirements which, especially if they are expressed in the form of competence profiles, provide the information and a common language that can link together such key areas of HRM as organisation, human resource planning, selection, performance management, employee development, and reward. The new approaches to pay and job evaluation that we identified through our research create processes which emphasise flexibility and competence in broad-banded structures in which the progress of individuals is governed by their capacity to develop and successfully apply new skills and competences and to demonstrate the capacity to adapt to new demands and expand their roles. This is the case at some forward looking companies in which it is recognised that the design of new pay processes and structures and the creation of new concepts for employee development go hand in hand and are mutually reinforcing. If, for example, the organisation wishes to concentrate on developing competence, then this will be a major factor in introducing competence-based pay.

Secondly, job evaluation can help to ensure that line managers take full responsibility for the management of their people by applying the process themselves and using it as a guide on pay decisions. Job evaluation should not be regarded as being solely within the domain of the HR or personnel department. HR specialists can help to initiate and implement a job evaluation process; they can provide help and training and administrative services, and they can be guardians of the process in the sense that they do their best to ensure that it is applied consistently and fairly throughout the organisation. But it is not their scheme.

Thirdly, if job evaluation is introduced and operated with the full involvement of employees and their union representatives (if any), it can be a vehicle for discussing and agreeing the key values concerning people and the rewards that exist in the organisation. It can bring management and trade unions together in a partnership that exists to develop a fair and equitable pay structure on the basis of mutual agreement. Some managements and some trade unionists may find it difficult to act together in this way, but our research demonstrated that when they do, the results are beneficial to all concerned.

Perhaps the most important lesson we learned from our research was that job evaluation must not be regarded as just another personnel technique or system imposed on organisations in isolation. Instead it should be treated as one of a range of interrelated and interactive personnel processes that are integrated with the major business processes. In other words, the approach to job evaluation should be governed by how the business functions in its constantly changing environment. Cultural change, organisation development, and business process re-engineering programmes come first; job evaluation follows. If, for example, the priority is flexibility and teamworking in a process-based organisation, then the approach to valuing jobs must be based on these requirements.

Jobs and roles

Is job evaluation concerned with jobs, or roles, or both? The terms *job* and *role* are often used interchangeably, but there is an important difference.

□ *A job* consists of a group of finite tasks to be performed (pieces of work) and duties to be fulfilled in order to achieve an end result.

□ *A role* describes the part played by people in meeting their objectives by working competently and flexibly within the context of the organisation's objectives, structure and processes.

When describing a job, the traditional approach has been to concentrate on why it exists (its overall purpose) and the activities it requires to be carried out. The implication is that these are fixed and are performed by jobholders as prescribed. On the face of it, there is no room for flexibility or interpretation of how best to do the work. Jobs are the same – in fact, should be the same – whoever carries them out. This may still apply to people on assembly-lines or those whose work is entirely governed by the machines or processes they operate. Elsewhere it represents the bureaucratic view of jobs as defined by Weber (1946), who stated that one of the features of an ideal bureaucracy is 'close job definition as to duties, privileges and boundaries'. It is a view that still seems to pervade traditional approaches to job evaluation, but it bears little relation to reality for many of the roles carried out in today's organisations, although public and private bureaucracies still exist, and bureaucratic enclaves sometimes persist inside otherwise more fluid and less structured businesses.

The concept of a role is much wider because it is people- and behaviour-oriented – it is concerned with what people do and how they do it, rather than concentrating narrowly on job content. When faced with any situation – eg carrying out a job – individuals have to enact a role in order to perform effectively within that situation. People at work are, in a sense, often acting a part; they are not simply reciting the lines but are interpreting them in terms of their own perceptions of how they should behave within their work context. Role definitions cover the behavioural aspects of work – the competences required to achieve acceptable levels of performance and contribution – in addition to the tasks to be carried out or the results to be attained. They emphasise the need for flexibility and multiskilling, and for adapting to the different demands that are made on people in project- and team-based organisations where the focus is on the system rather than on a hierarchical structure.

To a degree, individuals who are not in production-line or machine-controlled jobs can determine how they are going to play their parts, and some roles provide for much more freedom to act than others. But it is still necessary to define broadly what roles people are expected to play, and role definitions will refer to competences which cover such aspects of behaviour as leadership, teamworking, interpersonal relationships, caring, communication and innovation.

Organisations may identify generic roles – for example, process leader, team leader, process implementor/operator, supporter, professional adviser, designer/developer. Generic or core competences could then be established for each of these roles, more specific work-based competences being defined for individual roles.

The significance of this distinction between jobs and roles is that in the new process-based organisation, horizontal processes (which may have been defined in a business process re-engineering exercise) cut across organisational boundaries. Managements are beginning to regard their organisations in some fundamentally different ways. Rather than seeing them as a hierarchy of static jobs, they think of them, in the words of Ghoshal and Bartlett (1995), 'as a portfolio of dynamic processes . . . They see core organisational processes that overlay and often dominate the vertical, authority-based processes of the hierarchical structure . . . They see another process that builds competence across the organisation's internal boundaries.'

In this type of organisation and, indeed, any organisation that has had to cut back its hierarchy and operate more flexibly, it is necessary to value the roles people play, not just the jobs they are required to do. The way ahead has been summarised by O'Neal (1994) as follows:

> In the future, the basic unit of work will shift from the job to a role (eg supporter, contributor, business strategist), to blended task positions such as 'team leader'. Compensation objectives will shift from paying for jobs to paying for skills, knowledge and critical behaviours.

Job evaluation must recognise, as noted by Hillage (1994), that 'The product of a job is seen as a combination of the skills and attributes the person brings to it (ie supply) and the tasks required of them (ie demand).' As he points out, the emphasis has therefore shifted to role rather than job evaluation: 'With the increased interest in workplace behaviours and their impact on performance, evaluation may move even further from its roots in outputs, ie tasks, towards inputs, ie skills and personal attributes.'

Jobs and people

By focusing on jobs rather than roles, traditional job evaluation deliberately avoids considering the value of people. Human beings seem to be treated as unnecessary intrusions in the pure world of job hierarchies with which job evaluation is concerned. Of course, the reason behind the parrot-cry 'Job evaluation measures the value of jobs, not people' is to avoid contaminating the process of evaluation with considerations of the performance of individual jobholders. And it would indeed be undesirable for job evaluators to get involved in performance assessment, which is a separate matter.

But the traditional view still implies that people have nothing to do with the value of the job they perform, and this is clearly ludicrous. It is equally misguided to make the universal assumption that people adapt to the fixed specification of their jobs rather than believe that jobs should be adapted to fit the characteristics of the people in them. As Plachy (1987b) comments, 'Jobs are created according to the strengths and limitations of the people who design and fill them.'

The case for focusing job evaluation on people as well as jobs was put by Lawler (1986):

> The job evaluation approach is based on the principle that people are worth what they do. In many cases this may not be the most desirable cultural value for an organisation. It tends to de-personalise people by equating them with a set of duties rather than concentrating on what they are and what they can do. It tends to de-emphasise paying for their skills and for their performances . . . If an organisation's key assets are its human resources, a system that focuses on people rather than on jobs is the better fit.

What is emerging is a strongly expressed belief amongst some job evaluation practitioners and consultants (especially in the United States) that the emphasis should be more on people than on jobs. Edwards *et al.* (1995) have suggested that traditional job-based evaluation leads to:

☐ inappropriate focus on promotion – People are led to believe that a job is more important than the individual in the job. This implies that the only way to get on is by being promoted rather than maximising contribution and competence in the present role.

☐ inability to reward knowledge workers – Traditional job-based pay systems which reward position in the job hierarchy and the number of people supervised generally do not work well for knowledge workers whose performance is based on specialised applied learning rather than on general skills.

☐ inability to keep pace with high-speed organisational changes – In the new flexible and fast-moving organisations, in which the emphasis is on process and the use of self-directed teams that carry out variable project assignments, employee roles often do not fit traditional job-evaluation methodologies.

The importance of adopting a people- as well as a job-based approach was stressed by the Director of Remuneration Consulting at Hay Management Consultants (Derek Pritchard, 1995):

> A major feature of today's more fluid organisations is that the work that people actually do is determined not just by a conventional idea of a 'job', but also by their own capability – 'people make jobs'. A basic tenet of traditional job definition and evaluation is the separation of jobs and people; this may no longer be possible in a flexible organisation.

To sum up, it is people who create value, not jobs.

2

JOB EVALUATION:

HOW IT WORKS

The aim of this chapter is to build on the concepts discussed in Chapter 1 by concentrating on how job evaluation works – the basic approach and, in summary, the main types of job evaluation schemes. Consideration is also given to the number of schemes required, job evaluation for manual workers, the attitude of trade unions to job evaluation, the ways in which the reliability and validity of job evaluation can be established, and the fact that job evaluation schemes can decay or become out of date. Finally, the case for and against job evaluation is reviewed before conclusions are reached on the way forward.

The basic approach

The process of job evaluation begins by identifying how many and which jobs are to be evaluated. A decision also has to be made on whether there should be one scheme for all employees or whether there should be separate schemes for different levels or categories of people. The next step is to choose one of the methods summarised later in this chapter and described more fully in Chapters 3 to 7 (the considerations that affect the choice are discussed in Chapter 12). The final stages are:

☐ to select the representative 'benchmark' jobs that are to form the basis for comparisons

☐ to decide on the factors to be used in evaluating the jobs

☐ to analyse the jobs and roles

☐ to evaluate the jobs

☐ to develop a pay structure – This usually means designing a grade structure and then deciding on the rates or ranges of pay in the structure through internal comparisons and market pricing.

Benchmark jobs

Benchmark jobs are those identified as representative of the range of jobs to be considered. They serve initially as the basis for the design or modification of a job evaluation scheme, and then function as reference points for the internal assessment of job relativities in order to help in the understanding and evaluation of less obvious jobs. They are also used in the external process of matching jobs with those in other organisations in order to make market rate comparisons. See also the section on the selection of benchmark jobs in Chapter 12.

Job evaluation factors

Job evaluation is essentially about comparing the different characteristics or elements of jobs in order to establish relativities. When jobs are evaluated, even if there is no formal evaluation scheme, those concerned always have some criterion in mind, even if it is only some generalised concept of the level of responsibility compared with other jobs, or a comparative assessment of the impact of the job on end results, or its critical dimensions (eg turnover, output, resources controlled). In analytical schemes, such characteristics are termed *factors* (in the United States the term 'compensable factor' is used). Even in non-analytical schemes where 'whole jobs' are compared with one another – ie they are not broken down into their separate elements or factors – there may be explicit or implicit assumptions about the factors to be taken into account when making comparisons for ranking them or slotting them into a grade structure.

Factors are thus the main characteristics or elements which are common to the range of jobs being evaluated but are present to a different degree in those jobs. They are used as the basis for assessing relative values. If, in common parlance one job is held to be more responsible than another, responsibility is being used as a factor, however loosely responsibility is defined. The selection and definition of factors is one of the key processes in any analytical form of job evaluation and is discussed fully in Chapter 5.

Role analysis

Role analysis provides what is intended to be the factual data about the roles people play, upon which the evaluation is based. The information is collected systematically and presented in a structured form. Typically, it is presented in the form of a job description or role definition, but it can be recorded as answers to a structured questionnaire which directly provides the information for job evaluation.

The job evaluation process

This comprises the methods used to decide on the rank order of a job, its position in a job grade, or its comparative worth. In point-factor schemes it indicates how jobs will be scored. The process outlines how comparisons are to be made, in one or other of the following ways:

- *job to job*, in which one job is compared with another to decide whether it should be considered of more, less, or the same value (ranking, factor comparison, and 'internal benchmarking' processes)
- *job to scale*, in which judgements are made by comparing a whole job with a defined hierarchy of job grades (job classification) or comparing the different factors or elements of a job with a graduated scale of points for each of these factors (point-factor rating).

Grading

Most job evaluation systems are linked to job grades. The job evaluation process may simply enable jobs to be slotted into a predetermined hierarchical structure. Alternatively, a job evaluation exercise may lead to the design of a new grade structure or the revision of an existing one.

Market pricing

Market pricing is the final stage in the process of valuing jobs and developing pay structures. It establishes market rates and external relativities as the basis for attaching pay scales to job grades or fixing individual rates.

Job evaluation schemes

Job evaluation schemes can be divided broadly into non-analytical, analytical, single-factor, and skill- or competence- based schemes, market pricing, and management consultants' schemes (the so-called proprietary brands).

Non-analytical schemes compare whole jobs with one another and make no attempt specifically to distinguish between the factors within the jobs which may differentiate them. Job ranking, paired comparison, and job classification are usually regarded as the three main non-analytical schemes, although paired comparison is simply a statistical method of establishing rank order. Another non-analytical approach, not generally dignified with the title 'scheme', is internal benchmarking. This may not be recognised as a proper form of job evaluation but it is, nevertheless, practised by a lot of organisations, even if they do not refer to it by that name. And once they have carried out their initial analytical job evaluation exercise, many organisations do in effect slot in jobs by internal benchmarking whenever they perceive a close affinity between the job in question and a benchmark job.

☐ Job ranking is a non-analytical job-to-job method which simply places jobs in rank order.

☐ Paired comparison is a technique of ranking which involves evaluators comparing each job in turn with all the others being evaluated.

☐ Job classification is a non-analytical job-to-job method in which job grades are defined and jobs are slotted into the grades by comparing the whole job description with the grade definition.

☐ Internal benchmarking is also a non-analytical job-to-job method in which whole jobs are compared with benchmark jobs which, it is assumed, have already been correctly graded. They are then slotted into the same grade as the benchmark jobs if judged broadly comparable.

The *analytical schemes* are point-factor rating, as it is universally known in the United States (in Britain it is often called simply points rating or a points scheme), and factor comparison.

☐ Point-factor rating plans assess jobs in terms of the degree to which several specifically defined factors are present in the job being evaluated. A factor-by-factor assessment is carried out, each factor divided into degrees with a low-to-high scale of point values. Jobs are assigned a degree and a corresponding point value for each factor, and their overall 'value' is determined by totalling the assigned points for all the factors.

☐ Factor comparison plans start by evaluating benchmark jobs against a range of what are regarded as universal factors. This is converted directly into money values.

Skill- or competence-based schemes value people rather than jobs in terms of their attributes and competences.

☐ Competence or skill-based schemes determine the competences or skills required at various levels and relate these to the competences or skills required by individuals to carry out their roles at these levels.

Market pricing is used in conjunction with other internally-oriented evaluation schemes to price jobs by reference to market rates. Market pricing can also be used as the sole means of valuing jobs and placing them in a pay structure. Many people do not classify this as job evaluation, but it can be used to provide guidance on internal relativities and is therefore a means of valuing jobs for the purpose of developing a pay structure. Market pricing approaches are often associated with internal benchmarking.

☐ Market pricing establishes the market rate of jobs and uses this as the basis for fixing the rates of pay for those jobs and the differentials between them in accordance with the pay policies of the organisation.

The single-factor schemes are decision-banding and time-span of discretion.

☐ Decision-banding uses decisions as the single factor. There are six bands, each of which refers to a different level of decision-making in the job. The rationale for the system, which was developed by T. T. Paterson (1972), was that the ultimate factor for valuing jobs was the level and quality of decision-making involved.

□ Time-span of discretion – This approach was developed by Elliott Jaques (1958) on the basis of his hypothesis that the longest period of time for which jobholders can exercise discretion about their work without supervision correlated with the demands of the job and people's perceptions about relativities. It is an appealing concept but difficult to apply in practice, and has been little used.

The principal features of the basic schemes referred to above, with the exception of decision-banding and the time-span method, are described in more detail in Chapters 3 to 7, and the choice of approach is discussed in Chapter 12. The main evaluation packages or 'proprietary brands' offered by management consultants are described in Appendix A.

The number of schemes

Increasingly, organisations are introducing integrated pay structures which are supported by a single job evaluation scheme, although this often does not cover executive directors. Many employers still slice the organisational horizontally, however, utilising separate schemes for manual and for office workers. Some distinguish between managers-and-professional-staff and the rest of the employees in offices or laboratories. Others have schemes that apply only to certain categories of staff. Manual workers may be covered by a negotiated wage structure which, it is felt, does not need to be supported by job evaluation.

On the other hand, some employers slice the organisation vertically, utilising job evaluation schemes that cater for different job families or occupational groups. For example, there may be one scheme for office-based staff and a separate scheme for research-and-development scientists or engineers.

When different analytical schemes are used, the factors may be varied. Schemes for manual workers may include factors for dexterity, physical effort and working conditions. Where there are diverse groups of employees – as in the National Health Service – there may be strong arguments in favour of tailoring schemes to different job family or occupational group requirements. This ensures that all the factors are covered without overloading a common scheme with factors that might apply to only some of the jobs. In these circumstances, consideration could be given to linking the schemes in order to achieve consistency by overlapping evaluations – benchmark jobs covered by two distinct occupational schemes could be evaluated by both the schemes.

The considerations that affect decisions on the coverage of job evaluation schemes are discussed in Chapter 12.

Job evaluation for manual workers

Research covering 350 respondents conducted by Torrington and Hall (1992) showed that the number of firms using one or other of the different methods for evaluating blue-collar jobs was:

grading or classification	31
points-factor rating	26
factor comparison	21
ranking	13
Hay Management Consultants' method	9
other	4

Organisations with integrated pay structures (ie one structure covering all employees) do not generally have separate schemes for manual workers. If they do have one analytical scheme, however, it must include such factors as physical effort, manual dexterity, stamina and working conditions. Alternatively, they may have a factor plan which incorporates certain core factors applying to all employees but branching into groups of specialised factors for different groups of people – eg manual workers as distinct from office/administrative staff and 'knowledge workers'. Some organisations and categories of employers (such as local authorities) have entirely separate schemes with their own sets of factors for manual workers.

Manufacturing firms on the other hand tend not to have a formal analytical job evaluation scheme for manual workers, often because there is a well-defined skill hierarchy which, in their view at least, clearly establishes grades and rates of pay. These are determined by negotiation with trade unions, by reference to rates in the local labour market and, in the case of grades, by custom and practice. The result is 'spot rates' (ie specific rates for the job) for a hierarchy of work in such categories as skilled, semi-skilled, and unskilled. There may be established rates for special types of workers, such as toolroom turners and storekeepers, or 'plus rates' for extra skills. It is the prevalence of this approach in industry that explains why the Workplace Industrial Relations Survey (Millward *et al.*, 1992) found a much smaller number of formal job evaluation schemes in manufacturing concerns than has been established by the general surveys covering all levels of employees and sectors.

Other manufacturing companies, especially Japanese manufacturing firms, have deliberately decided not to use job evaluation. At Nissan this decision was made because they wanted complete flexibility of working practice with common terms and conditions for everyone. Peter Wickens, who was instrumental in developing the system at Nissan, believes that job evaluation creates artificial restrictions. He bases this view on his original experience at Continental Can Company where, as he told us, 'We took a leap of faith and abolished job evaluation,' relying instead on the identification of broad categories of jobs such as engineers and secretaries/receptionists.

At Nissan, then, there are no job descriptions, only generic job titles. Engineers, for example, carry out some simple, some complex, and some routine work. Instead of breaking this up into tasks for junior, middle and senior engineers, they have a philosophy that 'an engineer will do everything an engineer is required to do'. In other words, each engineer has the potential to undertake all levels and types of engineering work, capability being the determining factor. The next position up, the senior engineer, supervises half a dozen engineers, and the division between the jobs is based on management responsibility, not job complexity. Every shopfloor worker is at the same level. There are no special allowances. Nissan wants people to get involved in other work that adds to their job, and to do everything that is necessary with no restrictions.

Another approach is to use skill-based schemes, as described in Chapter 6, which relate pay to the level of skill acquired and used. They are most frequently introduced in companies where flexible and multiskilled methods of working are important – for example, in a cellular manufacturing system. Such schemes have replaced the previous arbitrary divisions into levels of skill and have contributed to the removal of demarcation lines between different jobs, thus making a major contribution to the achievement of flexibility.

Trade union attitudes to job evaluation

Many trade unions have traditionally been suspicious of job evaluation. They have felt that job evaluation might erode their traditional negotiation rights and that management is trying to blind them with pseudo-science. They are concerned about the level of transparency in a scheme devised and operated by management. They have also suspected job evaluation schemes, especially some of the 'proprietary brands', as being management-oriented. We came across one example where a union refused to co-operate in the introduction of a particular proprietary brand. Our discussions with trade union officials, however, indicated that there was an increasing degree of acceptance of the need for the unions to co-operate with management on job evaluation, especially to ensure that equal-value considerations are taken fully into account.

Trade unions may work with management in the development and application of job evaluation as a means of establishing internal relativities and comparable worth, but they reserve their right to negotiate on any revisions to the pay structure as it affects their members at the end of the exercise. Strong unions may challenge management with their own evidence on internal and external relativities, which could be just as comprehensive as that collected by management. It might well be interpreted differently but there is considerable scope for interpreting job evaluation and market rate data.

Steve Bloomfield of UNISON has said that UNISON and its predecessors have historically preferred factor-based job evaluation schemes because they are analytical and as objective as possible. He suggested that unions traditionally resisted job evaluation, but because it promotes equal pay, much of that traditional resistance has evaporated. The trade union philosophy is that employers should be paying for output and, as the unions are very committed to equal pay, they believe there must be some form of job evaluation plus payment for output. He also commented that employers wanted to reward those who bring quality and depth to the job, and there is an immediate conflict thus between paying for the job or for the person. UNISON remains sceptical about competence-based job evaluation because of the risks of gender bias, although it is seen as potentially an advance on performance-related pay. However, the union does not favour any system that does not relate to what people actually do.

Eric Mead of GMB told us that his union generally supported job evaluation, although it was beginning to get in the way of new developments such as teamworking and flexibility. In his view there was a need to reduce the number of grades to increase flexibility. GMB was generally in favour of new forms of job evaluation, including those based on competences, as long as they were well thought out.

As MSF explains in its publication on job evaluation in the National Health Service (MSF, 1994): 'Job evaluation . . . is important. It has a fundamental influence on the pay structure of an organisation. We cannot afford to ignore it.' The publication emphasises that 'MSF representatives should try to make sure the decisions to begin a job evaluation exercise, the basis on which it will proceed, and the procedures for choosing and implementing a scheme, should all be matters for joint discussion and negotiation between the trust and the unions.' MSF stresses the need for transparency, and its publication also makes the important point that 'The acid test for any job evaluation scheme any MSF member can apply is "Does it evaluate *all* the significant aspects of my job accurately and fairly?" '

Assessing the reliability and validity of job evaluation

Job evaluation processes should be both reliable and valid. Reliability is the degree of consistency or stability of an evaluation over time, or when used by different raters. Validity is the degree to which the job evaluation process truly measures job value.

Reliability

The reliability of a job evaluation process can be assessed by determining if it consistently assigns a job to the same job grade. This depends initially on the reliability of the job content data. It is very difficult in practice to assess reliability. Job evaluation is usually believed to be reliable if it is *felt* to be reliable (the 'felt-fair' principle).

Conceptually, a reliability study requires that jobs are evaluated by two or more evaluators using the same job content information. Research carried out in the United States by the National Academy of Sciences as reported by Risher (1989) has indicated that errors can arise which in some pay structures could mean more than a 20 per cent difference in pay.

Validity

As pointed out by Arvey (1986), it is important to understand that when people talk about validity in job evaluation they are not necessarily referring to the specific scores resulting from the use of a job evaluation instrument. Instead they are referring to the kinds of inferences and decisions made on the basis of those scores: 'There is nothing inherently valid or invalid about a set of scores – they are simply a set of scores.'

Three approaches can be adopted to validating job evaluation:

☐ Criterion-related, which attempts to determine the degree of correlation between the evaluation and the market rate. The problem is that accurate market rate data is not always easily obtained and, in any case, the fact that internal relativities correspond with external relativities may not necessarily have any real meaning. The market rate relativities could thus be misleading and irrelevant.

☐ Content validity, which attempts to show that the factors included in the scheme are representative of all the important job characteristics. But whether they do or not is a matter of opinion – it cannot be proved.

☐ Construct validity, which is related to the degree to which factor ratings give an accurate indication of perceived job value – a construct is a theory created to explain and organise existing knowledge. Job value is a construct. A test for construct validity can in theory be conducted by evaluating a set of jobs in an established hierarchy (ie one in which relative values have been agreed) using two or more evaluation methods. But this can be expensive and still lead to inconclusive results, even if the established hierarchy is correct, which may not be the case.

It is contended by Risher (1989), however, that 'The only measure of system validity is management's assessment: "Does it meet our business needs?" From this perspective each system should be uniquely configured to "fit" the employer's compensation strategy, organisation structure and planned career paths.'

The felt-fair principle
The validity assessment method that is most generally used is the highly subjective 'felt-fair' approach. This principle was formulated by Jaques (1958) and in essence states that if people feel an evaluation or a rate of pay is fair, then it *is* fair. He suggested that 'There exists an unrecognised system of norms of fair payment for any given level of work, unconscious knowledge of these norms being shared among the population engaged in employment work.'

Ultimately, as Armstrong and Murlis (1994) wrote, 'The acid test of the validity of any scheme is whether it produces results that are seen to be fair and reasonable.' The objective of job evaluation is to provide a sound basis for making such judgements. The problem is that some people make pre-judgements; they support the results of job evaluation that confirm those judgements and reject those that do not. A 'felt-fair approach' by management may simply reproduce the existing hierarchy, with which they are perfectly happy, having been living with it for some time.

Decaying, outdated and cumbersome job evaluation schemes
Job evaluation schemes can decay. People learn how to manipulate them to achieve upgradings, and this is most likely to

happen in hierarchical organisations that have narrow grade structures and where the best way to get more money is to be promoted. This leads to the phenomenon known as grade drift – upgradings that are not justified by a sufficiently significant increase in responsibility.

Job evaluation schemes can also become out of date: values that dictated the choice of factors some years ago may no longer be appropriate. Significant changes may have taken place in jobs or roles, organisation structure, or the corporate culture. New chief executives or personnel directors may wish to get rid of the old system to replace it with something they believe will fit the new organisation much better and, indeed, will help in achieving the changes they want. A business that is now more concerned with horizontal processes and teamwork may want to replace a job evaluation scheme that is essentially hierarchical and does not recognise new flexible methods of working. It may be felt that the existing scheme is discriminatory and needs to be replaced by one that is more likely to ensure equal pay for work of equal value. An organisation in which the personnel strategy is focused on skills development may wish to change to a skill-based approach.

Another reason for abandoning a job evaluation scheme, as was mentioned by several of the organisations we visited, is that it is perceived to be too cumbersome – ie complex, bureaucratic, or time-consuming.

The case for job evaluation

A case for job evaluation does not have to be made. No organisation has any choice. It is impossible to avoid making decisions on rates of pay, and, if they are not negotiated, pay decisions will be made on beliefs or assumptions about where the job fits into the organisation, the contribution made by jobholders, and the market rate for the job or the market worth of the individual in the job. However, the use of formal methods of job evaluation needs to be justified.

The arguments in favour of a formal approach are powerful – most people believe that they are indisputable. They can be summarised as follows:

☐ An equitable and defensible pay structure cannot be achieved unless a structured and systematic process is used to assess job values and relativities.

☐ A logical framework is required within which consistent decisions can be made on job grades and rates of pay.

☐ Equal pay for work of equal value can be achieved only through the use of formal analytical methods of job evaluation.

☐ A formal process of job evaluation is more likely to be accepted as 'felt fair' than informal or *ad hoc* approaches – and the degree of acceptability will be considerably enhanced if the whole process is transparent.

The case against job evaluation

Job evaluation is one of the most familiar personnel management techniques and apparently has everything going for it. It is the only management technique enshrined in a UK Act of Parliament (The Equal Pay Act, 1970). But over the years it has been heavily criticised, especially in its most common form, point-factor rating.

As long ago as 1964 McBeath and Rand wrote that 'These [points] systems attempt to bring science and accurate measurement to a situation in which the relevant criteria, factors, are not always clearly defined, and scales of measurement can only be arbitrarily established. Blind faith in the accuracy of any points system of evaluation is clearly and utterly misplaced.' In 1970 Graef Crystal suggested that 'all systems of job evaluation essentially boil down to organised rationalisation'. At an Institute of Personnel Management conference in 1972 a former President of the Institute, Bernard Ungerson, suggested to general acclaim that most job evaluation techniques are fundamentally unsound. And in 1973 the then head of the Civil Service, Sir William Armstrong, was reported as saying of an exhaustive study concerned with the grading of senior civil servants that 'We did a tremendous exercise of job evaluation in that area and I, at least, emerged from it very sceptical about the real objectivity of job evaluation and the real possibility of comparing jobs in different occupational settings.'

A politician's view about job evaluation was expressed by Kenneth Clarke in 1987 when he was Employment Secretary. He dismissed job evaluation as a 'bogus science'.

There have also been a number of attacks on traditional methods of job evaluation from academics, two of the most spirited having been made by Ed Lawler and Maeve Quaid.

Ed Lawler (1986)

Ed Lawler's major contentions about point-factor job evaluation are that:

☐ because it was originally developed to support traditional bureaucratic management, the point-factor approach discourages organisations from changing – 'the kind of work it takes to create job descriptions and job evaluations generates a high investment in the status quo'

☐ job evaluation can create unnecessary and undesirable pecking orders and power relationships in organisations

☐ the point-factor approach emphasises doing the job as described rather than doing the right thing

☐ virtually every point-factor system creates an internal wage structure in which promotion is the main way to increase compensation

☐ point-factor schemes reward people for creating overhead and higher cost to get more points and thus more pay

☐ people tend to go in for point grabbing – they realise that creatively written job descriptions can lead to pay increases

☐ job evaluation schemes are expensive to administer.

He concluded his attack by stating that 'These criticisms of the point-factor approach highlight that it is more than just a pay system. It reinforces a particular value system and a particular orientation to management. The decision to adopt it should therefore not be taken lightly.'

However, as Plachy (1987a) has commented, 'Much of Lawler's criticism revolved around the way in which job evaluation is used in today's organisation . . . Although these criticisms damaged the facade of point-factor job evaluation, they did not disturb its internal structure.'

Maeve Quaid (1993)

Maeve Quaid bases her comments on job evaluation on her two years' experience as a job evaluation specialist helping to install the Hay system in a Canadian province. She then researched the subject at Oxford and went back to conduct research into how the Hay system had been applied in the same province, and how well it was working.

She suggests that job evaluation functions as a rationalised, institutional myth and believes that it 'provides organisations with a set of language, rituals and rhetoric that has transported an otherwise impossible and indeterminable process to the realm of the possible and determinable. In this way, what job evaluation seems to do is to code and recode existing biases and value systems to re-present them as objective data.'

A summary of the main criticisms

Research conducted by Towers Perrin in 1994 (unpublished) indicated that the major criticisms of job evaluation in large UK organisations revolve around

☐ inflexibility in reacting to business and work changes
☐ inefficiency in terms of time-consuming and expensive operation.

The criticisms of job evaluation made by other commentators are summarised below.

☐ *It relies on human judgement* – Job evaluation guidelines are subjected to different interpretations and varying standards among evaluators. Madigan and Hills (1988) say that criteria for establishing job worth often vary and that therefore 'objective' or non-biased measurement of that worth is impossible.
☐ *It is inflexible* – As Grayson (1987) points out, 'Job evaluation systems have usually been designed on the basis of traditional systems about work: the result is job evaluation schemes that are seen to be too slow, inflexible, unhelpful in implementing change, and more geared to preserving the status quo.' Emerson (1991) commented that job evaluation fosters rigidity 'by paying people to remain in positions that require and reward non-adaptive behaviour'.

Incomes Data Services (1991) asserted that 'The whole panoply of job descriptions, the scoring of jobs, grading appeals, evaluation teams, and so on, convey a message that is at odds with flexibility.' An aspect of flexibility that traditional job evaluation also fails to recognise is the increased emphasis on teamwork and the need for people to be multiskilled.

☐ *It unrealistically ignores market forces* – as Supel (1990) argues, 'From both rhetorical and empirical perspectives . . . the point-factor system is redundant vis-à-vis a market pricing system, and the case is extremely strong for firms to allocate resources so that market pricing is given a larger role in their pricing procedures.'

☐ *It focuses on jobs rather than people* – As Fowler (1992) noted, some organisations 'criticise job evaluation for its assumption that employees adapt to a fixed specification of the job, rather than jobs being adapted to fit the characteristics of employees'.

☐ *It cannot prevent* a priori *judgements* – there is a tendency for managements to judge the validity of a job evaluation exercise by the extent to which it corresponds with their preconceptions about relative worth. As Armstrong (1993) suggested, 'Despite emphasis on objective and balanced decisions based on job analysis assisted by a paraphernalia of points and level definitions, evaluators tend instinctively to pre-judge the level of a job by reference to their own conception of its value. The information presented to them about the job is filtered through these preconceptions and the scheme is used to justify them.'

Conclusions

The case for formal job evaluation procedures may be strong, if only, as Madigan and Hills (1988) believe, because they 'simply make the criteria of value explicit and structure the judgement process'. But there are powerful counter-arguments, as described above. Admittedly, most of these are related to traditional point-factor schemes, but this is, after all, by far the most popular form of job evaluation. Job evaluation has indeed been heavily criticised because it creates or perpetuates hierarchical pecking orders but, as Hillage (1994) comments, 'The counter-argument is that this is a criticism of how job evaluation is conducted and not an inevitable consequence of the process.'

The point has been made by Armstrong and Murlis (1994) that:

> Job evaluation methodologies which emphasise place in hierarchy, numbers of people supervised or resources controlled, without taking into account technical expertise or complex decision-making, have little to contribute. Indeed, in more flexible environments, *it is frequently not the scheme itself which is at fault but the way it is applied* [italics added].

As suggested by Pritchard and Murlis (1992), job evaluation should be regarded as a process rather than a system – a process that consists of a series of steps each of which 'can be designed and when necessary modified, simply and practically, to meet specific needs and the changing of these needs'.

Job evaluation processes in fluid and adaptive organisations must, therefore, be designed and operated flexibly. Job evaluation schemes continue to be used, and there are strong arguments for using them, because they are perceived to be logical, systematic, fair, and a good basis for handling issues relating to equal pay for work of equal value. But job evaluation should

☐ not be applied too rigidly to support or create inappropriate hierarchies

☐ reflect the degree of flexible working that is now taking place in most organisations, which increasingly have to cater for individuals in dynamic roles, not static jobs, who are expected to behave adaptively and to extend their capacity to use their skills and competences effectively to deal with new work requirements and challenges

☐ be demonstrably concerned with the contribution of people, not just the demands of a job

☐ take account of the increased emphasis on teamworking

☐ not rely on elaborate, constricting and misleading job descriptions

☐ not involve the organisation in expensive and time-consuming routines

□ be reasonably simple to operate so as to facilitate the devolution of job evaluation decisions

□ provide a framework for making consistent judgements on comparable worth

□ be amended or replaced if a scheme has decayed or is no longer appropriate

□ be transparent – everyone concerned should know how it works and how it affects them

□ be acceptable as equitable and fair, and this is more likely if employees and their representatives have been involved in the development and implementation of the scheme.

Job evaluation does no more than provide a framework within which judgement can be exercised. It does not remove the necessity for that judgement. And it should be accepted that although job evaluation is concerned with the inputs provided by people in the shape of their knowledge and skills, it should also focus strongly on outputs – the contribution people can make in their roles. Ultimately, people are rewarded for what they do and what they achieve – their delivered performance – not just for their attributes.

In spite of all the reservations about traditional methods of job evaluation in this chapter, however, there are strong arguments in favour of adopting a formal approach that aims to provide a structured framework for the design and operation of pay systems and the management of relativities. And this is what the rest of this book is about. But the way forward must be based on an appreciation of the fact that there are many ways of evaluating jobs and roles, and none of these is 'scientific' or wholly objective. Every organisation has to make its own choice about what to do in the light of its business and HR strategies, its environment, its climate of employee relations, and its culture. Further choices have to be made as to how that approach should be applied in a way that increases the objectivity and consistency of decisions about job grades and pay. There is no one 'best way'.

We shall be exploring the criteria for choice in Chapter 12 after describing job evaluation methodologies and approaches to the achievement of equal pay for work of equal value in the next part of the book.

PART 2

JOB EVALUATION
METHODOLOGY

3

NON-ANALYTICAL JOB
EVALUATION SCHEMES

Non-analytical schemes examine and compare whole jobs without analysing them into their constituent parts or elements. The main schemes described in this chapter are:

□ job ranking
□ paired comparison
□ job classification
□ internal benchmarking.

Job ranking

Ranking is the simplest method of job evaluation. It is what everyone does, perhaps intuitively when deciding on the relative position of a job in a hierarchy and the rate of pay that should be attached to it. This in turn is what happens when the pay has not been predetermined by the price needed to attract or retain someone, or where there are no negotiated or generally accepted rates for the job.

The process of job ranking

Ranking is the process of comparing jobs with one another and arranging them in order of their importance, their difficulty, or their value to the organisation. In one sense, all evaluation schemes are ranking exercises because they place jobs in a hierarchy. The difference between ranking and analytical methods such as point-factor rating is that job ranking does not attempt to quantify judgements. Instead, whole jobs are compared – they are not broken down into factors or elements although, explicitly or implicitly, the comparison may be based on some generalised concept such as the level of responsibility. Sometimes ranking is carried out more analytically by considering a number of aspects of each job when comparing it with others, for example:

☐ the scope and impact of the job, in terms of the size of the resources controlled (people and/or money), impact on end results, amount of discretion allowed, and the level and range of contacts made

☐ the complexity of the job, in terms of the number and variety of tasks to be carried out and the range and difficulty of the problems to be solved

☐ the level of knowledge and skills required to carry out the job, in terms of business, technical or professional knowledge, managerial and leadership skills, interpersonal and communicating skills, or manual skills and dexterity.

This list of points to be considered is helpful in that it steers thinking towards distinct and definable aspects of the content of the job rather than dealing in what might appear to be over-generalised concepts such as responsibility. But there are dangers. Rankings may be distorted if evaluators attach different weights to the factors, emphasizing some at the expense of others. It is, in fact, a half-way approach to an analytical points evaluation system, offering all the snags without obtaining many of the advantages. Ranking on one overall factor may appear to be more intuitive, but if it is based on detailed factual information the results obtained could be just as valid as a more artificial analysis of a number of factors, each of which demands intuitive judgements. A multiplicity of intuitions added together do not necessarily produce a better result than one overall intuitive decision.

Ranking may be carried out by identifying and placing in order a number of clearly differentiated and well-defined benchmark jobs at various levels. The other jobs can be ranked by comparing them with the benchmarks and slotting them in at an appropriate point. The benchmark comparisons may be made between jobs in very broad categories, as at the Pirelli plant in Wales (Yeandle and Clark, 1989), where the groupings were simply 'producers', 'maintainers' and 'administrators'. Avoiding narrow definitions in this way promotes flexibility.

Alternatively, ranking may simply involve first identifying

the jobs perceived to be the ones with the highest and lowest value, then selecting a job midway between the two, and finally choosing others at lower or higher intermediate points. The remainder of the jobs under review are then grouped around the key jobs, and ranking carried out within each sub-group. This achieves a complete ranking of all the jobs, which should be subjected to careful scrutiny to identify any jobs that appear to be 'out of line' – wrongly placed in the rank order.

The final stage is to divide the ranked jobs into grades. To do this, an initial estimate should be made of the number of grades likely to be required, on the basis of an assessment of the range of jobs to be covered and any natural boundary lines in that range, coupled with an analysis of the present or pro-posed structure of the organisation – the number of levels in the hierarchy or any natural ladders of promotion. Grade boundaries may be drawn between groups of jobs with common features, the aim being to separate the groups to achieve a real distinction between the content and levels of jobs in adjacent grades. This is easier said than done, and drawing the boundary lines is always a matter of judgement which may involve reconsidering the initial estimate of the number of grades required. It is often an iterative process pur-sued until a 'felt-fair' result is achieved. Pay ranges have then to be allocated to the grades by reference to existing scales and market rate information. The presentation of an acceptable sequence of pay ranges may involve further iteration and adjustments of scales and the allocation of jobs to grades. This is by no means a scientific procedure, as is explained at greater length in Chapter 9. One of the advantages claimed for point-factor rating, as discussed in Chapter 5, is that it pro-vides better guidance on grade boundaries.

Subsequent gradings or re-gradings are usually carried out by internal benchmarking – comparing the descriptions of the jobs to be graded with any benchmark jobs that appear to be broadly similar in regard to the level of responsibility, and then slotting them into the appropriate grade. It may some-times be necessary to carry out a special ranking exercise for a selection of jobs to establish where a new or a changed job should be slotted into the hierarchy.

This method is easily understood by those affected, and does not make heavy demands on time or on administration. But it gives no measure of the difference between jobs, and this makes the allocation of boundary jobs into grades even more arbitrary than it usually is. Neither does it achieve the same impersonality as analytical methods because it has no defined standards of judgement. It thus leaves assessors more open to influence by their familiarity with the existing grades and pay levels and the personal qualities of individuals currently occupying the jobs.

Ranking can also be criticised on more technical grounds. As Moroney (1953) pointed out, 'It is often questionable whether ranking is a legitimate procedure at all. It can often be the case that we sensibly have a preference for one item rather than another without being able to show logical justification for a ranking procedure.' The problem with ranking is that the judgements become multi-dimensional when a number of jobs have to be placed in order of importance. Inconsistencies in judgement arise between people because they give more weight to one aspect of jobs than others, and because they do not know what complex of factors and what balance of them is operating at any moment. Moreover, although it is easy to establish the extremes in a rank order, it may be difficult to distinguish between middling jobs. To overcome this problem it may be better to limit comparisons to pairs of jobs (as described below) because, as Moroney notes, 'It is well known that direct comparison between two items is far more sensitive and discerning than actual measurement on a scale of values.'

Summary of the advantages and disadvantages of job ranking

The *advantages* of job ranking are that

- it is in accord with how people instinctively value jobs
- it is simple and easily understood
- it is quick and cheap to implement, as long as agreement can be reached on the rank order of the jobs without too much argument
- it is a way of checking the results of more sophisticated

methods to indicate the extent to which the hierarchies produced are 'felt fair' – but this may simply reproduce the existing hierarchy and fail to eliminate gender bias. The question is: 'felt-fair by whom?'

The *disadvantages* are that

☐ there are no defined standards for judging relative worth – and therefore no rationale to defend the rank order – it is simply a matter of opinion (although it can be argued that even analytical schemes do no more than channel opinions in certain directions)

☐ ranking is not acceptable as a method of determining comparable worth in equal-value cases

☐ evaluators need an overall knowledge of every job to be evaluated, and ranking may be more difficult when a large number of jobs are under consideration

☐ it may be difficult, if not impossible, to produce a felt-fair ranking for jobs in widely different functions where the demands made upon them vary significantly

☐ it may be hard to justify slotting new jobs into the structure or to decide whether or not there is a case for moving a job up the rank order – ie re-grading

☐ the division of the rank order into grades is likely to be somewhat arbitrary.

The use of job ranking

Because of the disadvantages listed above, job ranking is little used in large or sophisticated organisations except as a check on the results of an analytical evaluation exercise or to provide guidance on weighting in a point-factor scheme. Job ranking in its crudest form is more often used in the relatively informal environment of small or uncomplicated businesses, where everyone has a clear notion of relativities.

Paired comparison ranking

Paired comparison ranking is a statistical technique used to provide a more sophisticated method of job ranking. It is based on the assumption that it is always easier to compare one job with another than to consider a number of jobs and attempt to build up a rank order by multiple comparisons.

The technique requires the comparison of each job separately with every other job. If a job is considered to be of a higher value than the one with which it is being compared, it receives two points; if it is thought to be equally important, it receives one point; if it is regarded as less important, no points are awarded. The scores are added for each job and a rank order is obtained. At Cummins Engine (IDS study, 1992,) a derivative of the technique is used to slot jobs into one of five grades by reference to broad job descriptions. This is another example of a firm's seeking to enhance flexibility and skills development through its job evaluation processes.

The procedure for paired-comparison ranking consists of the following steps:

☐ Select benchmark jobs.
☐ Analyse the benchmark jobs and produce job descriptions.
☐ Enter the names of the jobs on a paired comparison ranking form as illustrated in Table 3.1.
☐ Complete the form (typical instructions for members of a panel or working party carrying out the job evaluation are set out below).

Procedure for completing the paired-comparison ranking form

1 Compare each job listed on the vertical column of the form and indexed with capital letters (A, B, C, etc.) with each job listed across the page and indexed with lower-case letters (a, b, c, etc.).

2 Score each comparison (eg Job A with Job b) in the section of the form above and to the right of the diagonal line as described in steps 3 to 5 below.

3 Start with Job A, compare it with Job b, and if you consider that Job A should be ranked higher (ie is of greater value) than Job b, enter 2 in square Ab.

  ☐ If you consider the Job A is of equal value to Job b, enter 1 in square Ab.

Table 3.1
PAIRED COMPARISON RANKING FORM

| Company: XYZ Ltd | | | Division | | Headquarters | | | | | | | |

| Evaluator | Name: J. Smith |
| | Job Title: Company Secretary |

| Job Letter | | a | b | c | d | e | f | g | h | i | j | | |

Job Letter	JOB TITLES	a Accounts Assistant	b Bought Ledger Controller	c Computer Operator	d Customer Service Officer	e Marketing Assistant	f Personnel Officer	g Postroom Assistant	h Receptionist	i Sales Executive	j Secretary	TOTAL SCORE	OVERALL RANKING
A	Accounts Assistant		0	1	0	1	0	2	2	0	0	6	8
B	Bought Ledger Controller	2		2	2	2	0	2	2	0	2	14	3
C	Computer Operator	1	0		1	1	0	2	2	0	0	7	7
D	Customer Service Officer	2	0	1		2	0	2	1	0	1	9	4=
E	Marketing Assistant	1	0	1	0		0	2	2	0	2	8	6
F	Personnel Officer	2	2	2	2	2		2	2	0	2	16	2
G	Postroom Assistant	0	0	0	0	0	0		1	0	0	1	10
H	Receptionist	0	0	0	1	0	0	1		0	0	2	9
I	Sales Executive	2	2	2	2	2	2	2	2		2	18	1
J	Secretary	2	0	2	1	0	0	2	2	0		9	4=

- □ If you consider the Job A is of less value than Job b, enter 0 in square Ab.

4 Continue comparing Job A with the other jobs listed across the page (c, d, e, etc.) in the same way.

5 Repeat the procedure with Jobs B, C, D, etc.

6 Compete the section of the form below and to the left of the diagonal line by reference to the scores for the equivalent box above and to the right of the diagonal line. For example, compare Ba with Ab, Ca with Ac, Cb with Bc, etc., and continue this process for every job until the

boxes below the diagonal line are all filled. The scores in the two sections of the forms divided by the diagonal line are mirror images of one another; for example, in Table 3.1,

- If 0 is recorded in Ab, 2 should be recorded in Ba.
- If 1 is recorded in Dh, 1 should be recorded in Hd.
- If 2 is recorded in Fe, 0 should be recorded in Ef.

7   When both halves of the form have been completed, add up the total points scored for each Job A, B, C, etc., and enter in the right-hand column headed total points

8   Rank as 1 the job with the highest score and enter the rank number in the column headed Overall Ranking. Rank the remaining jobs in sequence according to their points score.

Advantages and disadvantages of paired comparison ranking

The *advantages* of the paired comparison method of ranking are that

- it is easier to compare one job with another rather than having to make multi-comparisons
- greater consistency can therefore be obtained in ranking
- comparisons between dissimilar jobs are facilitated.

The *disadvantages* are that:

- paired comparisons do not overcome the fundamental objection to any form of whole-job ranking – that it does not provide any defined standards for judging relative worth
- as a non-analytical process it is not acceptable as a means of measuring comparable worth
- there is a limit to the number of jobs that can be ranked even with the help of computers – to evaluate 50 jobs involves 1,225 comparisons.

The use of paired comparison ranking

If ranking is used as the basic process of job evaluation, in spite of the disadvantages paired comparisons will produce a more acceptable result and more easily. If ranking is being carried out simply as a check on the ranking produced by an analytical scheme, or to provide guidance on weighting, it is always preferable to use paired comparisons. But even with the assistance of computers, it is difficult to deal with more than 50 or so jobs.

Job classification

Job classification, or job grading, is a non-analytical method that slots jobs into grades by comparing the whole job with a scale in the form of a hierarchy of grade definitions.

The process of job classification

Job classification is based on an initial definition of the number and characteristics of the grades into which jobs are to be placed. The grade definitions refer to such factors as the key tasks carried out, skill, competence, experience, initiative and responsibility. The number of grades is usually limited to between four and eight, between each of which there are clear differences in the demands made by any job in its respective grade. Each grade therefore represents a threshold that must be crossed before regrading occurs. Classification systems with more than eight grades become unmanageable because of the difficulty of defining clear differences between successive grades. If there are fewer than four grades it may be just as hard to produce a sensible definition that clearly distinguishes one grade from another, although this may not be a problem in a broad-banded structure (see Chapter 9).

For example, definitions of the first two levels in a five-grade classification scheme for office and administrative staff could be expressed as follows:

Grade 1: The work involves standard routines such as maintaining straightforward record systems or operating simple office machinery. No previous experience is required and an acceptable level of proficiency can be attained after a few days' training and experience in the job. Fairly close supervision is exercised or the work is easily controlled by self-checking. Tasks are clearly defined and the choice of action is within narrow limits. Contacts are limited to routine matters of exchanging information with other members of the organisation.

Grade 2: The work involves maintaining fairly complex records, operating office equipment such as word-processors, loading data into a computer, or dealing with routine enquiries. Prior experience of up to six months carrying out similar work may be required, or a period of concentrated training for a few weeks. An acceptable level of proficiency can be attained after up to about six weeks' training and experience within the organisation. A fair proportion of the work is standardised but there are some non-routine elements. General supervision is exercised but the work can be controlled mainly by self-checking. Contacts may be made with people outside the organisation to provide standard information or to answer routine enquiries.

Definitions such as these can be amplified by lists of the typical tasks and duties carried out by people in jobs within the grade, and by reference to generic competence profiles.

Advantages and disadvantages of job classification
The *advantages* of job classification are that

☐ standards for making grading decisions are provided in the form of the grade definitions
☐ explicit account can be taken of the training, experience, level of responsibility, and specific duties demanded by a job in comparison with other jobs
☐ jobs can quickly be slotted into the structure
☐ it is easy and cheap to develop, implement and maintain
☐ its simplicity means that it is easily understood.

The *disadvantages* of job classification are that

☐ it cannot cope with complex jobs that do not fit neatly into one grade
☐ the grade definitions tend to be so generalised that they may not be much help in evaluating border-line cases, especially at more senior levels
☐ it often fails to deal with the problem of evaluating and grading jobs in dissimilar occupational or job families, where

the demands made on job holders are widely different – eg technical and administrative job families

☐ grade definitions tend to be inflexible and unresponsive to technological and organisational changes that affect roles and job content

☐ the grading system can perpetuate inappropriate hierarchies

☐ because it is not an analytical system it is not effective as a means of establishing comparable worth and is unacceptable in equal-value cases.

Use of job classification

Because of its simplicity, job classification is sometimes used by organisations which want to introduce job evaluation and a grading system easily and cheaply. Some organisations with broad-banded structures may use a form of job classification. The responsibilities attached to the typical roles in the band are defined and may be amplified by reference to the generic competences applicable to those roles. One of the varieties of competence-based job evaluation mentioned in Chapter 6 uses competence profiles as the prime means of defining bands and the levels of pay that can be earned by people according to the competences they use to deliver the required level of performance in whatever roles they are capable of carrying out.

The problem of producing meaningful and properly differentiated grade definitions covering the entire staff of an organisation has led some businesses to develop special job classification systems for different job families. Others have abandoned the idea of job classification altogether and, if they do not want to use an analytical method, adopt the relatively informal approach of internal benchmarking.

Internal benchmarking

Internal benchmarking is what people often do intuitively when they are deciding on the value of jobs, although it has never been dignified in the job evaluation texts with the formal title of job evaluation.

The process of internal benchmarking

Evaluation by internal benchmarking simply means comparing the job under review with any internal benchmark job that is believed to be properly graded and paid, and slotting the job under consideration into the same grade as the benchmark job. The comparison is usually made on a whole job basis without analysing the jobs factor by factor. However, internal benchmarking is likely to be much more accurate and acceptable if it is founded on the comparison of role definitions which indicate key result areas and the knowledge, skills and competence levels required to achieve the specified results.

Advantages and disadvantages of internal benchmarking

The *advantages* of internal benchmarking are:

- □ it is simple and quick
- □ it is realistic – it recognises that this is a natural way of valuing jobs
- □ it can produce reasonable results as long as it is based on the comparison of accurate job or role descriptions.

The *disadvantages* of internal benchmarking are:

- □ it relies on judgement that may be entirely subjective and could be hard to justify
- □ it is dependent on the identification of suitable benchmarks which are properly graded and paid, and such comparisons may only perpetuate existing inequities
- □ it would not be acceptable in equal-value cases.

Uses of internal benchmarking

Internal benchmarking is perhaps the most common method of informal or semi-formal job evaluation. It can be used after an initial analytical job evaluation exercise as a means of slotting jobs into an established grade structure without going to the trouble of carrying out a separate analytical evaluation (although if there is an agreement with employees or representatives that all jobs should be properly evaluated, this would not be feasible).

In a sense, the graduated factor comparison method described in Chapter 4 provides a way of internal benchmarking on an analytical basis if the comparisons are made between jobs under review and the benchmark job(s) on a factor-by-factor basis. And this approach could be acceptable in equal-value cases.

Internal benchmarking can be combined with market pricing (see Chapter 7) to provide additional evidence on pay levels. This could be described as external benchmarking.

4

FACTOR COMPARISON

The factor comparison method was originated by Eugene Benge and further developed by Benge, Burk and Hay (1941). The traditional (and little used) form of factor comparison, as described below, compares jobs factor by factor using a scale of money values to provide a direct indication of the rate for the job.

A derivative of this traditional approach that is more commonly used, especially in equal-value cases, is graduated factor comparison, which requires comparisons to be expressed on a graduated scale (eg low, medium, and high) although the factors are not weighted. This method is described at the end of the chapter.

Both techniques are analytical and involve the comparison of jobs to a scale.

The traditional method

Basis

In the traditional factor comparison method, jobs are broken down into their component elements or factors. To prevent the scheme from becoming too unwieldy, Benge (1944) suggested that it should be limited to the following five factors, which he believed were the 'universal' factors found in all jobs:

☐ mental requirements
☐ skill requirements
☐ physical requirements
☐ responsibilities
☐ working conditions.

The main difference between traditional factor comparison

and point-factor rating is that in factor comparison monetary values are ascribed directly. In point-factor rating only points are assigned to factors. The conversion of these points into rates of pay or definitions of the pay brackets in a graded structure comes later. Point-factor schemes do not translate points directly into national currencies although a formula may be used to convert points into pay ranges for jobs, taking account of market rates.

Methodology

A factor comparison job evaluation exercise is usually conducted by a job evaluation panel in stages:

1 *Select benchmark jobs* – This is a crucial step in all job evaluation methods but is even more important in factor comparison. Benchmark jobs must not only meet the criteria set out in Chapter 13 but there must also be agreement that the jobs are correctly paid. This is because they will be the base from which the pay of all other jobs is derived. The rate may be the current prevailing level of pay, the rate that the organisation believes to be appropriate on the basis of a survey of market rates, or the rate resulting from joint negotiations.

2 *Agree factors* – The five 'universal' factors listed above are generally used for manual workers. For office workers, technical and supervisory staff, Benge recommended the following factors:

   □ mental requirements
   □ skill requirements
   □ physical factors, including working conditions
   □ responsibility for supervision
   □ other responsibilities.

3 *Analyse benchmark jobs* – The benchmark jobs are analysed to produce a job description in terms of the factors.

4 *Rank benchmark jobs by factors* – The benchmark jobs are ranked successively by reference to each of the factors. If the evaluation is being conducted by a panel, each of its members decides on his or her own ranking and consensus

is then reached on the panel's final decision. How this ranking is achieved is illustrated by the simplified example of four benchmark jobs shown in Table 4.1.

Table 4.1
FACTOR COMPARISON – RANKING JOBS BY FACTORS

Job	Skill	Mental require-ments	Physical require-ments	Respon-sibilities	Working conditions
Tool-maker	1	1	4	1	4
Craft worker	2	2	3	2	3
Process operator	3	3	2	4	2
Maintenance assistant	4	4	1	3	1

5   *Determine the relative importance of factors in each job* – The jobs are taken in turn and each factor is assigned a percentage figure representing its proportional impor-tance in getting the job done, as shown in Table 4.2.

Table 4.2
FACTOR COMPARISON – RELATIVE IMPORTANCE OF FACTORS

Job	Skill require-ments	Mental require-ments	Physical require-ments	Respon-sibilities	Working	Total cond-itions
Tool-maker	35	30	5	20	10	100
Craft worker	30	25	15	15	15	100
Process operator	30	30	15	10	15	100
Maintenance assistant	20	15	25	15	25	100

6   *Allocate money values to factors* – The rate of pay for each benchmark job is broken down and distributed among

the factors. This is based on the assessed relative importance of the factors, and indicates how much each factor is believed to contribute to the total 'price' for the job, as shown in Table 4.3.

Table 4.3
**ALLOCATION OF MONEY RATES
(FOR EXAMPLE, IN POUNDS STERLING)**

Job	Skill require-ments £	Mental require-ments £	Physical require-ments £	Respon-sibilities £	Working £	Total cond-itions £
Tool-maker	91	78	13	52	26	260
Craft worker	66	55	33	33	33	220
Process operator	54	54	27	18	27	180
Maintenance assistant	32	24	40	24	40	160

7   *Evaluate other jobs* – The remaining non-benchmark jobs are slotted factor by factor into each job factor column on a factor comparison schedule. For example, the job of an assembler could be slotted into the skill column as shown in Table 4.4.

Table 4.4
SLOTTING NON-BENCHMARK JOBS

Job	Benchmark jobs £	Non-benchmark jobs £
Tool-maker	91	
Craft worker	66	
Process operator	54	
Assembler	42	
Maintenance assistant	32	

This slotting process is conducted for each column, and the total of the five figures gives the rate for the non-benchmark job. The rate for an assembler could thus be built up as shown in Table 4.5.

Table 4.5
BUILD-UP OF RATE FOR NON-BENCHMARK JOB

	£
Skill	42
Mental requirements	50
Physical requirements	30
Responsibility	22
Working conditions	22
	166

Advantages of factor comparison
The *advantages* claimed for the traditional factor comparison method as described above are:

- [ ] it is analytical in the sense that it compares jobs on a factor-by-factor basis
- [ ] rankings are made by comparing jobs directly with another in respect of a defined factor; this avoids the need to produce level definitions which are often imprecise and can be understood only by reference to benchmark jobs
- [ ] it leads directly to a price for the job – it is not necessary to convert points into pounds, which in point-factor schemes is always a judgemental process.

Disadvantages of factor comparison
The disadvantages of factor comparison are:

- [ ] it depends absolutely on selecting benchmark jobs that are believed to be properly paid – but (a) how can anyone be certain that this is the case? and (b) how is it possible to avoid simply reproducing the existing pecking order, which may contain serious inequities?
- [ ] it is complex and difficult to understand

□ although analytical it still requires a considerable amount of subjective judgement on where jobs slot in

□ it could be held to be discriminatory in an equal-value case.

The disadvantages completely outweigh any of the claimed advantages, and for this reason factor comparison in its traditional form as described above is little used in the UK (if it is used at all – we have come across no examples).

Graduated factor comparison

Pure factor comparison plans linked directly to pay rates may no longer exist in British companies, but modifications of the original concept are in use and involve comparing jobs factor by factor with a graduated scale. The scale may have only three levels – for example, low, medium and high – and in this case no factor scores are used and the factors are not weighted.

These graduations may be scored, as is sometimes the approach adopted by the independent experts called in to report to industrial tribunals hearing equal-value cases (see also Chapter 11) on their evaluation of the jobs under consideration. In such cases, graduated factor comparison resembles the point-factor method except that the number of levels and range of scores are limited, and the factors may be unweighted.

Schemes used by independent experts are concerned only with comparative value between a few jobs, and the factors they select are relevant to the semi-skilled or unskilled jobs with which they have usually been concerned (examples are given in Chapter 11). This is in contrast to conventional analytical job evaluation schemes, which are designed to establish relative values by placing a substantial number of jobs in an order that indicates the extent of the differences in value between them.

For this reason graduated factor comparison is not used generally within organisations. But it is an approach that could be used if there is a problem of comparable worth and there is either no analytical job evaluation scheme or the existing one contains gender bias. It could also be used as a means of linking separate job evaluation schemes that cover different categories of employees or for providing a 'read-across' between job families.

5

POINT-FACTOR RATING

The point-factor rating method as devised by Lott (1924) was the first quantitative form of job evaluation. Our survey established that 35 per cent of the organisations in the sample that have their own formal job evaluation scheme use point-factor rating. The method is popular because it is perceived to be

☐ more objective because it is analytical
☐ more acceptable as being fair
☐ a better basis for designing and maintaining grade and pay structures
☐ a good basis for comparing internal and external rates of pay
☐ a defence against equal-value claims because it is analytical.

The last point is particularly important.

Overall operation

The point-factor method is straightforward although it has a multiplicity of elements.

A number of job factors are selected and defined – eg skill, responsibility, and effort. These are considered to be common to all or nearly all the jobs in the organisation, or to clusters of jobs in job families, and it is believed that the different levels at which they are present in jobs will indicate relative job value.

The levels or degrees at which each factor can be present in the organisation's jobs are defined.

Each factor may be assigned a percentage weighting to indicate its relative significance, and therefore value, in the job. This weighting is translated into the maximum points score that can be given for any factor, and the sum of the scores for each factor indicates the maximum score that can be allotted to any job. However, some schemes deliberately avoid weighting on the grounds that it is always arbitrary and subjective in addition to being potentially discriminatory. The designers of such schemes aim to create a factor plan in which all the factors are equally important.

The maximum points for each factor are divided between the levels or degrees for that factor. Each level thus has a points score or range of points assigned to it.

Benchmark jobs are selected and analysed in terms of the factors (methods of selecting benchmark jobs are considered in Chapter 13).

The level at which each of the factors is present in the benchmark jobs is determined by reference to the factor plan (see below).

Scores are allotted for each factor in accordance with the factor plan and added together to produce a total score for the benchmark jobs and a ranking of jobs in accordance with those values.

A grade structure is designed which divides the rank order into a number of grades defined in terms of points brackets.

The remaining non-benchmark jobs are then evaluated and slotted into the grade structure.

The job grades are priced by reference to market rates and/or existing rates of pay and relativities.

The factor plan

The factor plan consists of the factors themselves, the factor level definitions, and the scores allotted to each factor and factor level in accordance with the factor weighting (assuming the factors *are* weighted) – this is the factor scale.

An example of a typical weighted factor plan is shown in Table 5.1, and an example of a conventional point-factor scheme is given in Appendix B.

The particular points to be considered in selecting and defining factors, defining factor levels and weighting the factors, and defining factor scales are considered in the next three sections of this chapter.

Table 5.1
FACTOR PLAN

	Factors	Levels					
		1	*2*	*3*	*4*	*5*	*6*
1	Knowledge and skills	50	100	150	200	250	300
2	Responsibility	50	100	150	200	250	300
3	Decision-making	40	80	120	140	180	220
4	Complexity	25	50	75	100	125	150
5	Contacts	25	50	75	100	125	150

Selecting and defining factors

A job evaluation factor is a characteristic which occurs to a different degree in the jobs to be evaluated, and which is used as a basis for assessing the relative value of those jobs.

Choice

The choice of factors is critical because

- □ it expresses the values of the organisation on how people should be recognised and rewarded
- □ it can significantly influence the extent to which the scheme provides a fair basis for assessing relative values
- □ it can affect the degree to which the scheme may be held to be discriminatory in equal-value cases.

The factors selected will depend on the nature of the organisation and the jobs to be covered by the scheme. The choice will be strongly influenced by the values of the business. For example,

- □ If the emphasis is on measurable results, the key factors will be concerned with impact, influence, contribution and, sometimes, the effect of errors – although the latter factor may indicate that a 'blame culture' exists.
- □ If flexibility is important, the factors will cover such aspects as multiskilling, versatility, and the variety and complexity of the tasks.
- □ If professional skill and competence is the key, this would

be treated as a distinct factor.

☐ If priority is given to widening the skill base and focusing generally on levels of competence and continuous development, skill and competence factors will be prominent.

☐ If customer or client relations are the key to success, interpersonal skills and the levels and types of contacts and communications made or carried out by jobholders will be stressed.

☐ Organisations which depend largely on knowledge workers will include relevant skill and competence factors in the plan.

☐ Organisations where creativity is a key consideration will include factors referring to innovation, initiative, and the management of change.

☐ Some organisations will continue to concentrate on levels of responsibility as measured by the size of resources controlled and the degree to which jobholders are autonomous.

☐ Organisations involved in health care or caring for people with disabilities will include caring relationships and skills as a key factor.

☐ Organisations for which the factor plan has to cover people who operate office equipment or machines, or manual workers generally, will incorporate factors covering manual skills, dexterity requirements, physical effort, stamina, working conditions, and hazards.

☐ Organisations which are particularly concerned about equal value will take steps to achieve gender neutrality in the factor plan and the way job evaluation is carried out. (The considerations to be taken into account in developing a gender-neutral plan are discussed fully in Chapter 11.)

In selecting factors, organisations are making explicit the values they believe to be important when assessing job worth. And the fact that this declaration has to be made is one of the virtues of job evaluation, which can be used either to underpin existing values or to change values if they are no longer functional. The process of selecting factors must also take account of equal-value considerations, as discussed in Chapter 11.

There is plenty of choice. Our research revealed that the 15 point-factor schemes we studied had between them 50 different factors, although many of these undoubtedly overlap. The types and numbers of factors, and the ways in which they can be combined in different schemes, are discussed below.

Types of factors

Job evaluation factors break down the key components of jobs and, collectively, represent each of the most important elements of those jobs. In devising a factor plan it is necessary to remember that job evaluation is essentially about valuing work and the contribution made by the people who carry out that work. The criteria or factors chosen for this purpose should therefore represent the reality of what that work is all about. If the key aspects of the work are not covered in the factor plan, it will be inadequate as an instrument for comparing relative worth. The plan must therefore cover all the key characteristics of the jobs to be evaluated, and it must not discriminate against women or men.

To ensure that the factor plan is comprehensive it is helpful to base it on the *input-process-output model* for describing work, which is illustrated in Figure 5.1.

Figure 5.1
THE INPUT-PROCESS-OUTPUT ROLE MODEL

input ──────────▶ process ──────────▶ output

Work is carried out to fulfil a purpose defined in terms of the contribution expected from jobholders and the impact they make on their end results – their *output*. The output is initiated by the job holders' *input* – what they bring to the job in the form of skills, knowledge and expertise. All work is essentially about transforming inputs into outputs, and this is the *process* aspect of a job in which jobholders use skills and knowledge and bring to bear their competences in such areas as decision-making, problem-solving, innovation, interacting with people, or carrying out a complex or diverse range of tasks. In addition, jobs can make mental and physical demands on people and may have to be carried out in unpleasant or demanding working conditions. An analysis of the 50 factors used in the 15 job evaluation schemes mentioned earlier in terms of this model is given in Table 5.2.

Table 5.2
ANALYSIS OF FACTORS USED IN 15 JOB EVALUATION SCHEMES

Input factors	Number of schemes in which factor occurs
education	1
education and training	1
experience	2
knowledge	3
knowledge and experience	2
knowledge and skills	5
communication skills	3
demand for expertise	1
human relations skills	2
interpersonal skills	1
numerical logic and IT skills	1
personal qualities	2
physical skills	2
professional competence	1
qualifications and experience	1
skills	2
thinking and reasoning skills	1
Process factors	
communication	2
complexity	7
contacts	2
decisions	3
initiative	1
innovation and creativity	1
judgement	1
planning and organising	1
relationships	1
Output factors	
accountability	2
authority	1
autonomy	2
consequences of error	2
financial accountability/ responsibility	1

impact	3
influence	1
numbers supervised	1
responsibility	7
responsibility for confidential material	1
responsibility for information	1
responsibility for money	1
responsibility for own work and that of other staff	1
responsibility for people	1
responsibility for resources	2
span of control	1
supervision – direction and relationships	1
supervision received	2
supervisory responsibility	2
Demand factors	
effort	1
mental effort	2
personal demands	1
physical demands	1
physical effort	1
pressure and volume of work	1
unsocial hours	1

Numbers of factors

The number of main factors included in the schemes we analysed are shown in Table 5.3.

Table 5.3
NUMBERS OF FACTORS IN FACTOR PLANS

Number of factors	*Number of schemes*
4	2
5	6
6	2
7	1
8	2
10	2

In some of these schemes, however, the main factor was divided into a number of subfactors. For example, in one scheme, a responsibility factor was split into five subfactors:

- ☐ responsibility for others, including supervision received
- ☐ responsibility for product, process, materials
- ☐ responsibility for plant, premises, equipment
- ☐ responsibility for decision-making/problem-solving
- ☐ responsibility for cash and valuables.

This scheme had only four main factors but they were divided into 13 subfactors.

The number of factors required is a matter of judgement. If there are too few – say, less than four – the individual factors may cover too many aspects of the job and the level definitions may be confusing. If there is more than one criterion in a level definition – numbers managed and size of budget, perhaps – it may be difficult to decide between them. One approach used in some schemes is to deal with these factors through a matrix, a simplified example of which is given in Table 5.4.

Table 5.4
A FACTOR MATRIX

		Interpersonal skills			
		A	B	C	D
	a	10	20	30	40
Typical contacts	b	20	30	40	50
	c	30	40	50	60
	d	40	50	60	70

If there are too many factors – say, more than 12 or 13 – there is a risk of overlap and duplication, and the evaluation process may become unnecessarily complicated. This risk may, however, be reduced if subfactors are clustered together under main factor headings.

There is no absolute rule which decrees that one factor or set of factors is always better than another. Crystal (1970) quotes an experiment in which 47 different schemes were used to evaluate the same jobs. There were no significant differences in the evaluations although the number of factors used ranged from three to more than ten.

However, it can be argued that a larger number of factors facilitates more accurate comparisons, especially in equal-value (comparable worth) situations in which it is essential specifically to compare each facet of the jobs under consideration.

It cannot be emphasised too often that the factor plan should represent the assessment by an organisation of what it believes to be the key criteria for establishing the worth of jobs. For example, the focus could be on competences, especially those concerned with working flexibly in complex situations, interpersonal relationships, teamworking, and quality, in addition to the impact made by the job on organisational performance, the mental and physical effort involved, and working conditions.

Decisions on the types and numbers of factors are ultimately a matter of judgement, although influenced by equal-value requirements. Every organisation must make this judgement in accordance with its needs either when it is designing its own scheme (with or without consultants) or when selecting a proprietary brand. Methods of selecting factors are given further consideration in Chapter 13.

To summarise, a factor plan should ensure that all the characteristics of the jobs (male *and* female) are covered; that the factors are not duplicated – it is necessary to avoid any risk of double counting; and that as far as possible, only one criterion is included in each factor, although two related factors can be incorporated if a matrix format is used (as illustrated in Figure 5.4).

Defining factors

This is not always easy. As Arvey (1986) notes:

> On the one hand, there is a need to develop factors and factor definitions that can be applied across large numbers of different jobs – a situation that implies some flexibility and broadness in the factors developed. On the other hand, the factors developed and their definitions should not be so broad as to produce rating errors.

The guidelines on defining factors are:

☐ Include as few criteria and dimensions as possible; aim for one criterion per factor.

☐ Ensure that each key criterion is included only once in a set of factors; do not include any very similar criterion in another factor.

☐ Be as precise as possible about what the factor is intended to cover – wherever possible refer to specific measures, observable conditions, and types of behaviour or competences that can easily be linked to the demands made on actual jobholders, to the requirements they must meet to satisfy those demands, and to the results they are expected to achieve by meeting the requirements.

☐ Make the definitions as succinct as possible: too many words confuse.

☐ Remember that the aim is as far as possible to ensure that the factor has the same meaning for all those who carry out evaluations.

Examples of factor definitions include:

☐ *Knowledge* – This factor considers the company, industry and professional knowledge required to undertake the role requirement successfully.

☐ *Human relations* – This represents the degree to which a person needs the ability to communicate, exercise influence, and use leadership skills.

☐ *Care skills* – This factor assesses the skills used to exercise care and rehabilitate residents.

☐ *Physical and manual skills* – This refers to the dexterity and manual and manipulative abilities necessary to the performance of the job. It includes the use of hand tools and equipment, instruments, machinery, and other mechanical aids.

☐ *Numerical logic and IT skills* – This quantifies the degree to which a person is required to use, understand, and produce numerical information, or to apply information technology skills.

☐ *Decision-making* – This factor looks at the decision-making aspects of the job, in terms both of decisions for which the individual is personally responsible, and of the individual's impact on the decisions of other people in the organisation.

☐ *Contacts* – This reflects the extent to which the work requires making personal contacts inside and outside the organisation. Consideration should be given to the level and importance of the contacts, the frequency with which they are made, and the degree to which they involve exchanging information, answering queries, dealing with complaints, exerting influence, or persuading people to take a course of action.

☐ *Complexity* – This quantifies the range of activities and variety of tasks to be carried out, and the diversity of the problems that have to be solved.

☐ *Physical effort* – This covers the need for physical strength applied continuously or at intervals, and the effect of fatigue caused by continual limb or hand operations.

☐ *Mental, visual and allied effort* – This concerns the fatigue sustained through continuous visual examination, concentration, precision and co-ordination in hand and eye. It also covers the stress of working at speed, with small or delicate items, and of working to deadlines or specified standards.

☐ *Flexibility* – This exhibits the extent to which a jobholder is expected to be flexible in terms of using different skills, taking on additional responsibilities, or carrying out different tasks.

☐ *Teamworking* – This quantifies the demands made on a jobholder in terms of working as a member of a team.

☐ *Responsibility for the work of other people* – This factor measures the extent to which the job involves the organisation, guidance, and direction of others.

☐ *Resources controlled* – This reflects the size of the resources controlled in terms of the number of staff and the size of the budget.

☐ *Impact* – This attempts to measure the contribution made by a jobholder to achieving organisational, departmental or team objectives.

□ *Accountability* – This quantifies the degree to which a job-holder is answerable for delivering results.

□ *Autonomy* – This covers the degree to which work is prescribed – the extent to which a jobholder takes independent action, exercising discretion in making decisions, prioritising work and interpreting policy guidelines or advice.

□ *Influence* – This concerns how much the actions and decisions of a jobholder impact on the behaviour of others and on the results they achieve.

□ *Creativity* – This quantifies the extent to which a jobholder is expected to originate, design, formulate or develop new ideas, concepts, plans, policies, products, procedures, or systems.

Examples of factor lists

Examples of factor lists include:

HM Treasury Job Evaluation for Senior Posts (JESP) Method

1 Managing people
2 Accountability
3 Judgement
4 Influence
5 Professional competence

Motorola

1 Knowledge
   □ education
   □ experience
2 Communications
   □ interpersonal skills application
   □ typical contacts
3 Complexity
   □ thinking environment
   □ job challenge
4 Impact
   □ decision-making latitude
   □ results of action
   □ degree of effort
5 Span of control

- □ subordinate levels/number
- □ breadth of responsibility

Ross Youngs (Manual employees)
1   Physical effort
- □ effort
- □ stamina
- □ paced work
2   Mental effort
- □ concentration/recall
- □ decision-making
- □ initiative – independent action
3   Knowledge/skills
- □ manual/motor skills
- □ knowledge of product/production process/operating skills
- □ mental skills
- □ communication skills
4   Responsibilities
- □ for plant/machinery/equipment
- □ for product quality
- □ for safety
5   Working conditions
- □ temperature
- □ unpleasant conditions

Royal National Institute for the Deaf
1   Knowledge
2   Education, care and rehabilitation skills
3   Manual (non-oral) communication skills
4   Responsibility
5   Personal demands
6   Complexity
7   Unsocial hours
8   External contacts

Clark's Shoes
1   Knowledge
2   Communication skills
3   Complexity
4   Responsibility for decisions

Factor levels

Two things have to be done when designing a traditional point-factor scheme:

□ decide how many factor levels are required
□ define them.

How many levels?

The number of levels required clearly depends on the range between the highest and lowest incidence of the factor in any of the jobs and the degree to which it is possible to differentiate between the levels in that range. There is no rule which decrees that all factors must have the same number of levels. The scope or range of the different factors may vary considerably. The minimum number of levels is usually three, and the use of more than six or seven levels is rare. It is undesirable to impose too many levels because it could cause problems of differentiation between them.

Defining levels

This is perhaps the most critical, and it is certainly the most difficult, task to undertake when designing a traditional point-factor scheme. It is the level definitions that will be referred to most frequently when comparing the job analysis with the factor plan.

Guidelines for defining levels include:

□ Aim to capture all the differences in the nature, type, and extent of the work done relevant to each factor.
□ Define only the levels required to differentiate clearly between the degrees to which the factor might apply.
□ Define the levels so that there are obvious differences between them – it is helpful if this is seen as a series of steps, each of which represents a progressively greater amount or incidence of the relevant job criterion.
□ Do not duplicate the description of a criterion in another degree.
□ Focus on what the work actually entails at that level, or the specific outputs expected; avoid relying solely on a series of comparative adjectives or adverbs (eg small,

medium, large) without qualifying them with a description of what 'small' means, where possible expressed in quantified terms (frequency of contact, numbers supervised, size of budget, length of time required to become fully competent, weight of objects to be lifted, etc.).

☐ Define the levels in a way that facilitates the development of a structured questionnaire for job analysis purposes.

☐ Use language that expresses succinctly, directly, and unequivocally what is involved at that particular level, and that facilitates comparisons between the job analysis and the level definition.

These requirements are not easy to satisfy. The problem with defining levels is that it can become an exercise in semantics. It is too easy to fall into the trap of simply producing a series of comparatives and superlatives which have no meaning in themselves and which lend themselves to varied interpretations, as in the following example.

Mental concentration
1   Minimum of mental concentration
2   Light mental concentration
3   Normal mental concentration
4   Considerable mental concentration
5   Close mental concentration

What does 'normal concentration' mean? How can a distinction be made between 'considerable' and 'close' concentration?

The following are examples of factor level definitions which at least attempt to avoid the problem of loose comparatives by concentrating on the specific demands made on jobholders and on what the work actually involves.

Knowledge and skills
1   The ability to carry out certain tasks which can be acquired by means of a brief period of practical experience (days or a few weeks).
2   The knowledge and skills required to carry out the tasks which can be acquired by means of a longer period of practical experience (up to twelve months) or a period of concentrated training of up to six months.

3   The knowledge and skills required obtained only by up to five years' practical and relevant experience or by a period of intensive educational training lasting six to twelve months.

4   A high level of knowledge or skills in an area of professional or administrative work in which vocational training lasting one to three years is required, which could be coupled with two or three years' experience; or experience lasting five years or more which has led to the same level of professional or administrative knowledge and skills.

5   Advanced skills and knowledge demanding *either* a full professional qualification obtained after a period of over three years' education and professional training; *or* considerable experience gained over ten years or more, leading to the acquisition of a similarly advanced level of knowledge and skills.

6   The further development and application of the knowledge and skills gained at level 5 for a significant period – five years or more.

Note, however, that a heavily weighted factor which places considerable emphasis on education, training or experience could be regarded as discriminatory on the grounds that women's careers may be interrupted and they may have less opportunity to receive relevant training and experience.

Scope of responsibility
1   The following of prescribed instructions, procedures, or work routines without deviation.

2   General following of prescribed instructions or procedures with occasional deviations from work routines.

3   The selection of appropriate steps from obvious options.

4   The selection of appropriate steps from non-obvious options.

5   Freedom to act within broad company policy guidelines.

6   The development of company policy guidelines.

Physical effort
(based on the system used by the independent expert in Gill V. Starbeck Working Men's Club)

1   Generally unpronounced or sporadic physical effort, only moderate body movements, and occasional (less than 6 times a day) lifting or carrying light weights (under 10kg).

2   Fairly frequent (6–8 times daily) lifting or carrying of moderate weights (10 to 20kg), or continuously handling of light weights (less than 10kg) with occasional lifting of heavier items. Frequent (about 30–40 per cent of the time) physical activity such as bending or stretching.

3   Fairly frequent (6–8 times daily) heavy lifting (20kg or more) with more frequent lifting and carrying of moderate weights (10 to 20kg); or the continuous lifting or manoeuvring of lighter weights; or persistent (over 50 per cent of the time) bending, stretching or similar activity, including continuous limb movement causing fatigue.

4   Regular or continued (over 50 per cent of the time) heavy lifting; or continuous physical activity of a strenuous and highly fatiguing nature, such as pushing heavy loads or heavy digging.

The last example is reasonably explicit, but the earlier ones still leave plenty of room for interpretation. And any attempts to elaborate on such definitions may only lead to confusion. Level definitions can do no more than serve as guidelines; they cannot prescribe exactly what decisions evaluators should make: they are always subject to interpretation. That is why point-factor evaluation, although analytical, can never be a precise science. Yet factor level definitions can become more meaningful to evaluators as they gain experience in applying the schemes to jobs. The definitions can be exemplified by reference to other jobs to which the same factor level has been assigned.

Examples of the different factors and level definitions that could be incorporated in a wider-based factor plan than the one given in Appendix B are set out in Appendix C. This incorporates a number of competence-related factors, and the subject of competence-based job evaluation is discussed in more detail in Chapter 6.

Weighting and factor rating scales

The need to weight

The argument for weighting is that every organisation values the components of jobs differently. Because weighting can be both arbitrary and discriminatory, however, some factor plans are constructed with the aim of creating factors of equal value and are therefore unweighted (although a decision not to weight factors could be just as arbitrary as a decision to weight them). But the majority of points schemes are weighted using techniques such as those described below.

Weighting techniques

Weighting may be carried out by assigning to each factor a proportional value – a percentage of the total size of the job expressed as 100 per cent. This proportion is an indication of the influence exerted by the factor in determining relative values. For example, the factor plan given earlier in this chapter weighted the factors as shown in Table 5.5:

Table 5.5
FACTOR PLAN WEIGHTING

		Max. points	%
1	Knowledge and skills	300	27
2	Responsibility	300	27
3	Decision-making	220	20
4	Complexity	140	13
5	Contacts	150	13
		1110	100

There is nothing magical about the weightings in this example – every factor plan can and should have its own weighting pattern. What matters is that the weighting

☐ properly reflects the values of those affected by job evaluation – ie employees and their representatives as well as management

☐ does not discriminate against women or men (equal-value

considerations in designing factor plans are discussed fully in Chapter 11)

Weightings can be based on assumptions about the relative significance of the factors. There is much to be said for getting a group of people together to agree on a provisional weighting pattern. If the evaluation is being carried out by a working group, it is desirable to get the members of the group to evaluate and decide on the levels for each job first and then consider factor weightings.

Factor rating scales

Factor rating scales consist of the points assigned to each level. There may be just one point value per level, or the level may be defined as a range; or scope may be given for a three-point scale in each level (eg standard, standard plus and standard minus). Allocating a range to each level suggests a degree of accuracy in rating that is unachievable. Even allowing for three points in the level scale may be asking too much for the discriminatory powers of evaluators – although when they are deciding on levels they will often want to award a plus or a minus. People tend to dislike being constrained, and this feeling can be respected by allowing some variation upwards and downwards.

The simplest approach is to divide the total factor score equally between the levels giving an arithmetic progression like this:

Level	Points
6	300
5	250
4	200
3	150
2	100
1	50

Some organisations prefer the differences between the value of levels to widen progressively upwards like this:

Level	Points
6	300
5	230
4	170
3	120
2	80
1	50

This is based on the assumption that differences in the degree of responsibility and accountability, etc., are likely to be more at higher levels. But this could be just as arbitrary a belief as one which indicates that levels should be valued as if they were equidistant.

It is always advisable to test both the weighting and the factor scales. This can be done when an initial evaluation of the benchmark jobs has taken place according to the 'felt-fair' principle – ie do people feel that the result is fair and reasonable? If not, the weighting and factor scales are adjusted on a trial-and-error basis until the result looks right.

A more stringent test can be made by first scoring the benchmark jobs to produce a rank order. The same jobs are then ranked separately by the paired comparison method to determine the degree of correlation between the rank order produced by the points scheme and the rank order resulting from the paired comparisons. If the initial trial produces an unsatisfactory correlation, the weightings are readjusted until an acceptable figure is obtained.

This approach is clumsy and time-consuming, especially if the initial assumptions are seriously out of line. A more sophisticated approach is to use the multiple regression analysis technique. Multiple regression analysis is defined as the statistical method for investigating the relationships between independent and dependent variables, and obtaining a 'regression equation' for predicting the latter in terms of the former. In a factor weighting exercise the different factors are the independent variables for which points are assessed and added up for each of the jobs to produce the dependent variable of the overall rank order. A multiple regression analysis exercise consists of the following steps:

1   The whole jobs are ranked by paired comparisons – a computer can be used to calculate the rankings, especially if it is decided to increase the accuracy or acceptability of the results by using a number of different judges and reconciling their views for the final ranking.

2   Each factor is ranked separately for all the jobs by paired comparisons, again with the help of a computer.

3   The multiple regression analysis computer program then

establishes the degree of correlation between each of the independent variables (the factors) and the dependent variable (the overall rank order). The degree of correlation is a measure of the validity of the values or weightings assigned to the factors. If the paired comparison ranking list is replicated by the points score ranking list, it can thus be assumed that the factor values are probably right. If there is little correlation between the two lists, the values are probably wrong. The degree to which the two lists match can be established by calculating the coefficient of correlation – a statistical formula which if it produces a result of $+1.0$ indicates a completely positive correlation whereas a result of -1.0 indicates a completely negative correlation. Values between these extremes indicate the degree of positive or negative correlation. Experience of using this technique has shown that a correlation of $+0.75$ is acceptable, given the inevitable limitations of the original data, although a result of $+0.8$ or more would be better.

4   The program then:
   □ ranks each factor in turn (starting with the factor with the highest correlation and finishing with the factor with the least correlation) and then reconstructs the whole job ranking order by applying weightings to the ranking orders within the factors
   □ tests the independent variables by measuring the correlations between them to establish the degree to which they separately contribute to producing the overall rank order (a very high correlation between two factors would suggest a high degree of overlap and might result in one of the factors being eliminated).

As a result, the most important factors are identified and weighted in line with the degree to which they are significant. Unnecessary factors can be dispensed with.

Multiple regression analysis is a sophisticated technique that in theory produces better results than relying on trial and error, but this depends on the validity of the initial assumptions about the overall rank order. In this respect, the approach is just as specious as any other method. If the subjectively established overall rank order is wrong, what degree of confidence can be attached to the factor weightings? The technique has a circular look about it. But it all depends on the degree to which care has been exercised in choosing and analysing the benchmark jobs. This has to be done thoroughly to ensure that a soundly based scheme is developed for future use.

Advantages and disadvantages of point-factor job evaluation

Point-factor evaluation is the most popular non-proprietary brand approach because it is analytical and it at least gives the appearance of being rational and scientific, although the vision may differ from the reality. But it has come under heavy attack in recent years, not least from Ed Lawler (1986), as summarised in Chapter 2.

Advantages of point-factor schemes
The *advantages* of point-factor schemes are:

☐ Evaluators are forced to consider a range of factors which, as long as they are present in all the jobs and affect them in different ways, reduce the danger of the oversimplified judgements that can be made when using non-analytical schemes.

☐ Point schemes provide evaluators with defined yardsticks which should help them to achieve some degree of objectivity and consistency in making their judgements.

☐ They at least appear to be objective (even if they are not), and this quality makes people feel that they are fair.

☐ They provide a rationale which helps in the design of graded pay structures (see Chapter 9).

☐ They can assist in matching jobs when making external comparisons for market pricing purposes.

☐ They can be acceptable in equal-value cases as long as the factor plan is not discriminatory.

☐ They adapt well to computerisation (see Chapter 10).

Disadvantages of point-factor schemes
The *disadvantages* of point-factor schemes are:

☐ They are complex to develop, install and maintain.

☐ They give a somewhat spurious impression of scientific accuracy – it is still necessary to use judgement in selecting factors, defining levels within factors, deciding on weightings, and interpreting information about the jobs in relation to the definitions of factors and factor levels.

☐ They assume that it is possible to quantify different aspects of jobs on the same scale of values and then add them together. But the attributes and job characteristics cannot necessarily be added together in this way.

Apart from the complexity issue, however, this list of disadvantages simply confirms that we already know about any form of job evaluation. It cannot guarantee total objectivity or absolute accuracy in sizing jobs. It can do no more than provide a broad indication of where jobs should be placed in a pay structure in relation to other jobs. But the analytical nature of point-factor rating will at least give a more accurate indication than non-analytical methods. If this method is used carefully, the results are more likely to be acceptable (to be felt fair), and a sound basis for dealing with equal value issues will have been established. Additionally, and importantly, point-factor evaluation provides a good basis for designing a graded pay structure.

Conclusions

Point-factor rating is the most popular approach because people generally feel that it works. And so it does, in the sense that if carried out properly it is seen to be analytical, thorough, and fair as a means of determining internal relative values.

But it is still a big leap from the ranking produced by the evaluation to devising a grade structure – this can be mainly a trial-and-error process. And the jobs still have to be priced, which is largely judgemental. Furthermore, people can be well satisfied with the progress of a job evaluation exercise until they find out how it affects their pay. Whatever protestations are made by management to the contrary, employees usually feel that job evaluation equals more pay. This stage of the process can cause a lot of grief and has to be very carefully handled.

It is still possible to be uncomfortable about the impression of accuracy conveyed by scoring jobs. The quantification of subjective judgements does not make them any more objective and gives an entirely spurious impression of scientific accuracy. Emerson (1991) believes that 'The actual distinction between jobs in organisations are neither measured nor empirically accounted for in point-factor schemes.'

In considering evaluation points (or, indeed, any other quantified approach to summing up people) one can sympathise with the feelings of Paul Dombey (Dickens, 1846) who, after being force-fed knowledge at Doctor Blimber's academy, was confronted by Miss Blimber with an 'Analysis of the character of P. Dombey':

> 'I find that the natural capacity of Dombey is extremely good, and that his general disposition to study may be stated in an equal ratio. Thus, taking eight as our standard and highest number, I find these qualities in Dombey stated each at six three-fourths.'
>
> Miss Blimber paused to see how Paul received this news. Being undecided whether six three-fourths meant six pounds fifteen, or sixpence three farthings, or six foot nine, or three quarters past six, or six somethings that he hadn't learnt yet, with three unknown something elses over, Paul rubbed his hands and looked straight at Miss Blimber. It happened to answer as well as anything else he could have done.

Perhaps any attempt to reduce people to points is likely to have the same effect.

In spite of this possible reaction, those who introduce and live with any evaluation or assessment system seem to like structure, and frequently like to quantify everything within that structure. So point-factor schemes work for them.

As already noted in the first part of this book, however, job evaluation in its traditional points scheme form is being challenged as inflexible, bureaucratic, hierarchical, time-consuming, over-complex, expensive, and oriented to jobs rather than people.

Many job evaluation experts recognise that job evaluation has to be applied much more flexibility and treated as a process rather than a rigid system which, when the right buttons are pressed, produces the right answer. In addition, new approaches to job evaluation and grading are being advocated and introduced (more the former than the latter), as discussed in later chapters. These include:

□ the development of competence-based approaches (see Chapter 6)

□ the introduction of more flexible broad-banded pay structures (see Chapter 9)

□ the use of computer-assisted job evaluation (CAJE) techniques which cut out much of the tedium of the process and are claimed to produce better results than traditional manual methods (see Chapter 10).

6

COMPETENCE–BASED

JOB EVALUATION

It has been suggested by Edwards *et al.* (1994) that: 'Traditional job-based pay is evolving to people-based pay, which focuses on individual competences and demonstrated performance rather than job title or grade.' Ed Lawler in his article on 'What's wrong with point-factor job evaluation' (1986) believed that skill- or knowledge-based pay systems showed promise as an alternative to job-based pay.

Much greater significance is now attached to knowledge work in organisations, and more emphasis is being placed on flexibility, multiskilling, individual and team autonomy, and empowerment. These developments have combined with the thrust to extend and increase levels of skill and competence to meet new challenges in a highly competitive environment. The need is to reinforce the message that job evaluation is about people as well as about jobs.

People-related pay approaches are usually described as competence-based, skill-based or knowledge-based, and these terms are defined in the first section of this chapter together with a working definition of the concept of competence. The following aspects of competence-based job evaluation are then discussed: its aims, its methodology, its advantages and disadvantages, and its uses. The chapter concludes with a review of skill-based job evaluation.

Definitions

Competence
The concept of competence is all-pervading in personnel management circles today. But it is one that is bedevilled by jargon, semantics and many different definitions, some more

meaningful than others. For practical purposes it can simply be regarded as the ability to meet performance expectations in a role and to deliver the required results. Put another way, competence is about

☐ what you need to know
☐ what you need to do
☐ how you need to do it.

The concept of competence therefore refers to applied knowledge and skills, performance delivery, and the behaviours required to get things done well.

Competence-based pay

Competence-based pay relates grading and rewards to the achievement of defined levels of competence. Competence levels and achievements can influence pay in two ways:

☐ by defining the relative values of roles in competence terms and on this basis allocating jobs into grades or bands within an organisation-wide or job family pay structure – this may be described as *competence-based job evaluation* which assesses job worth wholly or partly by reference to the levels of competence required in the role

☐ by relating pay progression to competence only, or to a combination of competence and performance in achieving objectives – this may be described as *competence-based pay progression*, and is usually based on some form of performance management process.

This chapter concentrates on the job evaluation aspect of competence-based pay, although competence-based pay progression processes can be fitted into a pay structure which may or may not have been designed with the help of a conventional job evaluation scheme. Progression within the broad bands of such a structure (as described in Chapter 9) may be related to the development and successful application of competences in an expanding role.

Skill-based pay

Skill-based pay is a payment method in which pay progression is linked to the kind, number, and depth of skills that individuals acquire and use. It is a term which most frequently refers to manual workers' pay systems.

Knowledge-based pay

The term 'knowledge-based pay' is used mainly in the United States, more or less synonymously with 'skill-based pay'. The distinction between knowledge and skill often seems to be confused in US definitions. For example, Ziskin (1986) describes knowledge-based pay (KBP) thus:

> Unlike traditional pay systems that affix a rate or range of pay to a particular job, KBP systems call for the assignment of a pay rate to the individual employee. This pay rate increases as the employee acquires additional skills. Because of the emphasis on measurable skill acquisition, KBP is most commonly found in production-oriented environments.

To avoid confusion we are using the term 'skill-based pay' to embrace knowledge-based pay.

The aim of competence-based job evaluation

Competence-based job evaluation aims to value the work people do in terms of the competences required to perform effectively in different roles and at different levels in the organisation. It measures both the value of roles and the contribution of people against the same criteria. So if an analytical process determines that a role requires a particular level of competence in, say, leadership, then that could be translated into a standard of competent performance for the individual in that role. This standard of leadership together with standards developed for other aspects of the role could become yardsticks by which pay progression can be determined and performance, potential, and training and development needs assessed. They can also form the basis for role and person specifications to be used in making recruitment and promotion decisions.

A competence-based approach can thus help in the development and implementation of integrated human resource management processes. Job evaluation becomes – as it should be – an integral part of those processes, not just an 'add-on' administered by the personnel department.

Using the concept

Within an organisation the value of a role can be measured ultimately only in terms of the performance delivered by the person in that role and the impact of that performance on business results. This is the output part of the input-process-output model described in Chapter 5. The level of performance achieved depends on the behaviour of individuals, however, and that represents the process part of the model. And because the concept of competence embodies the ability to use knowledge and skills effectively, these should be included as representing the input aspect of the model – the attributes required of individuals to perform well.

The question could be asked: 'What is the difference between this model and any other type of analytical scheme which incorporates input, process and output factors?' And the answer is: 'Precious little, *as long as those factors refer to relevant behavioural dimensions and cover the key output areas in a way that reflects the expectations of performance in terms of the standards and results required in those areas.*' This is exactly what should be incorporated in a good factor plan. But it is also precisely what many traditional plans do not contain.

The value of a competence-based approach to job evaluation is that it captures what people in their roles are expected to do and to achieve, taking into account the dynamic elements of those roles. It is not imprisoned within the cramped confines of a belief that evaluation is just about static jobs. According to this concept, competence-based evaluation enhances rather than replaces conventional analytical forms of evaluation. Although it is concerned with the input/process elements of roles, it recognises that the purpose of a role is to achieve results; it therefore focuses attention on output (required performance) as well as the competences and skills needed to deliver it in the context of a flexible working environment.

Typology

Competence-based job evaluation concentrates on people in their roles, not jobs. There are three varieties, as described below, two of which resemble traditional methods (point-factor and job classification schemes), except that the emphasis is on competences rather than the traditional factors or criteria used in such schemes. The third type is far more radical, in that there is no 'scheme', only an approach which evaluates people in their roles on an individual basis.

Point-factor competence-based evaluation

This is the most common approach. It is, broadly, the one adopted by the National & Provincial Building Society and currently being developed at Triplex Safety Glass. The headings in the factor plan consist entirely or mainly of core or generic competences included in a competence framework. The levels at which the generic competences can be applied in roles are defined and scores are allocated to each level. The competence-based factors may not be weighted. Individual role competence profiles are defined, and are compared with the generic competence level definitions and scored in exactly the same way as in a conventional point-factor scheme. A broad-banded structure is likely to be adopted, the bands defined in points terms and roles allocated to bands accordingly. Within the bands pay is related to market rates, and progression depends on individual levels of competence and contribution. There may be no upper limits – progress is governed by the capacity of individuals to develop their competences, expand their roles by taking on new responsibilities, and deliver performance to meet or exceed expectations.

Role classification competence-based job evaluation

In this approach the grades in a broad-banded structure are defined generally as in a job classification scheme, but the grade definitions are expressed in terms of the organisation's core or generic competences. Roles are slotted into bands on the basis of comparisons between individual competence profiles and the band definition. Progression within and between the bands takes place as described above. Alternatively, a job family structure is adopted in which the levels in the job family are defined in competence terms. Pay progresses within the job family along curves related to individual competence and contribution.

Individually based competence-related role evaluation

This approach is based on a broad-banded or job family structure. The bands may be designated very broadly by reference to generic roles – for example, process direction, process management, team leaders, process implementation – but no attempt is made to define them in competence terms. Progress within and between bands is related to individual competence and contribution, as demonstrated by the capacity to take on additional responsibilities and new roles.

Methodology

There are three approaches to developing competence-based job evaluation:

□ Take an existing analytical scheme and modify the factor plan to make it more competence-related by reference to an existing competence framework.

□ Take existing competence frameworks and adapt them to develop a competence-based scheme.

□ Conduct a special analysis of generic and job-specific competences to produce a competency framework and develop a scheme from this analysis.

The first approach would lead to a competence-based approach covering all the employees catered for by the existing job evaluation scheme. The second and third approaches could be used to produce either a competence-based scheme covering the whole organisation or one that applies to job families within the organisation.

Adapting an existing scheme

The first step to take when adapting a scheme by reference to an existing competence framework is to analyse the scheme's factors to identify those that appear to fit the framework (possibly with some modification) and those that do not fit at all. It is then necessary to review those factors that do fit within the competency framework and decide whether any additional factors are required.

Adapting an existing competence framework to create a job evaluation plan

This method starts by taking the existing competence framework as a basis for a factor plan which, apart from the inclusion of competence headings, would resemble a conventional point-factor scheme. It is most unlikely that the plan would follow precisely the elements in that framework. The guidelines set out below on what constitutes a good competence-based factor would have to be taken into account. And to ensure that everything which contributes to establishing the value of a job is considered, additional headings might have to be introduced that were not covered by the existing framework and might not, strictly speaking, be competences at all. The result could turn out to be a hybrid set of competence-based and other input or output factors. And this is the most likely result, whether starting from scratch or adapting an existing scheme. Such schemes could be better described as competence-related than competence-based.

Alternatively, an existing framework of work-based or occupational competences could be analysed and adapted to fit into a job family environment in which each level in the family is defined in terms of competence levels.

Developing a completely new competence-framework and competence-related job evaluation plan

This is the most radical approach and requires the initial definition of generic competences, followed by the development of a method of evaluation, which may be computerised. Conceptually, the development process could proceed by starting with an analysis of corporate requirements and then developing generic competence frameworks.

At corporate level, this would be a matter of reviewing and analysing strategic plans and the external and internal environment. The organisation's goals and the critical success factors which determine whether or not those goals are achieved can then be identified. Critical success factors could cover such areas as the levels of competence required of members of the organisation, innovation, quality, customer service, cost, leadership and flexibility. It would also be necessary to analyse the core competences of the organisation in such areas of expertise as technical, scientific, professional, marketing, manufacturing and product development.

The generic competences required for people in roles as individuals or team members should be derived directly from the corporate analysis of strategic goals, critical success factors and core competences. The processes of competence analysis, profiling and mapping required to develop a competence framework must flow from these analyses at corporate level – competence has no significance in itself. It cannot be considered in isolation. It is only relevant if it contributes to delivered performance by being directed at the achievement of corporate goals, meeting critical success factors and underpinning the effective use of the core competences of the organisation.

But the analysis should not be confined to generic behavioural competences. What organisations must also concentrate on is the *work* required to deliver results – the occupation-related competences that determine the extent to which what is done achieves the required standards of performance and output.

The outcome of this analysis could be a point-factor competence-related scheme, a role classification scheme, or a job family structure as described in the next three sections of this chapter. Alternatively, it could form the basis of an individual competence-related approach as described above.

Developing a competence-related point-factor job evaluation scheme

The process of developing a competence-related point-factor evaluation scheme is much the same as that described in the last chapter for a conventional points scheme – ie a factor plan has to be produced, and this requires the selection of factors, the definition of factor levels, and the development of factor scales following a decision on how the factors should be weighted.

The difference is, of course, that competence-related job

evaluation is based on a competence framework which provides the starting-point for selecting factors and defining levels. The aim is to develop a plan that is related as closely as possible to that framework so that first, people factors are taken fully into account when valuing roles, and second, an integrated approach can be evolved which uses the competence framework for a number of interrelated human resource management processes, namely human resource planning, selection, performance management, training and continuous development, as well as reward. However, additions and amendments to the existing competence framework may have to be made to cover all the input-process-output factors required for a fully rounded evaluation to take place.

Identifying the factors

The first step in developing a competence-based factor plan for job evaluation purposes is to identify the factors. As McHale (1990) notes, some factors can easily be translated into a job demand and a statement of the skill or competence required. He suggests that a competence area such as analytical ability or strategic perspective easily lends itself to being turned into an evaluation area. But he dismisses the idea that a factor such as accountability can be translated into a competency: 'How can one recognise an accountancy competency or a number of staff reporting competency? It is these redundant factors that need to be replaced with dynamic competency-based ones.'

McHale also rejects the idea of including physical effort/skill as a factor: 'Including them in a competency approach is of no real value because it will only be used marginally to adjust an evaluation score.'

A competence-based approach may eliminate factors specifically referring to education, training and experience. What matters is the knowledge and skills acquired by these means, and what people do with them, rather than how they were acquired.

The factors included in a competence-based system should

☐ spell out the underlying skills and competences required
   to meet the demands of roles at different levels in the

organisation or within a job family – this implies that it is possible to define levels at which any particular competence or cluster of competences are required

☐ cover all the areas of behaviour and performance that need to be valued in order to establish the worth of a job

☐ contribute specifically to the creation of added value by people in their roles, taking into account the goals and critical success factors of the organisation

☐ reflect and reinforce the core competences and values of the organisation

☐ be able to cope with rapidly changing and flexible roles.

Selecting the factors

When deciding what competence-related factors should be included it is probably best to forget the semantics that seem inevitably to be associated with the competence industry. It is better to concentrate on a very simple overall notion of what sort of factors should be considered when measuring the value of jobs, roles and people. The possible factors include:

Input factors
☐ communicating skills, written and oral
☐ information technology skills
☐ interpersonal skills – customer relations, negotiating, selling and training, etc.
☐ numerical skills
☐ physical skills – manual dexterity etc.
☐ thinking and reasoning skills
☐ professional, scientific or technical knowledge
☐ knowledge of internal processes, systems, procedures, products and services
☐ knowledge of the business, and the economic and political environment in which the organisation operates

Process factors
☐ decision-making
☐ handling complexity
☐ innovating

- managing resources – people, money, equipment, etc.
- operating flexibly
- planning and organising
- problem-solving
- strategic perspective
- team leadership
- teamworking

Output factors
- contribution
- delivery of results
- impact
- influence

In addition a competence-based factor plan may have to include what might be termed demand factors, which refer to mental and physical effort and working conditions.

This is by no means an exhaustive list and every organisation can select from it or add to it in accordance with its own priorities and culture and the roles to be covered by job evaluation – there is no such thing as a standard set of competence-related factors. It is also important to take account of equal-value considerations.

Factor definitions should be prepared in accordance with the guidelines set out in Chapter 5.

Completing the factor plan

The factor plan is completed by defining factor levels, deciding on weighting, and producing factor level scales. The procedure is the same as that followed in designing conventional points scheme factor plans. And this is hardly surprising for a competence-related scheme based on factors is essentially a point-factor system. The only thing that is different is the type of factors used.

It has, however, been proposed by Tijou (1991) that in a competence-related scheme a simple split between the different levels could be

- the implementation of a competence in a particular role
- the management of that implementation

☐ the development of the resources and requirements of the organisation

☐ the definition of direction.

These broad bands could be subdivided to reflect the organisation's structure and the role categories covered by the scheme.

Tijou gives an example of level definitions for decision-making using this framework:

☐ *Operating* Uses available data to make good decisions within own area of work.

☐ *Managing implementation* Seeks quantitative and qualitative data to assist with decision-making within a team's area of responsibility.

☐ *Developing resources and requirements* Actively manages quantitative and qualitative data related to management function; makes good decisions affecting management unit activity within required time limits.

☐ *Setting direction* Expertly integrates quantitative and qualitative data from wide range of sources inside and outside the company; makes consistently sound decisions with impact upon corporate direction.

Examples of competence-based factor and level definitions are given in Appendix C.

Developing a role classification scheme

The first step in developing a role classification scheme is simply to decide how many bands are required. This decision should not be arbitrary. It should be based instead on organisational analysis to determine which are the distinguishable main levels of work carried out in the organisation under such headings as strategic and policy direction, managing functions and processes, leading operational, professional or support teams, and implementing as members of such teams.

The next step is to define each of the bands in terms of generic competences. Preferably, the band definitions should deal with each competence separately, and in this respect the method becomes analytical. For example, the leadership headings in a four-band structure could be defined thus:

1   Operate as a member of a work group or team, responding to leadership and working with the team leader to achieve team targets and standards.

2   Lead an operational, technical, or professional group or project team, or a support group in which leadership skills are required, to develop a committed and cohesive group capable of achieving its targets by processes of self-management and control.

3   Lead a department, function, or major project/process in which acute leadership challenges may have to be met involving real issues of managing change and relationships with people.

4   High-profile leadership role in which the leader faces tough challenges across the organisation in improving performance, getting results and dealing with employee-relations issues.

Finally, profiles for individual roles are developed under the same headings and used as the basis for matching the role with the band definition.

Competence-based job evaluation in job families

A job family is a group of jobs in which the essential nature and purpose of the work is similar but the work is carried out at different levels. The jobs within a family may be linked in any of the following ways:

□   the nature of the work undertaken – eg administration, data processing, customer relations
□   the technical or professional discipline – eg science, engineering, design, creative working, accountancy, personnel
□   a common function – eg production or sales management
□   a hierarchy in a regionalised organisation – eg regional, area and branch managers
□   actually the same job but a function at a different levels – eg branch manager.

Within each type of job family there are a number of common factors, but there are also differentiating factors that can be used to distinguish the various levels of work.

Traditional forms of job evaluation do not work well for roles in which the competences of individuals largely determine the level at which they operate, the impact they make, and the influence they exert on the delivery of results. In this type of environment it is difficult (if not impossible) to separate the job from the person. The level at which individuals operate may have everything to do with their knowledge, skills and competence, and nothing to do with the size of the resources they control (if any). This applies particularly to roles carried out by scientists, designers, development engineers, researchers, creative people, and professional and knowledge workers. In these circumstances a job family approach may be appropriate because it recognises through rewards that people within a job family have the opportunity continually to develop and expand their range of competences and, therefore, the level of their contribution.

Using competences to define job family levels

Competences can be used to define job family levels as long as they focus on actions and outcomes as well as personal attributes and behaviours.

Job family levels may be defined as a whole, and this becomes a form of job classification, except that the definitions are produced on the basis of a rigorous process of competence and functional analysis, as described in Chapter 8. To facilitate comparisons it may be useful to set out level definitions in a job family under a set of competence headings, as illustrated in Table 6.1.

Some job families are more diverse than others and may be divided into homogeneous groups. For example, a professional engineer job family could be divided into design, development, and project engineers. As Pritchard and Murlis (1992) suggest, this broad family approach is more appropriate when career development is not simply up a series of parallel ladders but includes diagonal moves as people gain experience in a variety of roles: 'What is wanted is a wide staircase or scrambling-net which can accommodate a diversity of roles and career paths.' An approach along these lines may alleviate what is perhaps the biggest drawback to job families – that

Table 6.1
EXTRACT FROM LEVEL DESCRIPTIONS FOR RESEARCH GROUP JOB FAMILY

	Level	Level 2	Level 3
Leadership	Leads teams of professional scientists and technicians	Leads project teams of professional scientists and technicians	Conducts scientific experiments as a member of a multi-disciplinary team
Project management	Coordinates and controls a number of research projects	Controls research project to achieve objectives and deadlines	Monitors own performance as a team member against project objectives and deadlines
Performance	Delivers and communicates results as agreed in overall development programme	Delivers and communicates results as agreed for project programme	Delivers expected results as a team member
Relationships	Maintains close links with (a) customer group managers, and (b) relevant external research institutions to ensure that (i) their needs are being met, and (ii) up-to-date information is obtained on latest developments and best research practice	Liaises with customer group team leaders to ensure that the project is meeting their needs	Contributes to building and maintaining good relationships inside the team and with colleagues in other units
Budgetary control	Exercises budgetary control for unit	Exercises budgetary control for project	Keeps within budgeted limits of expenditure for work on project

they confine people into separate categories and therefore inhibit flexibility in developing their capacity to take on different or wider responsibilities in other functions or occupations.

Rates of pay within job families can be fixed by comparison, level by level and factor by factor, with other job families. They also have to be aligned to market rates, and some organisations treat job families as separate market groups, their pay levels determined primarily by market forces.

This approach, however, could lead to internal inequities and equal-value problems when comparisons are made between job family rates of pay and those applied to the rest of the organisation. In these circumstances it may be appropriate to use a more conventional point-factor or other analytical form of job evaluation to provide a 'read-across'.

Advantages and disadvantages of competence-based job evaluation

As was made clear earlier in this chapter, the difference between competence-based and other types of evaluation – especially analytical methods – may be partly one of substance (ie a focus on competences) but it is not necessarily one of form. When considering the advantages and disadvantages of this approach it is therefore necessary to address the substance issue: what are the advantages of using competences in a point-factor, role classification or job family scheme, or as a general approach to valuing people?

Advantages
Competence-based job evaluation can

☐ direct attention to the things that really matter in delivering performance

☐ focus on roles

☐ provide for jobs and people to be measured against the same criteria

☐ clarify 'aiming points' – the requirements that need to be met to advance or broaden a career

☐ provide a framework for continuous development and self-managed learning

- help to extend the skill-base of an organisation
- play an important part in developing a coherent approach to human resource management in which policies and processes interact and are mutually supportive.

Disadvantages

Competence-based job evaluation

- depends on the definition of competences and competence levels through functional and other forms of analysis – but competence frameworks are too often developed without sufficiently rigorous analysis, and factor or level definitions are vague, obscure or irrelevant
- can be just as bureaucratic and difficult to introduce and manage as any other form of job evaluation
- requires competence frameworks to be constantly updated, and this is time-consuming and easily neglected
- could lead to problems with equal value – gender bias can just as easily creep into a competence-based pay system as into any other system and there could be real difficulties in assessing comparative worth unless a more conventional factor comparison scheme is used to supplement it (and why should the process of job evaluation be further complicated in this way?); it is also possible that generic role definitions could be discriminatory
- depends on a clear understanding of the slippery and often confusing language of competences
- can contain jargon and complexities which too easily become part of an 'over-engineered' system that is unacceptable to line managers (leaving it as the property of the personnel department)
- can lead to over-emphasis on inputs rather than outputs; knowledge, skills and behaviour rather than results.

The last point is important. Murlis and Fitt (1991) have expressed caution about the use of competences for job evaluation, warning that they can only serve as differentiators of job (or person) size if two provisions are fulfilled: first, they must relate to a particular set of accountabilities or role elements; and second, there must be management processes in place for assessing the acquisition of competences and the numbers of people required to deliver the total load. As they point out:

> If the second condition is not fulfilled, a competency-based approach runs the risk of getting out of control. Recommending competency acquisition for its own sake may be satisfactory for the individual manager who wants to reward this and encourage individual development, but it can be costly for any organisation because it may be paying for what it cannot use.

Users of competence-based job evaluation

Competence-based job evaluation can work in any type of business, but it is particularly appropriate in organisations with numbers of knowledge workers where the emphasis is on people in flexible and developing roles rather than on rigid job hierarchies. It can be relevant in project- and process-based organisations in which this type of role flexibility is important and where the contribution of people can be significantly and measurably enhanced if they acquire additional skills and competences *and* are able to use them to good effect. It can work well in job families.

A good reason for adopting this approach is the opportunity it gives to integrate organisational core competences and individual competences. But it can only function effectively if the business believes in the power of competence analysis, evaluation and assessment as a means of improving performance and of achieving added value and competitive advantage through people.

Above all, it should be remembered that competence-based job evaluation is often simply an enhancement of traditional job evaluation methods which can work in some circumstances but not in others. It succeeds if the organisation sees competence development as a priority. It fails if those introducing it are simply jumping on the competence bandwagon without appreciating the need for a rigorous approach to the development of competence frameworks and their translation into evaluation factors.

Competence-based job evaluation in action
The following case-studies arose from our research and describe approaches to developing and operating competence-based job evaluation.

Retail organisation
We found an example of a competence-based job evaluation scheme in a small retail organisation. There are five competence levels covering all staff.

Entry Level equates to the level of competence that staff are expected to have on joining. It is not necessarily specific to retail and is more about customer service and willingness to be flexible. Specific qualities looked for at entry level are an outgoing personality and team skills.

Operational Level is the level of competence which all joiners are expected to attain within three to four months.

Advanced Level includes some supervisory skills and means the individual can deputise for some management activities.

Deputy manager is the first level of management and includes all the competences needed to run a small team.

Manager includes the competences necessary to manage staff and take part in the management activities of the organisation. It also requires people to be flexible and mobile.

The competence levels build upon one another and it is possible, depending upon performance, to progress rapidly through them. Pay equates directly to level of competence, and each grade has a pay band. At managers' discretion, and with advice from personnel, high performers can be paid higher in the pay band.

National & Provincial Building Society
The National & Provincial Building Society has been going through a period of intensive change. Following an organisation re-design, which included a business process re-engineering exercise, the Society's organisation has been transformed from one based on functional hierarchies to one that is essentially process-based with an emphasis on team and project work. The Society reduced its 17 grades to the following four main role areas or levels:

- directing processes
- managing requirements and resources
- leading teams
- implementing in teams.

During this period the traditional analytical job evaluation scheme was effectively abandoned because, as the Chief Executive said, it reinforced hierarchy and encouraged empire-building. What has now been introduced is a competence-based approach. Competencies are defined as 'the knowledge, skills, attitudes and behaviour required to effectively carry out roles within N&P'. They are described in terms of behaviour – 'what an individual is seen to do, or what a role-holder should be able to do'. What has been evolved is a competency framework that supports a completely integrated approach to human resource management.

The intention was to design a competency framework that would both reflect the organisation design and 'how people behave when they are successful'. Role statements are produced for all roles. They are developed as appropriate from generic statements. The role statements are then used to create role competency profiles which describe the organisational and 'process-specific competencies' that are required by the roles.

This role competency profile is developed through a Role Competency Assessment Document by team leaders assisted by a role assessment adviser, usually an HR adviser. There are three sections in this document:

- *Style of play* – in which the measures are achievement, making the most of opportunities, learning/development, continuous improvement, challenge, openness, creating enthusiasm, and team play
- *Individual competencies* – in which the measures are conceptual thinking, creativity, resilience, clarifying issues, gaining commitment, ensuring understanding, agreeing contribution, prioritisation, optimising the use of resources, developing self and others, problem solving, measuring and improving
- *Business competencies* – in which the measures are under-

standing the external environment, applying analytical techniques, planning, process design and development and improvement, managing projects, developing customer requirements programmes, developing external relationships, meeting customer requirements, property management assessment and valuation, implementation processing, legal and regulatory concerns, human resource management, organisation support, systems, and accountancy and finance.

How competencies are demonstrated in different roles is indicated by a scale of seven points on each of the above 35 competency measures. The instructions for completing the document state that: 'You must score "what" and "how" the role is required to contribute, not what it is "nice" to have, or is only occasionally required. Your first question should therefore be – Is this competency required in this role? If it is required, then one of the seven descriptions will match what is needed in the role and the relevant box should be ticked.'

This 'role competency profile analysis' process is used to help in the allocation of roles to one of the four levels in the organisation. It is done by scoring each of the measures on a scale of from 1 to 7, and competency system software developed in-house is used to generate an overall score for each role. The scoring process produces clusters of roles that reflect the four organisational role levels (some roles fall between the clusters but they have been allocated to one or other of the adjoining clusters following further analysis and consideration).

There is a minimum salary for each level, but no maximum is defined. The aim is to make the structure as broad and flexible as possible so that individuals can progress and develop their competences in their roles. Individual progress is related to the development and application of the competences (the match between the individual's competence and the competency requirements of his/her role) and the contribution. Individuals are paid more as they develop and use additional competences, but it has to be demonstrated that the competences are required for the role. They can, in fact, progress as far as their role requires. There are no artificial limits. Market rate data is used to support managers and team leaders in making judgements about the appropriate reward for specific roles.

Roger Stones, Manager of Roles, Resources and Responsibilities, lists the aims of this process as follows:

□ to provide a picture/description of the competencies and abilities required to play a role (the role profile)

□ to provide an indication of the overall degree of competence required by the role through a 'scoring' process

□ to be able to assess the nature of a role

□ to support
  – team design
  – manpower resource planning
  – succession planning
  – individual development
  – career path planning
  – recruitment and selection.

He emphasises that role profiling and assessment is now only an indirect support to the reward process.

Pilkington Optronics

The foundation of the Pilkington Optronics scheme is a comprehensive and detailed company-wide analysis of competences. The competence analysis process begins at the top level in each of the functions within the company. The analyses of the other jobs in the function are regarded as sub-sets of the top job.

The technique used is functional analysis. It starts with a definition of the overall purpose or mission of the function – 'what it is there to do'. In effect the manager begins with a blank sheet and identifies all the skills and competences required to carry out the work. This covers

□ where the job best fits under the main functional area headings of technical, operations, commerce, operational management, and organisation management

□ the sub-functional areas – eg within the technical function these would be science, information systems, engineering, and technical expertise

□ the essential competences as derived from the functional

analysis – this defines the competences, indicating for each competence its frequency of use, criticality, and time to train, and grouping them under a major competence heading

☐ any other functional experience that would be useful in the job, and the competences required.

The analysis is agreed by the jobholder(s). An extract from the form used for competence analysis is given in Appendix D.

On the basis of the initial functional and competence analysis, the manager considers what jobs could be combined on the basis of an appropriate grouping of competences ('route-mapping'). This may involve the application in the redesigned job of a wider range of competences and, therefore, multi-skilling. For example, where there could have originally have been ten or so job-titles these could be amalgamated into one job-title and all the previous ten jobholders would now be assigned to the new job. (In fact, this was subject to a review at a later stage.)

The job evaluation is carried out by a panel chaired by a line-manager and comprising equal numbers of management and trade union representatives.

Expert Choice software is used as a decision-making tool by the panel to enable paired comparisons to be made on competence dimensions in the following manner:

1 Functional areas:
   ☐ evaluators assess the relative importance of each functional area on a verbal nine-point scale (from equal to extremely strong)
   ☐ *Expert Choice* converts the verbal evaluation into a numerical (percentage) weighting – 100 per cent overall divided between the functional areas – eg technical 70 per cent, operations 30 per cent

2 Sub-functional areas – the same process is used for sub-functional areas so that, for example, the 70 per cent weighting for technical could be divided into science 20 per cent, information systems 20 per cent, technical expertise 15 per cent, and engineering 15 per cent

3 Competence headings (up to seven) – each of these is assigned to a sub-function – eg engineering – and the

relative importance of each heading within that sub-process is again weighted with the help of *Expert Choice*; for example, design could be weighted as 10 per cent out of engineering's total of 15 per cent

4   Individual competences – these are weighted within each competence heading by the same technique.

The total sum of all the weightings calculated by the above process should add up to 100 per cent.

A computerised model has been created that defines all the competences which have been identified by the competence-mapping process described above. It sets out the weightings under each heading for all the amalgamated jobs established by this exercise.

Using the model, data is input by the manager on each individual jobholder in the newly defined jobs in terms of the competency/skill levels he/she possesses. This is done on a six-point scale:

- □ expert
- □ advanced
- □ skilled
- □ part-skilled
- □ little skill
- □ no skill.

This assessment is agreed with the jobholder and is used to produce a rank order. The rank order provides the basis for sorting jobholders into the new graded structure.

Triplex Safety Glass

At Triplex Safety Glass a new grade and pay structure is being developed following a business process re-engineering exercise. This resulted in the organisation's being re-structured and slimmed down. It also initiated a culture change programme which emphasised customer focus.

The pay and reward project prompted by these developments fully involved the four trade unions. The overall strategy was to improve the ways in which individual and team performance were recognised and to emphasise the acquisition and application of relevant skills and competences.

The pay and reward project was managed by a multifunctional steering committee which included trade union representatives. The project team was also multifunctional, with trade union members. It was facilitated by Anne-Marie Southall of Coopers & Lybrand.

Commitment and policy statements, as set out below, were produced by the senior management team and further developed by the project team.

Commitment statement

Skilled people committed to supplying the customer needs for Automotive Safety Glass extremely well and, as a result, earning rewards for both the company and themselves.

Pay and reward policy statement

Triplex Safety Glass Ltd is committed to understanding and satisfying customer requirements, empowering, involving and developing its employees, and providing a return on investment to its shareholders. This Pay and Reward Policy recognises that employees should receive fair and equitable reward and remuneration for achieving business objectives.

Pay and Reward should recognise individual competence and contribution whilst also rewarding work group performance at a level that is competitive to ensure that Triplex can attract, retain and motivate a capable workforce.

The project team works within the framework of those statements. Its aim is to develop a pay and reward structure that would enable the maximisation of the contribution, commitment and development of all members of the organisation, as individuals and as team members. This was amplified into a statement of what the overall objectives of the programme were.

The project team summarised the approach to the pay and reward study thus:

1   Best business practice
2   Employee involvement
3   Team approach

4   Other studies (eg training)
- □ attendance to one study only
- □ across the sites (business)

5   Make us better
- □ people
- □ in our roles
- □ for the future

6   Management commitment
- □ give direction
- □ enable positive results
- □ assist selling
- □ effect implementation.

These statements were disseminated to all employees as part of a comprehensive communications programme designed to achieve complete transparency for the project.

The team has proceeded to take part in the development of generic role profiles which spell out the purpose of the role, key accountabilities and competences.

A competence-based job evaluation scheme is being developed and implemented. The factors incorporated in the scheme are

1   professional knowledge/ experience
2   functional skills
3   organisational skills
4   communication (interpersonal) skills
5   initiative/problem-solving

Work is proceeding currently (June 1995) towards the development of a broad-banded integrated pay structure on the basis of the evaluations.

Skill-based pay

Skill-based pay is a payment system in which pay progression is linked to the number, kind and depth of the skills that individuals develop and use. It usually focuses on paying for the horizontal acquisition of the skills required to undertake a wider range of tasks. But it may also pay for the vertical development of the skills needed to operate at a higher level, or the development in depth of existing skills. Skill-based pay can be regarded as a form of job evaluation in that it relates job grades and pay to the acquisition and application of skills, mainly those exercised by manual workers.

Skill-based pay systems are introduced to enlarge the skills base of organisations and to encourage flexibility through multiskilling. They are people- rather than job-oriented. Individuals are paid for the skills they are capable of using (as long as those skills are necessary), not for the job they happen to be doing at the time. There may be a basic job rate for individuals with the minimum level of skills, but above that level they are paid for what they can do themselves and as members of teams.

How skill-based pay works

There are many varieties of skill-based pay, but a typical scheme for operatives is likely to have the following features:

☐ the scheme is based on defined skill blocks or modules – clusters or sets of skills which the organisation is willing to reward with extra pay

☐ the type and number of skill blocks that individuals need to learn and can learn are defined

☐ the successful acquisition of the skills contained in a skills block or module results in an increment to base pay

☐ the incremental skills payments are limited to a defined hierarchy or range of skills

☐ the order in which the skills must be acquired in a skills hierarchy may be defined, or more freedom is allowed to build up a range of skill blocks (this freedom may however be restricted by defining the basic skills that have to be acquired first)

☐ training modules and programmes are defined for each skill block to provide what is sometimes referred to as the necessary 'cross-training'

☐ the training and/or the acquisition of the skills within a module is usually accredited by organisations such as the National Council for Vocational Qualifications, the Engineering Training Authority, or the City and Guilds

Institute. Alternatively or additionally, the training may be certified by the company and/or an education and training institution.

Problems with skill-based pay

Skill-based pay systems are expensive to introduce and maintain. They require a considerable investment in skills analysis, training and testing. Although a skill-based scheme in theory only pays for necessary skills, in practice individuals do not use them all at the same time, and some may be used infrequently, if at all. Inevitably, therefore, payroll costs increase. If this is added to the cost of training and certification, the total of additional costs may be considerable. The advocates of skill-based pay claim that their schemes are self-financing because of the resulting increases in productivity and operational efficiency. But there is little evidence that this is the case, and there is some indication from the research carried out by Cross (1992) that companies which introduce skill-based pay schemes have underestimated the costs involved and are finding it difficult to quantify the benefits.

7

MARKET PRICING

Market pricing is the process of assessing rules of pay by reference to market rates – what similar organisations pay for comparable jobs. It takes two forms: it establishes external relativities, and it can act as a form of job evaluation in itself by using the relativities or differentials between the market rates for comparable jobs as the logic for defining internal relativities or differentials.

It also provides information on movements in market rates so that adjustments can be made to the organisations's pay structure or job rates to ensure that they remain competitive.

Market pricing is based on the assumption that it is always easy to get hold of comprehensive and accurate information on market rates. This assumption is ill-founded. The chapter therefore starts with a discussion of the concept of a market rate and the problems of obtaining accurate information. It continues with an assessment of methods of getting market rate data, and how such data can be used for the two purposes mentioned above.

The concept of a market rate

The first questions that arise when considering the concept of a market rate are: 'Which market?', 'Which jobs?' It is then necessary to answer the question 'Which market rates?'

Which market?

The market may be local, regional, national or international. It can be easier to get information about the local labour market, especially if this is for standard jobs in offices, on the shopfloor, in sales, or in retailing. Regional and national markets can be more difficult. It may not be possible to gain immediate access to information and it may instead be necessary to rely on special enquiries or published surveys and other data. The international market is the most difficult of all.

Which jobs?

Market rate data can be obtained more easily for some jobs than others. For typical jobs such as retail assistants, word processor operators, programmers, accountants and sales managers, even managing directors, there is plenty of information either in the public domain or accessible without too much difficulty from other sources. Jobs within a particular sector (such as the voluntary sector) may be easily priced because of the flow of information between charities and the accessibility of published survey material and even advertisements (although they should always be treated with caution).

But there are some specialised jobs for which information is always difficult to obtain without extensive enquiries – after all, some jobs within organisations may be unique or very rare indeed.

Which market rate?

The other problem is that the concept of a market rate is much more imprecise than most people think. There is no such thing as *the* market rate, except for a unique job. There is always a range of rates, even in the local labour market. Market rate data is usually expressed as a range, often the inter-quartile range – ie the difference between the lower quartile and upper quartile levels in the distribution of rates collected by the survey. (The lower quartile is a quarter of the way above the lowest figure in the distribution, and the upper quartile is a quarter of the way below the highest figure.) The inter-quartile range therefore covers the middle 50 per cent of the distribution, and the middle point of the total distribution, the median, is usually taken as the market rate.

A further difficulty is that the various published sources of data on market rates (these are listed in Armstrong and Murlis, 1994) often produce variations of as much as 25 per cent or even more between the median rates of the jobs covered by the survey or analysis. This is simply because the sample and the timing of these surveys are different, and the processes for matching jobs (comparing like with like) may in any case produce more accurate results in some surveys than in others.

When a number of sources are analysed the likelihood is that the data conflict. The temptation is to take an average, but this means committing the statistical sin of 'averaging averages', and the resulting figure will bear no relationship to any real data. But a decision has to be made on which rate to select as a datum point for comparative purposes, and this becomes a matter of judgement. What is produced may be called a 'derived market rate', the derivation being an interpretation of the likely relevance and accuracy of the different sources. Some of these are more accurate than others because of the size of the sample and/or the method of collecting information. Management consultants such as Hay, who use their own evaluation scheme as the basis for comparison, are likely to produce more accurate information on the range of market rates, but it is still necessary for organisations to decide where their own rates should be positioned. This is the pay policy of the business, sometimes called the pay stance or posture.

Pay policy

The pay policy or stance of an organisation is usually expressed explicitly or implicitly as where it wants its rates to be positioned relative to the market-place. The policy could broadly be to keep pace with the market and pay average (or median) rates. Or a business may want to be ahead of the market to enable it to attract and retain high-quality people. It may therefore pay above the median – somewhere between the median and the upper quartile, or even more. An organisation may alternatively and reluctantly have to accept that it cannot afford to pay at the median and must therefore position itself below that level.

Decisions on pay policy are influenced by the extent to which it is believed that the organisation

- □ must pay top rates to attract and retain top people
- □ can attract and retain the level of people it requires at, say, the median rate or even below the median rate
- □ cannot afford to pay more than the average and may even have to pay less.

Policy decisions on the pay stance may be made empirically on the basis of the experiences of the organisation in recruiting or losing people because pay levels are not competitive.

There need not necessarily be one pay policy extending across all occupations in the business. It may be decided for some 'market groups' that it is essential for pay levels to be highly competitive, while for others simply keeping pace with the average is sufficient. This approach could also apply to individual jobs where a deliberate decision may be made to recruit and to pay well above the average rate in order to get and to keep the right person. Such decisions, however, can erode internal equity and there is often tension between this principle and that of external competitiveness. It may also create equal value problems as discussed in Chapter 11.

Sources of market rate data

The sources of market rate data are

☐ general published surveys which cover a range of management posts and levels

☐ specialised published surveys which cover the members of a profession (such as accountants), an occupation (such as computer specialists), an industry (such as engineering), or a sector (such as charities)

☐ the database maintained by management consultants

☐ special surveys of national, local or sector employers conducted by the organisation with or without the help of consultants

☐ 'pay club' surveys – data obtained from groups of employers who exchange pay information between one another on a regular basis

☐ data in journals such as those published by Incomes Data Services and IRS Employment Review

☐ advertisements – readily available, although the data can be suspect because of the difficulty of ensuring that jobs are matched properly

☐ data from recruitment campaigns

☐ general market intelligence – keeping an eye on the marketplace by scanning newspapers and maintaining a network of personal contacts with whom information can be exchanged informally.

There is, in fact, a lot of data around. The problems are in assessing its validity and sorting out the often conflicting messages received. 'Market tracking' can be time-consuming and expensive but, in spite of the problems of getting absolutely reliable data, it is essential.

Establishing external relativities

When designing, modifying or updating pay structures that have been based on conventional job evaluation, market rate data needs to be obtained for the benchmark positions. The latter should include as many jobs as possible for which external comparisons can be made.

Such comparisons are most reliable if they are based on direct exchanges of information with other comparable organisations ('comparators') in special surveys or through a pay club. For this purpose the reliability of the data is increased if it is based on 'capsule' job descriptions which summarise the main characteristics of the benchmark jobs. It is even better if the comparison can be made by means of a form of job evaluation. This could be an existing point-factor scheme although that would probably be difficult and time-consuming to manage unless the comparators use the same scheme. This is where proprietary brands of job evaluation can help to achieve better job matches.

The alternative is to use some form of factor comparison. This means selecting a fairly small number of factors – say, knowledge and skills, responsibility, complexity, contribution, and mental and physical effort. The comparisons could then be made by reference to these factors along the lines described in Chapter 4.

When the information has been collected it is necessary to sort it and make an assessment of the messages it contains about relative external roles. This can be used to attach rates to jobs or pay brackets or scales to job grades as described in Chapter 9.

Market pricing as a method of job evaluation

Market pricing can function as a method of job evaluation. Many businesses operate a 'spot rate' structure in which the rate for the job is largely based on market comparisons (or the rate that has to be paid to attract and retain individuals on the basis of their personal 'market worth'). The positioning of the spot rates for the various jobs establishes the internal differentials which are, therefore, derived directly from the differentials established in the marketplace.

In practice this is what often happens even when a formal job evaluation exercise has taken place to establish internal relativities. It is no good sticking religiously to the latter if the external market forces dictate that they should be different. The extent to which an organisation submits to market pressures depends, of course, on the degree to which it believes that it has to be competitive in the open market, either generally or for particular jobs.

Market pricing as a method of job evaluation is also used by some organisations to 'anchor' the job ranges or zones in a broad-banded structure (see Chapter 9) or to indicate rates of pay at the various levels in a job family structure.

Market pricing evaluation can be conducted in the following seven stages:

1   The jobs to be evaluated are identified.
2   The jobs are analysed and described in terms of job content and characteristics. In a large organisation only a representative sample of jobs are analysed at this stage. They are the jobs for which external comparisons can be made and are designated as the benchmark jobs.
4   A pay structure is developed that incorporates pay ranges or scales to cover all the jobs. The limits of the structure are related to the highest and lowest market rates for those jobs. The number of grades between these limits depends on a) the size and complexity of the organisation, and b) the policy on the width of the bands (the amount of pay progression allowed within one job) and the overlap between bands. It may be necessary to have more than one structure to cover different market groups where jobs in some functions are subject to special market pressures.

They may then be grouped together in such a way that movements in pay for one job within the group are likely to be associated with movements for other jobs in the group, but not for those in other groups.

5   The benchmark jobs are provisionally slotted into the structure by reference to the information obtained on market rates for each of the jobs. If the policy is to pay at the upper quartile of the distribution of pay, the grading accords with the band into which this figure falls. This may be about the mid-point of the band to represent the target pay or reference point for the jobs in the grade. In practice it may fall at any point in the grade, and judgement would have to be used in borderline cases. The final decision should be made by comparing the benchmark job in question with others in the same or adjacent grades and placing it in the grade where there are broadly comparable jobs.

6   A final choice is made on the grading of the benchmark jobs by checking to ensure that the provisional allocation has not upset any well-established and appropriate internal relativities. In these circumstances, an overlapping graded pay structure should ease the making of fine adjustments. If Job B is obviously lower in the hierarchy than Job A, it can be placed in the next grade down, but a 50 per cent overlap between the grades would enable the pay of people in Job B to advance to a level that might be comparable with the market rates for similar jobs without the need to upgrade the job. Where such adjustments are not possible because of strong market forces operating on one or more jobs, it may be necessary to recognise them as exceptions or create separate market group pay structures for them. A structure with wide grades or pay ranges eases the accommodation of jobs into a single grade when the variations in market rates are confined within the pay range. In some broad-banded structures, however, the market rates anchor jobs in zones for particular occupations, and there is more flexibility in aligning internal pay ranges with market rates. Approaches to designing grade and pay structures are discussed more fully in Chapter 9.

7   The remaining jobs are slotted into the grades by comparison with the benchmark jobs. The greater the number and range of occupations or functions covered by the benchmarks the better.

Advantages and disadvantages

This approach has the merit of being practical, straightforward and quick, and many firms use it for those reasons. If jobs are analysed thoroughly, if the pay survey is comprehensive, and if good judgement is exercised in allocating jobs to grades, the results can be quite satisfactory. However, these are big 'ifs'. The drawback is that it relies on the accuracy of the market rate information, and this may not be easy to obtain, especially in companies in specialised fields that tend to grow their own staff. And judgement may be fallible in situations where no yardsticks are available and where it has not been possible to subject the jobs to comparisons based on detailed analysis of defined criteria.

Another drawback to this approach is that it can perpetuate discrimination against women. If market rates for jobs generally held by women are depressed because of long-standing gender bias, then this will be reflected in the pay structure. This may produce tensions between the principle of internal equity and comparable worth and the perceived need to be competitive. Pay structures often do incorporate compromises between the competing imperatives of internal equity and external competitiveness but these compromises may clearly discriminate against women. A market pricing system of job evaluation is not analytical and as such may be discriminatory.

If, however, an organisation is satisfied that this approach is non-discriminatory, it could adopt it as the simplest and most realistic method of valuing jobs in financial terms, although it would always have to remember that it may be building its pay structure on the shifting sand of a number of doubtful assumptions about what are the true market rates.

8

ROLE AND COMPETENCE

ANALYSIS

The reliability and validity of job evaluation depends largely on the quality of the analysis of roles and competences that provides the factual information upon which the evaluation is based. This analysis provides the data for a number of key personnel processes, including organisation design, human resource planning, recruitment, performance management, and training and development. It is therefore an important aid to the creation of coherent personnel plans and practices.

This chapter first defines role and competence analysis and the concept of generic roles. It then deals with the techniques of role and competence analysis and the preparation of role descriptions for job evaluation purposes.

Definitions

Role analysis

Throughout this chapter we talk of role analysis rather than job analysis. The terms 'jobs' and 'roles' are often used interchangeably, but there is a distinction, as defined in Chapter 1. 'Role' is preferred to 'job' because it incorporates the more dynamic elements of what people do and how they do it. Role analysis covers the collection of information about job content and job demands as in job analysis, but it goes beyond these details to look at the part that people play in carrying out their roles rather than the tasks they carry out. In other words, it is concerned not only with job content but also with the broader aspects of behaviour expected of role-holders in achieving the overall purpose of their role – for example, working with others, working flexibly, and the styles of management they use. Role analysis for job evaluation purposes focuses on the particular characteristics of roles that indicate relative value – the job evaluation factors that include input and output requirements and the demands made on people in the role.

Role definitions

Role definitions describe the part to be played by individuals in fulfilling their job requirements. They expand on the job content information contained in a job description by setting out the behavioural competences that characterise the role and describing the context within which the role is carried out. In job evaluation, role definitions are used as the prime source of information about the demands made on role-holders, the outputs expected from them, and the levels of competences they need.

Competence analysis

Competence analysis can be part of the overall role analysis process. It is concerned with functional analysis to determine work-based competences and behavioural analysis in turn to establish the behavioural dimensions that affect job performance.

Work-based or occupational competences refer to expectations of workplace performance and the standards and outputs that people carrying out specified roles are expected to attain. *Behavioural or personal competences* are the personal characteristics of individuals that they bring to their work roles.

Generic roles

Role and competence analysis may be concerned with individual roles but it can concentrate on obtaining the information required to produce generic role definitions. These refer to characteristic roles in the organisation such as team leader, scientist, production or development engineer, and production team member. Each definition describes the common elements of a role in output terms – ie what people in the role are expected to achieve. It may also incorporate behavioural requirements in the form of a generic competence profile for the role. Generic role definitions are a means of enhancing flexibility. They indicate that although everyone in that role is expected to meet the common requirements, specific activities that individuals carry out in their roles are not prescribed, yet the particular expectations of performance in the role may be agreed in the form of objectives and individual performance development plans. Scope is therefore provided for the role to expand as new opportunities arise and additional competences are acquired.

However, the use of generic role definitions as the basis for job evaluation could be regarded as unfair or discriminatory if they did not adequately differentiate between the values of particular roles because key characteristics had not been distinguished and compared.

Role analysis techniques

Role analysis gets the facts about a role from people in the role, their manager or team leader, and colleagues or fellow team members. It is not a matter of obtaining opinions or making judgements. What goes into a role definition should be what actually happens and why, not what people would like to think happens.

The facts can be obtained by interviews and/or by questionnaires. These may be structured to produce generic or individual role definitions.

Interviews

The aim of an interview should be initially to obtain the basic facts about the role:

☐ the title of the generic or individual role
☐ organisational details – reporting relationships, team membership
☐ a brief description (one or two sentences) of the overall purpose of the role
☐ a list of what people in the role are expected to achieve – these may be described as key result areas, principal accountabilities or main responsibilities.

These basic details can be supplemented by questions designed to elicit information about the characteristics of the role, the level of responsibilities, and the demands made on people in the role. Where appropriate, these questions should be linked explicitly to the factors included in the evaluation scheme. They could cover such aspects of the role as:

Inputs (knowledge and skills)
    ability to carry out specified tasks or administrative routines
    ability to process data
    the skills required to plan and organise activities
    the interpersonal skills required to lead teams, work effectively as a team member, relate to internal and external customers and clients, network, persuade people to take a course of action, communicate, take care of people, handle people problems, and assess, train and develop employees
    the skills required to analyse and interpret data and to arrange and present complex information in a clear and logical manner which facilitates understanding and decision-making
    the skills needed to use equipment and machines, covering what individuals have to know and be able to do to operate them effectively
    the manual skills required, including dexterity and the skills required to carry out particular tasks
    the information technology knowledge and skills required to understand and make use of computer applications and integrated or computer-controlled systems (manufacturing, design, financial, administration, etc.) including data-processing skills, electronic communication systems, managing databases, and working in distributed data-processing systems and automated offices
    the skills required to handle numerical and financial data
    the level of knowledge required of company policies, procedures, technical processes, systems, products, services, customers or clients, and sources of supplies
    the level of understanding required of the business, economic, social and political environment in which the organisation functions.

Process

responsibilities – accountability for managing resources (people, money and plant and equipment) and/or handling confidential information

the degree to which the work is routine or repetitive

the extent to which the role involves making independent decisions requiring the exercise of judgement

the amount of supervision received and the degree of discretion allowed in making decisions

the typical problems to be solved and the amount of guidance available when solving the problems

the range of tasks to be carried out or responsibilities to be fulfilled

the diversity of skills used

the relative difficulty of the tasks to be performed.

Outputs

the contribution made by jobholders to achieving the objectives of their team, department or organisation

the impact jobholders make on results

the degree to which jobholders exert influence over activities and decisions and the effect of that influence

the extent to which jobholders are accountable for results and the effective management of resources.

Job demands

the physical effort that has to be exerted by jobholders in terms of lifting, carrying, manoeuvring heavy weights, or other physical exertions and activities such as digging, bending, stretching, etc.

the stamina required by people in the role – working for long periods on physically demanding tasks, standing or working in confined conditions or in situations where movement is restricted

the mental, visual and allied effort associated with work involving continuous visual examination, concentration, precision, and the co-ordination of hand and eye

the stress of working at speed, with small or delicate items, and the stress/pressures caused by frequent changes or discontinuities, the need to re-schedule work and the requirement to work to deadlines, schedules or exacting standards, or to achieve ever-increasing targets

the extent to which the work is carried out under disagreeable conditions

the type of hazards associated with the work

the special requirements in such aspects of the role as unsocial hours, lengthy shifts, and travelling.

Conducting the interview

Role analysis interviews should be conducted with the following agenda:

☐ Work to a logical sequence of questions that may help interviewees to order their thoughts about the role.

☐ Probe as necessary to establish what people really do – answers to questions are often initially vague, and information may be given by means of untypical instances.

☐ Ensure that people do not give imprecise or inflated descriptions of their work.

☐ Sort out the wheat from the chaff: answers to questions may produce a lot of irrelevant data which must be sifted before preparing the role definition.

☐ Obtain a clear statement from people in the role about their authority to make decisions and the amount of guidance they receive from their manager or team leader – this is not easy: if asked what decisions they are authorised to make, many people look blank because they think about their role in terms of duties and tasks rather than abstract decisions.

☐ Avoid asking leading questions (which make an expected answer obvious).

☐ Allow every individual ample opportunity to talk by creating an atmosphere of trust.

It is helpful to use a check-list derived from questions such as those listed above when conducting the interview. Elaborate check-lists are not necessary: they only confuse people. The essence of the art of role analysis is 'Keep it simple'. The questions should be structured specifically to obtain the information required for evaluation purposes. They must therefore cover each of the main factors to be referred to when evaluating the job. The points to be discussed should vary according to the occupation and level of the individual and the job evaluation factors.

It is always advisable to check the information provided by individuals with their managers or team leaders. Different views can be held about the role, and these should be reconciled. Role analysis often reveals such differences in addition to any organisational problems. This information can provide a useful spin-off from the analysis process.

When preparing generic role definitions it can be helpful to conduct role analyses by means of discussions with groups of people in the role. In this way, different points of view can be aired and a better overall picture obtained.

A major advantage of analysing roles by means of interviews is that they can be carried out flexibly. Properly handled, they can provide a picture of what the role is really like, including its more subtle aspects (eg interpersonal relationships). But interviewing can be time-consuming, and the results are not always easy to analyse. Much depends on the skill of the analyst to get to the facts and to appreciate the significance not only of these facts but also of the behavioural requirements of the role. And job analysts can consciously or unconsciously be prejudiced. That is why, in large evaluation exercises, general or structured questionnaires are often used, speeding up the interviewing process, minimising prejudice (as long as the questionnaire itself is not prejudiced), or even replacing the interview altogether – although this may mean that it may not be able to capture the 'true flavour' of the role.

General questionnaires
Questionnaires covering such points as those included in the check-list above can be completed by individuals and approved by their manager or team leader. They are helpful when a large number of roles are to be covered. They can also save interviewing time by recording purely factual information and by enabling the analyst to structure questions in advance to cover areas that need to be explored in greater depth. Questionnaires can produce information quickly and cheaply for a large number of jobs. They can be phrased in non-discriminatory ways. But a substantial sample is needed and the construction of a questionnaire is a skilled job that

should be carried out only on the basis of some preliminary fieldwork. It is highly advisable to pilot-test questionnaires before launching into a full-scale exercise. The accuracy of the results also depends on the willingness and ability of individuals to complete questionnaires. Many people find it difficult to express themselves in writing about their work, however well they know and do it.

Structured questionnaires

There are two problems with general questionnaires:

1   Analysing the facts – However carefully the interview or questionnaire is structured, the information is unlikely to come out neatly and succinctly in a way that can readily be translated into a role definition. It is often necessary to sort out, rearrange, and even rewrite the information.

2   Using the information for evaluation purposes – Too many questionnaires provide only generalised data, even if they follow the points listed above. Evaluators therefore have difficulty in aligning their answers to level or grade definitions.

To avoid these problems, there is much to be said for developing structured questionnaires that provide answers which can be used to prepare role definitions set out explicitly under the evaluation scheme factor headings. This could reduce the extent to which evaluators have to exercise judgement in interpreting the data, although it can never replace that judgement.

Such questionnaires can eliminate the need for role definitions as the basis for job evaluation, and therefore reduce the lengthy and often tedious time usually taken in preparing such descriptions – one day per role is a typical amount of time if allowance is made for checking and the repetition involved. Use can be made of computer-assisted job evaluation systems as described in Chapter 10 to produce evaluations direct from the questionnaire. It is possible to reduce the amount of work involved even further if the individual and his or her manager input the data about the job direct into the computer. A program has been devised which asks the questions and processes the answers to deliver a score. This eliminates the need for written questionnaires and job description. The GAUGE job evaluation system, developed by the Burnley Health Care Trust (as described on pages 170–73), comes into this category. A number of the organisations we visited used various forms of structured questionnaires, and extracts from some of them are given in Appendix D.

Structured questionnaires are often offered by consultants as part of their computerised job evaluation package, and save considerable time and effort. The design of such questionnaires is not easy: they should always be pilot-tested to ensure that they can be completed easily by jobholders and that the information can readily be translated into a job evaluation score.

Competence analysis

Competence analysis is, of course, primarily used to produce competence profiles and frameworks for human resource planning, recruitment, performance management, training and development activities. But it can also provide the information required for competence-based pay processes as described in Chapter 6, and the results of the analysis may be incorporated in a role definition.

The most commonly used methods of competence analysis are expert opinion, workshops, structured interviews, and functional analysis. Critical-incident techniques or repertory grid analysis are sometimes used to produce behaviourally-oriented lists of competence dimensions, but the techniques are probably too elaborate for most competence-based pay applications.

Expert opinion

The simplest method is for 'experts' (members of the personnel department and representatives of line management) to get together and draw up a list from their own understanding of 'what counts', possibly by reference to other published lists. This certainly saves time and trouble, but it may not be particularly analytical, and reliance on other people's ideas could result in a list that is irrelevant to the real needs and requirements of the business. When defining the core, generic, or individual role competences it is essential to ensure that they flow directly from the core competences of the business, so that people competences are fully integrated with and support business competences.

Workshops

A more structured approach through a workshop is likely to produce better results. Such a workshop usually begins by defining the job-related competence areas – the key functions in terms of the outputs required for the roles under consideration. Using the competence areas as a framework, the members of the group develop examples of effective and less effective behaviour, which may be recorded on flip charts.

The workshop facilitator's task is to help the group to analyse its findings, to prompt, to provide examples, and to assist generally in the production of a set of competence dimensions that can be illustrated by behaviour-based examples. The facilitator may have some ideas about the sort of headings that should emerge from this process, but should try not to influence the group to come to a conclusion that it has not worked out for itself, with or without guidance.

Structured interview

This method starts from a list of competences drawn up by experts or a workshop and proceeds by subjecting a number of individuals to a structured interview. The interview begins by identifying the key activities or result areas of the role, and goes on to analyse the behavioural characteristics that distinguish performers at different levels of competence.

The basic question is: 'What are the positive or negative indicators of behaviour that are conducive or non-conducive to achieving high levels of performance?' These may be analysed under such headings as

- □ personal drive (achievement motivation)
- □ impact on results
- □ analytical power
- □ strategic thinking
- □ creative thinking (ability to innovate)

☐ decisiveness

☐ commercial judgement

☐ team management and leadership

☐ interpersonal relationships

☐ ability to communicate

☐ ability to adapt and cope with change and pressure

☐ ability to plan and control projects.

In each area instances should be sought that illustrate effective or less effective behaviour.

One of the problems with this approach is that it relies on the ability of the interviewer to draw out information from people. It is also undesirable to use a deductive approach which pre-empts the analysis from a prepared list of competence headings. Far better to use an inductive approach which starts from specific types of behaviour and then groups them under competence headings. This can be done in a workshop.

Functional analysis

Functional analysis is the method used to produce competence-based standards for NVQ frameworks, but it can equally well be applied to the definition of work-based or occupational competences within an organisation. Functional analysis starts by describing the overall purpose of the occupation and then identifies the key *functions* undertaken.

In NVQ language, a distinction is made between *tasks*, the activities undertaken at work, and *functions*, the purposes of activities at work. The distinction is important because the analysis must focus on the outcomes of activities in order to establish expectations of workplace performance. This is the information required to define standards of competence at the various levels in job families or for individual roles.

When the units and elements of competence have been established, the next question asked is 'What are the qualities of the outcomes?' in terms of the performance criteria at each level that can be used to judge whether or not an individual's performance meets the required standards. This feeds information into the performance management process.

Functional analysis can also lead to definitions of the

behavioural dimensions of competence, especially when generic definitions are required for a whole occupational area – for example, managers or team leaders.

Role definitions

Structured questionnaires can sometimes replace role definitions for job evaluation purposes, but role definitions still remain the main means by which information about jobs is communicated to evaluators. It is therefore necessary to give some consideration to how they should be laid out.

The format for role definitions depends upon the requirements of the organisation. There are many varieties, but one that is used fairly commonly is presented below.

Purpose

This is a short statement of why the role exists. It should be expressed in a single sentence. When defining the purpose of a role it is helpful to consider questions like:

- What part of the organisation's or team's total purpose is accomplished by this role?
- What is the unique contribution of this role that distinguishes it from other roles?
- How would you summarise the overall responsibility of individuals in this role?

Organisation

This section explains where the role fits into the organisation. It sets out the role or job title of the person to whom the individual is responsible, and the role or job titles of the people who are directly responsible to the role-holder.

Key result areas

Key result areas are statements of the end results or outputs required of the role. They answer the question: 'What are the main areas in which people in this role must get results to achieve its purpose?' For most roles from eight to ten headings are sufficient to cover the major result areas. Fewer than four or five headings probably means something is missing;

more than ten may mean that the role definition is going into far too much detail.

The complete key result area schedule should always be expressed on the proverbial one side of one sheet of paper. The emphasis should be on contribution and outcomes.

Key result area statements should have the following characteristics:

☐ Taken together, they represent all the major outputs expected of the role.
☐ They focus on what is required (results and outputs) not how the role is fulfilled (detailed tasks and duties).
☐ Each key result area is distinct from the others and describes an important aspect of the role in which results are to be achieved.
☐ They suggest (but need not state explicitly) measures or tests that could determine the extent to which results are being achieved.

A key result area statement is written in the form: 'Do something in order to achieve a stated result or standard.' It should point clearly to performance measures. Each statement is made in one sentence beginning with an active verb (such as *prepare, produce, plan, schedule, test, maintain, develop, monitor, ensure*). For example:

☐ Prepare marketing plans which support the achievement of corporate targets for profit and sales revenue.
☐ Control manufacturing operations to achieve output targets, quality specifications and delivery to time requirements within cost budgets.
☐ Maintain a stock control system which optimises inventory levels.
☐ Deal promptly and accurately with queries from customers on products and prices.
☐ Provide an accurate, speedy, and helpful word processing service to internal customers (fellow team members).

Context

The context section is designed to add 'flavour' to the bare list of key result areas. It describes the role's working environment and, importantly, how the role is carried out in terms of interactions with other people, the amount of flexibility required, the sort of problems that have to be regularly solved, the decisions people have to make, and the skills, knowledge and behavioural competences required. For job evaluation purposes this section can be structured in line with the factors used in an analytical scheme under such headings as 'skills', 'competences', 'responsibilities', 'complexity', 'interpersonal relationships' and 'mental and physical demands'.

Alternatively, it can be expressed in a structured narrative covering

- the impact made by the person in the role on end results – the contribution made to achieving the objectives of the organisation, function, department or team
- the amount of influence the individual is expected to exert on policy-making, planning, and the decisions or actions of other people
- where the role fits in with other key aspects of the work of the organisation or team
- decision-making authority
- how work is assigned, reviewed, and approved
- the particular knowledge, skills and experience required
- the complexity of the job – the degree of flexibility needed to undertake different tasks or use different skills
- the particular demands of the job in such areas as communicating skills, customer relations, interpersonal skills, quality management, team leadership, teamworking, planning, project management, etc.
- the major problems individuals are likely to meet in carrying out their work
- the pressures on people in the role – to meet deadlines, achieve exacting targets and quality standards, keep pace with a production line, cope with constantly changing priorities, deal with potentially difficult interpersonal situations, etc.
- physical conditions – the requirement for physical effort and stamina, prolonged standing, using VDUs, working in

confined or uncomfortable conditions, etc.
- □ the extent to which the work involves manual dexterity
- □ the plant, equipment or tools used.

Competences

If there are generic competence profiles, these should be referred to in the role definition. The definition ought also to set out the specific competence profile for the role if one is available.

Critical dimensions

The critical dimensions of a role include any quantitative data that indicate its size and the range of responsibilities involved. For example: output, number of items processed, sales turnover, budgets, costs controlled, numbers supervised, and number of cases dealt with over a period.

Examples of role definitions are given in Appendix E.

9

DESIGNING GRADE AND

PAY STRUCTURES

Perhaps one of the most interesting of our research findings was that although many organisations go to elaborate lengths to devise and implement complex job evaluation processes, the final and most important decisions on grading these jobs and attaching pay scales or ranges to the grades are still largely a matter of judgement.

This chapter examines how such judgements are made, first by describing grade structures, second by discussing methods of grading jobs in those structures, and third by examining how graded structures can be priced.

Grade structures

Some organisations use spot rates (a single rate for a job) or pay curves (pay progression along a curve in relation to competence and contribution). But most have some form of graded structure, whether as a series of grades with pay ranges attached, or a pay spine divided into grades defined in terms of incremental pay points.

The main features of grade structures

A typical graded pay structure is illustrated in Figure 9.1.

There are a number of important features in such a structure.

☐ A hierarchy of job grades exists. These may be defined in any of three ways:
   (i)   in terms of the level of jobs that are allocated to each grade (as in job classification evaluation schemes);
   (ii) by reference to internal benchmark jobs already allocated to the grade (as in internal benchmarking processes of job evaluation); or

Figure 9.1
A TYPICAL GRADED PAY STRUCTURE

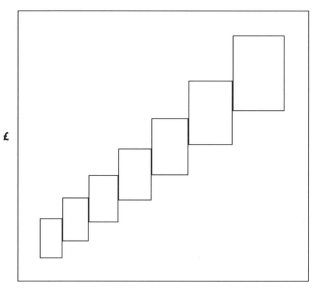

Grades

(iii) by a range of points derived from a point-factor evaluation exercise.

☐ A pay range or scale is attached to each grade. This is
defined as the width of the range expressed as a percentage
of the lowest point, or the percentage spread on either
side of the mid-point. Thus a range of £20,000 to £30,000
may be expressed as either a 50 per cent bracket or as an
80–100–120 per cent range. The width of the range is a
matter of choice (see below).

☐ The pay range is aligned to market rates in accordance with
the pay stance of the organisation (ie how it wants its rates
of pay to be related to market rates).

☐ The jobs allocated to each grade are assumed to be of equal
worth.

☐ Individuals may progress through the whole or part of a
range in accordance with their level of contribution or

competence (through variable increases), or their time in the job (through fixed increments).

☐ There are differentials between ranges, the size of which depend on policy and practice in relation to the job hierarchy and the number of grades.

☐ The pay ranges may overlap to provide for more flexibility and to recognise that a top performer in one grade may be worth more than a new starter in the grade above.

Advantages and disadvantages of graded structures

The *advantages* of graded structures are:

☐ they are easy to explain to employees

☐ they clearly indicate pay relativities

☐ they provide a framework for managing those relativities and for ensuring that jobs of equal value are paid equally

☐ they enable better control to be exercised over fixing rates of pay and pay progression.

The *disadvantages* are:

☐ defining grade boundaries is a matter of judgement which may not always be easy to defend

☐ if there are too many grades, there will be constant pressure for upgrading, leading to grade drift

☐ pay ranges create expectations that everyone is entitled to reach the top of the scale

☐ graded structures can create or maintain hierarchical rigidity which is at odds with the requirements for flexibility in new team- and process-based organisations.

Choices

There are several choices to be made when designing or updating graded pay structures. These relate primarily to the number of grade structures, the number and width of the grades, and the differentials and overlaps between them.

Some organisations are introducing a *number of integrated grade structures* to cover all levels of employees. But many slice their organisation horizontally, having one structure for manual workers and another for salaried staff. Others slice the organisation vertically and have structures for different job families or market groups – in the latter case separating occupational groups subjected to strong market rate pressures from the basic structure.

The *number of grades* is influenced by the organisational structure (flatter organisations need fewer grades), the corporate culture (is it essentially hierarchical?), and the amount of flexibility required in organisations based on team or project work or in those where the emphasis is on horizontal processes, possibly following a business process re-engineering exercise.

A conventional structure in a typical hierarchical organisation may be designed with differentials increasing from 15 per cent in the lower grades to 20 per cent at the top, whereas the width of the ranges or bands may increase from 30 per cent to 40 per cent. This could result in an eight-graded structure if salaries of from £10,000 to about £50,000 had to be covered, with overlaps between grades of the order of 35 per cent to 40 per cent.

An arrangement along these lines, which could be termed a medium-banded structure, is fairly typical. But there are many variations to this pattern. There is plenty of choice – no rules state that any one type of structure is 'best' – it all depends on what the organisation wants and needs.

However, much interest has been expressed recently in *broad-banded structures* in which the width of ranges is more than 50 per cent and could be 100 per cent or more. A 100 per cent band structure would need only three bands to cover jobs ranging from £10,000 to £50,000, allowing for a 25 per cent overlap. The 'architecture' of a broad-banded system can vary considerably. Our research revealed that some systems are more structured than others. One approach we identified is to decide in advance that what the organisation wants is, say, no more than four or five bands to cover all its employees. These could be described simply in terms of generic roles – for example, team member, team leader, process manager, and process director. Generic role definitions are prepared and individual roles slotted into the bands with reference to those definitions.

Another closely related approach we came across was to define each band in terms of the level of work people within the band carry out, and, importantly, the competences they need to have. Jobs are slotted into the band by reference to those definitions. In other words, a type of job classification system is used but the band definitions are more generalised than in a conventional narrow-banded job classification structure.

A more structured and analytical approach is to define the limits of the bands by means of a conventional point-factor evaluation scheme. Any job that is 'scored' within those limits is allocated to the band. Clearly, the points brackets are much wider than in the more conventional graded structure.

Within the band, 'zones' may be established for groups of related occupations of which the market rates are broadly similar – the zones are sometimes said to be 'anchored' by these rates. Progression through the zone can be related both to competence and to contribution. There may be some indication of the upper limit, but the understanding is that people can go beyond that if they develop and use their competences in a way that results in a significantly higher level of performance delivery and/or they take on new or wider responsibilities. What is emphasised in such a structure is that pay progression is managed more flexibly in relation to contribution and competence. It does not depend on promotion up a narrowly defined ladder. Broad-banded structures provide the means positively to reward people who perform flexibly in a process- or project-based organization to good effect.

One of the characteristics of the organisations we came across with broad-banded structures was the considerable amount of authority being devolved to line managers to make pay decisions. This was, of course, always within budgets, and guidelines were made available on market rates. The distribution of pay increases could also be monitored and managers asked to justify any unusual patterns.

The *advantages* claimed for broad-banding is that it allows for a much more flexible approach to managing pay and relativities, and that it removes the pressure for upgrading as a means of gaining increases in pay. Broad-banding is often associated with competence-based pay by which progression depends on the levels of competence attained as well as on contribution. It can be linked to policies of continuous development, and it can ensure that people are rewarded for enlarging the scope of their role to meet new situations and demands. Progression in a band is not simply related to the 'size' of a job in terms of the number of people or other resources controlled. People who have been rewarded for achieving high levels of competence in one role may be rewarded more for taking on the challenge of a new role and developing the additional competences required to carry out that role effectively. This happens even if in strict job evaluation terms the 'size' of the new role is smaller. What counts is continuous development, adaptability, and flexibility, not 'job size' measured in crude job evaluation terms.

The criteria for upgrading may include the requirement for individuals to have demonstrated adaptability and flexibility in taking on new challenges and increasing their level and range of competences.

The *disadvantages* of broad-banding are first, that individuals may feel adrift (people like structure), and second, that the organisation may find it more difficult to manage progression and provide for consistent and fair treatment, although budgetary control can be exercised over payroll costs. In a broad-banded system, some processes need to be provided for managing pay determination and progression by creating 'zones' or 'spot rates' that are anchored by market rates as described above. Processes for assessing competence and performance must also exist.

Designing grade structures

People involved in designing or re-designing a pay structure are usually faced with a situation in which there is either no structure at all or one in which the existing elements have become unmanageable. In either case, the first requirement is to define the problem. The next steps are to set objectives and plan a development programme.

Defining the problem

Where there is no structure at all it is necessary to establish

☐ the existing arrangements – rates of pay and how they are determined

- the extent to which the pay arrangements are incoherent and/or inequitable
- the impact this situation makes on the attitudes and performance of employees as evidenced, for example, by high levels of turnover or by poor motivation
- any problems of recruiting or retaining good staff
- actual or potential problems in ensuring that work of equal value is paid equally
- any additional expense arising from problems in controlling payroll costs and getting value-for-money from the pay system.

Where there is an existing pay structure the same questions need to be answered to establish the nature of the problems and the present arrangements. The reasons for the structure's becoming more or less unmanageable then needs to be identified. These could include problems arising from

- a decayed job evaluation scheme in which the factors may no longer be relevant or which is subject to manipulation by managers and employees alike
- too many grades
- inflexibilities in the way in which job evaluation is applied and pay is managed
- unjustifiable pressure for upgrading leading to grade drift
- serious inequities in the pay for jobs of comparable worth
- uncompetitive rates of pay.

Setting objectives

The objectives of a design or re-design exercise could be expressed along the lines of: 'To develop an equitable and competitive pay structure that enables fair and consistent decisions to be made on job grades and rates of pay, facilitates the management of relativities, and ensures that proper control of payroll costs can be maintained.'

Defining the programme of work

The programme of work should include

- communicating to employees the intention to carry out the exercise and, as appropriate, setting up processes for their involvement
- selecting or designing a new job evaluation scheme or re-designing the existing scheme
- evaluating or re-evaluating benchmark jobs
- conducting a market pricing survey
- designing the grade structure
- attaching pay ranges or scales to job ranges
- allocating jobs to the new grades
- dealing with any anomalies
- informing employees of the results of the exercise and how it affects them.

Developing a grade structure

There are basically two approaches to developing a grade structure: (1) to decide in advance the number of grades required, and then to define the basis upon which jobs are to be slotted into those grades (the pre-emptive approach); (2) to conduct a job evaluation exercise and to design a structure on the basis of the job rankings or points scores produced by the exercise (the empirical approach).

The pre-emptive approach involves prejudging the grade structure on largely subjective grounds. If this simply involves replicating an existing well-defined and elongated hierarchy, the danger is that flaws already present in the structure may be perpetuated. There are situations, however, where jobs fall into natural groupings which clearly establish the grade hierarchy.

A pre-emptive approach may be based on a fundamental reorganisation which could follow a business process re-engineering (BPR) exercise and decisions to de-layer and increase operational flexibility. In these circumstances it may be decided that a completely new structure is required. This could be a broadbanded structure as described above. Such structures are often designed pre-emptively on the basis of any new approaches that have emerged from a BPR project – for example, flatter organisational structures and changed concepts about roles in organisations where the new emphasis is on teamwork, projects, and horizontal processes.

Having decided on the design of the structure, the next stage is to establish how jobs should be slotted into it. This can be achieved in any of three ways:

□ using point-factor evaluation to score benchmark jobs and then defining the width of the grades in points terms

□ defining the characteristics of each grade so that jobs can be allotted to grades by comparing job descriptions with the grade definition – this is the job classification approach

□ simply allocating benchmark jobs to the grades and slotting other jobs in by a process of whole job comparison (internal benchmarking).

Each of these approaches can produce a grade structure in which gradings are 'felt fair', but this is only possible when great care is taken over definitions and the benchmarking process. And pre-empting the structure may produce illogicalities that could only be avoided by adopting a more empirical and preferably analytical approach.

The empirical approach to grade structure design is based on the outcome of a ranking or point-factor job evaluation study. Designing a job grade structure after a ranking exercise involves listing the jobs in rank order and then drawing in grade boundaries wherever seems appropriate. This is entirely a matter of judgement, and the criteria against which that judgement can be tested are listed below.

The point-factor evaluation method is basically similar in that it involves drawing grade boundary lines at appropriate places in the rank order of points scores for benchmark jobs. However, the points scores do provide an indication of the difference between jobs in quantified terms, and this in theory makes it easier first to establish the extent to which similar jobs are clustered together, and secondly to identify gaps between clusters where grade boundary lines can be drawn that clearly distinguish between adjacent grades.

Criteria

The criteria for judging whether correct grade boundaries have been drawn are:

☐ the existence of clusters of jobs with natural breaks between them, so that when there is a distinct difference between the levels of the clusters the jobs are allocated to separate grades

☐ the degree to which jobs of a similar size and with common features as indicated by the job evaluation factors are grouped together

☐ the extent to which the structure reduces the risk of boundary problems by not placing jobs that are nearly the same size on either side of a grade boundary – there should ideally be a distinct gap between the highest-rated jobs in one grade and the lowest rated jobs in the next grade above.

These criteria are quite exacting and are often difficult to satisfy, especially when the width of grades is fairly narrow – wide grades do not eliminate boundary problems but there are likely to be fewer of them and they may be easier to manage.

The first attempt at producing a grade structure is often unacceptable and alternative configurations therefore have to be considered. This process is made easier by the use of computer software to model different alternatives. At a later stage the same programmes can be used to cost the various options so that the most affordable alternative is selected – affordability is an extremely important consideration.

It is at this stage that any pretence that defining job grades is a scientific process has to be abandoned. Even with computerised assistance it now becomes a matter of judgement, often based on trial and error. Grade structure design usually involves repetition, trying something out, testing against various criteria and, if necessary, trying something else until it feels right. And the operative word is *feels*. There is no objective scientific test of the rightness or otherwise of a grade structure.

One approach is to try a number of different configurations based on alternative grade widths, as illustrated in Figure 9.2.

Figure 9.2
ALTERNATIVE GRADE STRUCTURES

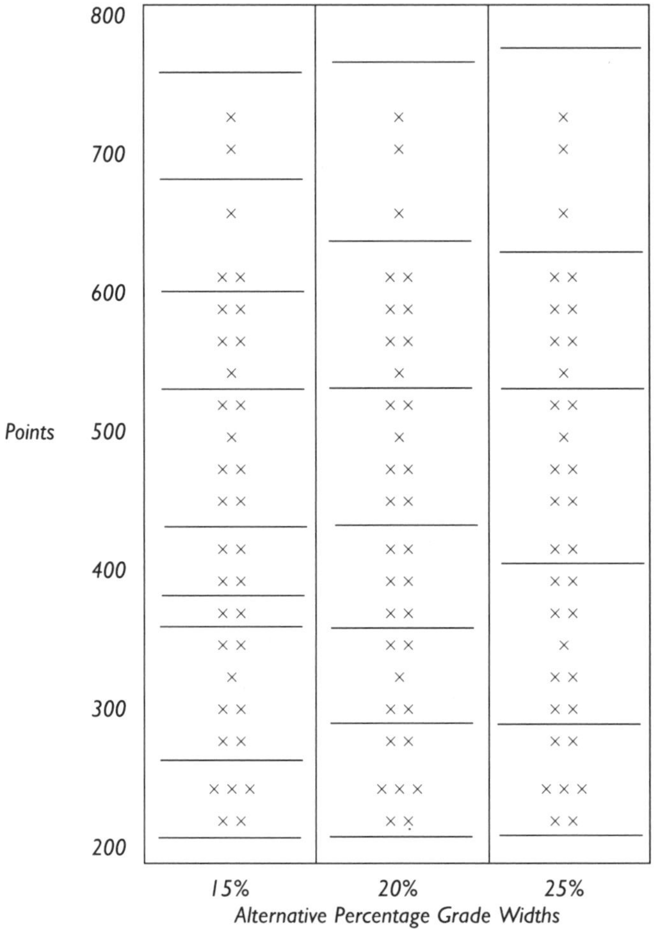

Alternative Percentage Grade Widths

This example assumes that all grade widths should be equally sized in percentage terms. But there is no rule that says this should be the case. Range widths and scales can vary according to the type of jobs allocated to the grades.

Each alternative can be evaluated against the criteria listed earlier until one emerges that feels right. And, ultimately, the 'felt-fair' principle is the only one that can be used to judge whether or not a sensible grade structure has been developed.

Pricing grade structures

Following the design of a graded structure as described above, decisions have to be made on pricing the structure – ie attaching pay ranges or scales to the grades.

Basic pricing considerations

Pricing decisions are made by reference to both internal and external considerations.

Internal considerations come first. These refer to internal relativities, the differentials between grades, and the scope for pay progression within grades – the size of the pay range or scale. Differentials must be large enough properly to reflect increases in job sizes between adjacent grades. The size of the differentials varies according to the number of grades in the structure and the level of each grade. It will probably be not less than 10 per cent in the lower grades, and it could be much more at higher levels.

The extent of the range depends on policies on the amount of pay progression that should be allowed in a grade through some form of performance- or competence-related pay. The greater the scope for improving performance, developing competence levels and working flexibly in a role, the greater the width of the range. But this, as so many other aspects of pay structure design, is a matter of judgement.

External relativities also have to be considered. These are concerned with the relationship between market rates and the rate for the job in the organisation. Market rate pressures vary but there are generally some jobs for which competitive rates must be paid if key people are to be attracted and retained. In these circumstances market rates cannot be ignored and it is necessary to resolve the competing claims of internal equity and external competitiveness. However, there is still the problem, as mentioned in Chapter 7, that the concept of a market rate is less precise than it seems.

Developing the pay structure

The first step is to check on internal relativities, which can be done by plotting the results of the job evaluation exercise and the job grades emerging from that study against existing rates of pay for the benchmark jobs. This is illustrated in Figure 9.3, which incorporates points scores. (A similar approach can be adopted if the basis of the structure is job ranking.) A trend line of actual pay has been drawn to show the relationship between points and pay.

Figure 9.3
SCATTERGRAM OF ACTUAL PAY DATA

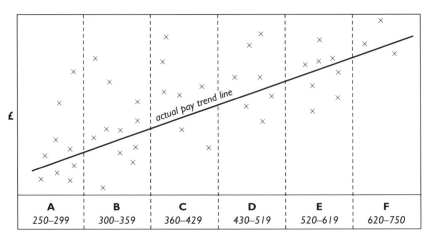

A	B	C	D	E	F
250–299	300–359	360–429	430–519	520–619	620–750

Grades and Points Ranges

The trend line usefully reveals how the existing pay structure relates to the differentials established by job evaluation. But it should not necessarily be accepted as the correct relationship. Allowance must be made for market rates, and in any case it may be desirable to rethink the basis on which pay should be related to the worth of the job as measured by job evaluation. The relativities may need to be changed and some account taken of the principle of comparable worth – equal pay for work of equal value – which may be prejudiced if too much attention is given to the existing pattern of pay relativities.

Subject to this proviso, the trend line gives a broad and preliminary indication of the pay ranges needed to accommodate the jobs that are reasonably close to it. But a final conclusion cannot be reached until an assessment is made of market comparabilities. The trend line also highlights any apparent anomalies – jobs for which the rate of pay is some distance above or below the line. These have to be investigated to establish the extent to which result from such causes as individuals being overpaid in relation to the work they do, market rate forces, or incorrect job evaluation outcomes.

The next stage is to consider market rate implications. To do this, valid and reliable market rate data for benchmark jobs can be plotted on the scattergram and a market rate trend line drawn, as shown in Figure 9.4. This may well only refer to median rates, but upper and lower quartile lines could also be shown.

Figure 9.4
SCATTERGRAM OF MARKET RATE DATA

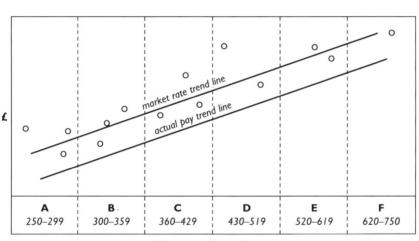

A	B.	C	D	E	F
250–299	300–359	360–429	430–519	520–619	620–750

Grades and Points Ranges

A policy decision is then required on how internal rates should relate to market rates. It might be decided, for example, that they should broadly be matched. The implications on the pay structure would then have to be considered and decisions made on where the range limits should be placed, taking into account policy on the width of the ranges and the desirability of having ranges which, as far as possible, accommodate the market rates for all the jobs in the grade. Clearly, the wider the range, the greater the likelihood of fitting in all the jobs. But there may well be some jobs for which market rates are much higher than the pay range for the grade into which they have been allocated on the basis of internal comparisons. In such cases, market rate premiums may have to be added to the rates for those jobs – it is undesirable for jobs to be placed in a higher grade than that indicated by internal equity factors simply because of market rate pressures.

If there are a number of jobs in a job family for which market rates are significantly higher, it might be appropriate to set up a separate market group structure. In the event of market rates being significantly lower than the scale, internal relativity imperatives should prevail.

Finalising the structure

Information collected, presented and analysed as described above is now put together to produce a final version of the structure as illustrated in Figure 9.5. In this example the mid-points of each grade broadly correspond with the median market trend line. This is a policy decision that is based on how the organisation wants to relate the rates for its jobs with market rates. For instance, a high-paying organisation might want to align its mid-points with the upper-quartile market rates. Alternatively, such an organisation might align the median market rate to a position somewhere between the lowest point in the range and the mid-point. The chart identifies any anomalies – in this example mainly underpaid jobs that need to be brought up to the minimum for the grade, possibly in stages.

Figure 9.5
GRADE STRUCTURE

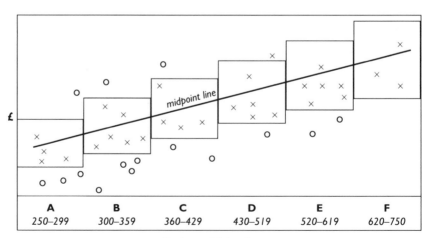

A	B	C	D	E	F
250–299	300–359	360–429	430–519	520–619	620–750

Grades and Points Ranges

Further iteration may take place while the structure is fine-tuned and while methods of dealing with anomalies (jobs for which rates of pay are outside grade limits) are considered. The structure is then presented to management (although it would be wise to have tested earlier versions of it and raised any difficult points during the process of design and re-design). Finally, plans are made for implementation and the costs of doing so are assessed, preferably through computer pay modelling.

At this stage the questions to be answered before accepting the new structure are:

☐ Does it meet the objectives set for the exercise?

☐ Does it generally look reasonable – ie is it 'felt-fair'?

☐ Is it likely to be acceptable to all concerned? if not, can it at least be justified?

☐ More specifically, do jobs appear to be correctly grouped together in the grades?

☐ Are there any anomalies, and if so, why?

☐ Are there any likely boundary problems arising because jobs of nearly equal value have been placed on the opposite sides of a grade boundary?

☐ Does it ensure that jobs of equal value are paid equally?

☐ Can higher rates of pay because of perceived market pressures be objectively justified?

☐ Will it be manageable?

☐ Will the cost of implementation be acceptable?

If the earlier work was thorough, and, importantly, key issues were raised in advance with those concerned (management and employees), it should be possible to answer these questions satisfactorily. If not, then it is back to the drawing-board!

10

COMPUTER-ASSISTED

JOB EVALUATION

Computer-assisted job evaluation (CAJE) supports job evaluation in two ways:

☐ It helps with the administration and maintenance of a job evaluation scheme – keeping evaluation records and auditing the operation of the scheme.

☐ It helps with the whole process of evaluating jobs rather than simply administering the scheme.

The second of these two applications embraces the first, and when reference is made to computer-assisted job evaluation this is what most people are talking about.

Aims

The aims of computer-assisted job evaluation are:

☐ to set up and maintain a database of job analyses and evaluations

☐ to assist in the process of making judgements about job values by functioning as an expert system, one that captures the knowledge of experts in the domain of job evaluation and that emulates the reasoning processes of such experts

☐ to help to achieve consistency in evaluation judgements by reference to the database of previous evaluations

☐ to speed up the process of evaluation

☐ to reduce the bureaucracy often built into job evaluation systems and, incidentally, save paper.

Nonetheless, a full computer-assisted job evaluation system does not replace human judgement. It simply provides an efficient means of applying the evaluation criteria and values that have been incorporated by the designers into the system on the basis of their analysis of the reasoning processes and rules used by evaluators.

This chapter contains a brief summary of the two main applications of CAJE. Further examples are given in Chapter 17.

Administration and maintenance of CAJE systems

A CAJE system designed to help with administration and maintenance is in effect a database which holds records of evaluations. This database contains details of the scoring, ranking and grading of all benchmark and other jobs. The data can be held for each factor on a level-by-level basis so that information can be obtained on which benchmark jobs have been rated at a particular level in a factor, so facilitating comparisons.

The data can be used for

☐ evaluating company jobs, with reference to the overall scores and gradings given to benchmark jobs in similar occupations or functions, or to jobs elsewhere in the organisation (internal benchmarking on a whole job basis)

☐ comparing for validation the levels at which benchmark jobs have been evaluated for particular factors (internal benchmarking on a factor-by-factor basis)

☐ carrying out consistency checks on evaluations by different job evaluation panels or groups of evaluators

☐ conducting comparative audits of the evaluation scores and grade distributions of jobs on different functions, departments or units.

Evaluating jobs with the help of computers

A full CAJE system not only contains a database for the purposes listed above but also assists in the actual process of evaluating jobs. In the latter application it functions as an expert system – ie one based on 'rules' for processing, analysing and drawing conclusions from data that have been developed by experts in this area.

The basis upon which a CAJE expert system functions

A CAJE expert system simply replicates in digital form the thought processes followed by evaluators when conducting a 'manual' evaluation. What expert systems do is:

☐ to ask intelligent questions on the extent to which a particular factor is present in a job

☐ to compare the answers to these questions with the factor level definitions in the factor plan and decide which is the most appropriate level

☐ to continue to do this with each of the factors in the plan

☐ to add the scores for the levels given for each factor to produce the total score for the job

☐ to compare the total score for the job with the points brackets that define the grade in the pay structure and allocate a grade to the job.

The rationale behind any expert CAJE system is that there must be clear and discernible reasons for deciding on the levels to be allocated to a factor in any job. Indeed, if there were no apparent reasons or 'rules', the job evaluation process could not operate consistently. The 'rules' may, however, be quite complex.

In a CAJE system the evaluation decision rules are defined either quantitatively or qualitatively, or both, and built into the system shell. The system then operates as follows:

☐ Information about the job relating to each factor is entered into the computer in the form of answers to a questionnaire – the answers may first be recorded manually onto the questionnaire before loading them into the computer, or they may be generated by the software (ie displayed on the computer screen) and the answers input directly to the computer without the necessity of completing a separate questionnaire.

☐ The computer applies the rules to these answers and determines the factor scores.

☐ The total score is calculated for the job by the computer.

☐ The job is graded.

☐ The job information in the form of a factor analysis is stored in the computer.

The computer can also be used for consistency checks – for example, to establish internal consistency between the answers given to different questions. If one answer seems to be inconsistent with another (as in a high score on number of people managed and a low score on leadership skills), it could be highlighted by the computer and the evaluator directed to reconsider such answers. The computer can also carry out consistency checks with other benchmark jobs by displaying the scores for the job in question alongside those of a relevant benchmark job (or any other previously evaluated job) and highlighting the scoring differences.

The system can generate instant information in the form of print-outs. For example, the GAUGE system developed by Burnley Health Care NHS Trust, as described later in this chapter, provides for the code for each answer option selected during the evaluation of a job to be stated in sequence by the system which also has a pre-loaded phrase or statement for each answer code. The system can then assemble all the statements associated with the relevant answer codes and present these in a narrative form, reflecting the way in which the job has been described through the answers chosen. There is thus a full rationale on a factor-by-factor basis of how the overall score and the job grade have been derived.

Developing a CAJE system

A tailor-made CAJE system can be developed for an organisation from its existing point-factor scheme. This avoids the discontinuities that arise when an established system is being replaced, and means that the original investment in the scheme, and the expertise created over the years in its use, are not wasted.

It may, however, be decided that the existing factor plan needs to be modified or that an entirely new factor plan – possibly competence-based – has to be devised. The factor and subfactor definitions and weighting in this revised or new plan should provide the framework for the CAJE system.

The development process for a CAJE system, whether based on an existing plan or on a revised or new plan, consists of no fewer than 14 stages:

1   to identify and analyse benchmark jobs (even if the exist-
    ing plan is being maintained, it is still necessary to carry
    out this analysis and the subsequent steps)

2   to define and weight the factors and subfactors (this stage
    could be carried out along the lines described in Chapters
    5 and 6)

3   to analyse and define the different levels at which the fac-
    tors and subfactors apply in the benchmark jobs

4   to develop on the basis of this analysis a questionnaire
    aimed at establishing for individual jobs the levels at
    which the factors and subfactors apply

5   to use the factor plan and questionnaire developed in
    stages 2 to 4 above to score and rank the benchmark job

6   to assess the validity of the results obtained at stage 5 and
    the effectiveness of the questionnaire as a means of pro-
    ducing acceptable results; validity may be assessed by
    ranking the benchmark jobs using the paired-comparison
    method, and measuring the correlation between that
    ranking and one achieved by the use of the factor plan at
    stage 5

7   to modify the factor plan and questionnaire, and re-evalu-
    ate as necessary in the light of the assessment at stage 6

8   to define the evaluation rules for use in the system; this
    means developing an algorithm (ie a process containing
    rules which enables certain calculations to be carried out)
    which relates the dependent variable of the evaluation or
    ranking produced at stage 5, or modified at stage 7, to
    questionnaire responses so that the factors and jobs can
    be scored directly from the questionnaire responses

9   to test the evaluation rules (the algorithm) to ensure that
    it delivers satisfactory results for the benchmark jobs – ie
    results that correspond with those produced by the
    manual evaluation; modification of the algorithm and,
    possibly, the questionnaire may be necessary until a valid
    result is obtained (this is often an iterative process)

10 to configure the software to carry out the following func-
    tions:

    □   score factors and complete jobs

- grade jobs
- conduct consistency checks
- display results of evaluations and consistency checks on screens
- generate print-outs of results
- create and maintain the database
- enable authorised users to access the database
- enable authorised persons to modify the system (eg factors, weightings, questions)

11 to test and as necessary amend the program

12 to prepare a users' manual

13 to train users

14 to provide maintenance and support services.

The sequence of actions listed above assumes that a tailor-made system is being developed from scratch. But, as discussed below, consultants and software houses can introduce their own systems, which may be customised to a greater or lesser degree.

Responsibility for development

It is necessary to have expert help in developing the algorithm and software. This can be provided by management consultants and/or specialists from software houses with experience in CAJE systems. In theory, an organisation with a powerful systems analysis/programming department could develop a system in-house, assuming that there is sufficient job evaluation expertise within the personnel department. But this combination is rare.

If consultants are used, the project should be set up and controlled along the lines discussed in Chapter 14.

Clearly, whoever is responsible for job evaluation should be closely involved in the project from start to finish. If there are trade unions, it is also highly desirable that they should be consulted at the outset and that they should provide members of any project team set up to oversee and manage the development process. The whole programme should be project-managed as described in Chapter 13.

Advantages and disadvantages

The *advantages* of computer-assisted job evaluation are:

□ speed (especially if the questions are generated by the computer and questionnaires do not have to be completed manually and then entered into the computer)

□ simplicity – job evaluation panels are no longer necessary; the evaluation can be conducted by the job holder and his or her manager with or without a union representative as appropriate (a representative from the personnel department may not be needed except when evaluators are being trained)

□ consistency – the rules are applied consistently by the program on the basis of the information loaded into the computer.

The *disadvantages* are:

□ the quality and consistency of the results depend entirely on the quality of the information entered into the computer system – inevitably this quality varies, although consistency checks and audits can help to improve the reliability and validity of results

□ the evaluation process can appear to be mechanical (which to a degree is exactly what it is)

□ some people will view the 'black box' element of CAJE with suspicion: they may distrust the mysterious processes which generate scores, and it is not enough to say that all job evaluation methods have a touch of mystery about them (at least with manual methods the processes can be described without resource to jargon: it is much more difficult to describe what goes on inside an expert system – 'Just what is an algorithm?' is a question that might easily be asked, but not so easily answered).

The uses of CAJE systems

The advantages of CAJE systems outweigh the disadvantages as long as

□ it is appreciated that such systems cannot replace the judgements required in all job evaluation processes

□ they are introduced and explained with considerable care so that people broadly understand how they function – and this is possible without resource to jargon; ideally, it should be possible to demonstrate how the algorithm works

□ they are used carefully and with discretion; it should always .be understood that the scores and gradings produced by CAJE systems have to be interpreted and applied in the light of an understanding of what constitutes a felt-fair system.

Examples of CAJE systems

The Benefits Agency

The Job Evaluation Grading Support (JEGS) system used in the Benefits Agency was developed by HM Treasury with the intention of making it available for civil service departments and agencies to whom responsibility for pay and grading was being delegated.

The Treasury decided that this new civil service scheme, which replaced the out of date QFA system, should fulfil three criteria: it should be user-friendly, it should be fairly inexpensive to operate, and for these reasons it should be computerised to avoid the use of expensive job evaluation panels. Management consultants Towers Perrin helped the Treasury to develop the system, an analytical points scheme with eight factors: knowledge, skills, contacts and communications, problem-solving, decision-making, autonomy, management of people, and financial responsibility. Towers Perrin also designed the system's software by tailoring their standard job evaluation package to Treasury needs. The JEGS system allows for the computerised evaluation of jobs without a panel. It includes 'logic challenges' to test for any inconsistent answers.

The Benefits Agency has been using JEGS successfully to establish the grading of posts at a time when rapid and significant changes are taking place to job structure, content and culture within the Agency. It therefore represents a good example of how job evaluation can be used to support change programmes.

The system is used only to grade jobs. Pay determination is an entirely separate matter. The first step in the JEGS evaluation process is the completion of a job analysis form by the jobholder. This provides the agenda for an evaluation interview conducted by a trained analyst. Following the analyst's assessment of the post, he or she refers to the JEGS guidelines and completes a multi-choice questionnaire, requiring responses to 59 questions. These responses are then input into a PC and the JEGS software provides a score for the job. Once the score has been generated, analysts are encouraged to think whether it makes sense to them on the basis of their own experience and in relation to other jobs with similar scores. The JEGS guidance notes stress that 'the score produced by the system should not be seen as the final or sole arbiter of grading decisions'.

Burnley Health Care NHS Trust – GAUGE Job Evaluation System

The GAUGE Job Evaluation System was developed by Ken Hutchinson, Human Resource Director of the Trust with the help of Willie Wood, who at the time was the international job evaluation specialist for PA Consulting Group, and Fiona Johnson, Manpower Planning Manager of the Trust.

The process is based on the *JE Manager* software, developed by Monitor Systems Ltd. The software provides a job evaluation methodology that is totally computerised, removing the need for any paperwork or panels in its application.

A key feature of the design is that the system is effectively three linked job evaluation schemes with five core factors in common (each with two dimensions) and six optional factors, two of which are selected for each of three staff groups. The factor plan is given in Figure 10.1 below.

The evaluation process replaces both the job analysis, or other fact-gathering processes such as a structured questionnaire, and the evaluation panel deliberations. This is achieved by getting people who know most about the job to answer a series of logically interrelated questions. These questions, which are directly based on NHS jobs, are pre-loaded into the system and are intended to be the questions an experienced job evaluation panel would ask of itself in deciding what

Figure 10.1
GAUGE FACTOR PLAN

At the suggestion of Sue Hastings, Research Officer at the Trade Union Research Unit, a fourth leg is being developed to accommodate direct care-based support staff.

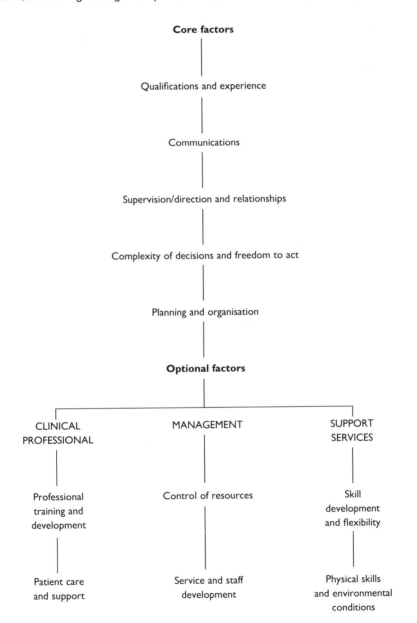

Core factors

Qualifications and experience

Communications

Supervision/direction and relationships

Complexity of decisions and freedom to act

Planning and organisation

Optional factors

CLINICAL PROFESSIONAL	MANAGEMENT	SUPPORT SERVICES
Professional training and development	Control of resources	Skill development and flexibility
Patient care and support	Service and staff development	Physical skills and environmental conditions

factor scores to allocate to the job being evaluated. The allowable responses are pre-set, as are the conclusions the panel would have drawn from each response and the most relevant follow-up question.

The conclusions take the form of 'eliminating' one or more of the possible dimension or factor levels from consideration. In this way no time is wasted and no irritation caused by asking superfluous or inappropriate questions. The questioning continues until every level except one has been eliminated. That level is then logically accepted by the system as the 'correct' level for the job being evaluated, and the questioning moves on to the next dimension or factor.

There are about 350 separate questions, but the system logic ensures that only those 40 to 50 that are most relevant to the particular job to be evaluated are actually posed during the evaluation. An extract from the list of communication questions incorporated into the system is given in Figure 10.2

Figure 10.2
EXTRACT FROM COMMUNICATION QUESTIONS

FOX01
Does the job require the explanation of complex situations and procedures to other people?
A. YES
B. NO

FOX02
Does the jobholder ever have to give complicated information or instructions to others?
A. YES
B. NO

FOX03
Is most of the information required from the jobholder available from books, papers, records, calculations, instruments, VDU screens, etc.?
A. YES
B. NO

FOX04
Are the things the jobholder has to explain technically or medically complicated?
A. YES
B. NO

FOX05
Are some of the more important things the jobholder has to explain or describe to others of a SENSITIVE nature, which the listener(s) may be unwilling to accept?
A. YES
B. NO

FOX06
Is most of the subject matter that the jobholder has to communicate in carrying out the main responsibilities of the job likely to be contentious?
A. YES
B. NO

Once the last question has been answered, the system generates a points score which it displays on the 'validation result' screen if that facility has been activated. This indicates whether the score is 'HI', 'OK', or 'LO' when compared with the expected points range. The latter is determined by the score of the most closely relevant benchmark job and the tolerance range allowed. There is a facility to go back and re-evaluate any factor.

A key feature of the *JE Manager* software is the creation of a 'job overview' for each job evaluated. This can be displayed on the screen and printed immediately in hard copy or called up for any previously evaluated job by someone with the required password level. There is thus a rationale on a factor-by-factor basis of how the overall points score was derived. This fully describes the demands made by the job on the jobholder and removes the need for any manual preparation of paperwork.

The GAUGE system can be used in conjunction with a pay modelling facility that provides pay structure costings and permits the integration of labour market pay information.

Cancer Research Campaign

The software used in the computerised system adopted by Cancer Research Campaign was developed by William M. Mercer, the pay and benefits consultants. It loads information from a job analysis summary sheet onto the computer and then calculates the points score for the job. Information from all the job evaluations is contained on the database. A particularly useful feature of this system is 'autocheck', which provides for consistency by checking the validity of new evaluations against previous evaluations for comparable jobs. This verifies the evaluation or highlights inconsistencies, readjusting the points score and, if necessary, the grading.

11

EQUAL PAY FOR WORK

OF EQUAL VALUE

As Robert Elliott (1991) stated, 'Discrimination arises when equals are treated unequally'. Discrimination in the determination of the relative rates of pay for men and women may not be so blatant as it was before 1975 when the 1970 Equal Pay Act came into force, but it still exists. The most recent *New Earnings Survey* (HMSO, 1994) showed that women's average gross hourly earnings (excluding overtime) were 79.5 per cent of men's. This was certainly better than in 1970 when women's earnings were 62.1 per cent of men's. But there is still a 20 per cent differential.

It seems that historic attitudes about the fundamental value of women in society compared to men continue to exert a powerful influence on their relative rates of pay. Undoubtedly this has arisen because the value of work undertaken by women has been insufficiently recognised. The demands their work makes in terms of knowledge and skill have consistently been undervalued compared with the work undertaken by men. Such undervaluation occurs right across the pay market, but has also arisen because of inherent gender bias in the design of job evaluation, grading and performance appraisal schemes, or in the application of such schemes.

In a comprehensive analysis of the economics of equal value, Jill Rubery (1992) suggested that the undervaluing of women's employment is caused by three interrelated factors:

☐ gender discrimination in the ways in which jobs are graded and paid

☐ widespread occupational segregation by gender

☐ differences in the labour supply and labour market conditions which allow these differences to be perpetuated.

Inequalities in pay exist because of inequalities of opportunity in selection, training, development and promotion. The overall differential in rates of pay is partly a result of the fact that, because of these inequalities, there are fewer women than men carrying out the more demanding jobs. The general subject of equal opportunity is outside the scope of this book, however, and in this chapter we concentrate on equal pay for work of equal value issues and the implications of these issues on job evaluation.

Equal pay for work of equal value: the legal framework

The equal pay for work of equal value legal framework is provided by the 1970 Equal Pay Act as amended by the Equal Pay (Amendment) Regulations (1983). There has also been a fairly limited amount of case law. The Act and its Amendment are implemented through industrial tribunals who may call for reports from 'independent experts' to carry out a job evaluation study.

The Equal Pay Act 1970

Under the Act, which came into force in 1975, an employee in the UK is entitled to claim equal pay with an employee of the opposite sex in the same employing organisation in two situations:

☐ where they are doing the same or broadly similar work (like work)
☐ where the work they do is work rated equivalent under a job evaluation scheme.

The basis of the Act is that every contract of employment is deemed to contain an equality clause that is triggered in either of those situations. The equality clause modifies any terms in a woman's contract that are less favourable than those of a male comparator. So if the woman is paid less than a man doing the same work she is nonetheless entitled to the same rate of pay. Claims under the Act are heard by industrial tribunals.

There are three important points to note about the original Act.

1   Because it was confined to like work and work rated as equivalent the scope of comparison was fairly narrow.
2   It did not make job evaluation compulsory, but did establish the important point (or made the important assumption) that where job evaluation did exist and valued two jobs equally there was a *prima facie* entitlement to equal pay.
3   The Act recognised that a job evaluation scheme could be discriminatory if it set 'different values for men and women on the same demand under any heading'. It gave effort, skill, and decision, as examples of headings.

However, the European Commission's Equal Pay Directive of 1975 stated that the principle of equal pay should be applied to work of equal value. The EC argued successfully before the European Court of Justice in 1982 that the UK had failed to implement the Directive because the Equal Pay Act enabled a woman to obtain equal pay for work of equal value only where her employer had implemented job evaluation. The UK Government conceded the point; the 1983 Equal Value Amendment to the Act was introduced, and came into force in 1984.

The Equal Value Amendment

Under the Equal Value Amendment, women are entitled to equal pay with men (and *vice versa*) where the work is of equal value 'in terms of the demands made on a worker under various headings, for instance, effort, skill, decision'.

This removed the barrier built into the original Equal Pay Act which prevented women claiming equal pay because they were employed to do jobs that no men were employed by the same employer to do. Equal-value claims could now be made even where there were no job evaluation arrangements – although the existence of a properly applied non-discriminatory job evaluation which indicates that two jobs in question are *not* of equal value remains a defence in an equal-value case.

The Amendment also provided for the assignment of 'independent experts' by tribunals to assess equality of value between claimant and comparator under such headings as effort, skill and decision, without regard to the cost or the industrial relations consequences of a successful claim.

Equal-value claims can be made across sites and across employers within an umbrella organisation, with potentially far-reaching consequences, provided applicant and comparator are deemed to be 'in the same employment'. This happens when they have common terms and conditions of employment. In *Leverton v Clwyd County Council (1989)* the House of Lords held that it was sufficient for applicants to be covered by the same 'Purple Book' agreement, despite differences in their individual terms and conditions.

The material factor defence

If an employer can show that a difference in pay is due to a material factor, a claim may be rejected even when the jobs have been shown to be of equal value. The term *material* means 'significant' and 'relevant'. The purpose of the material factor defence is to limit the right to equal pay to situations in which a difference in pay is due to discrimination that cannot be justified by the employer.

The following factors have been held in case law to justify a difference in pay, but in each case it is a question for the tribunal to decide whether the factor is 'material', and whether the difference in pay is due to that factor.

☐ *Market forces* – In *Enderby v Frenchay Health Authority (1993)* the European Court of Justice ruled that 'the state of the employment market, which may lead an employer to increase the pay of a particular job in order to attract candidates, may constitute an objectively justified ground' for a difference in pay. But tribunals will want clear evidence that a market forces material factor defence is based on 'objectively justified grounds', bearing in mind that the labour market statistically discriminates against women. They may view with suspicion evidence gleaned only from published surveys which they may hold to be inherently discriminatory because they simply represent the *status quo.*

☐ *Red circling* (cf *Snoxell v Vauxhall Motors Ltd 1977*) – this is when an employee's job is downgraded but the employee's pay is not reduced. Such protection may not last indefinitely. A tribunal might expect the pay of the red-circled employee to be frozen until the pay of other employees in the same grade catches up (cf *Outlook Supplies Ltd v Parry 1978*).

Employers cannot defend equal-value cases on the grounds of the costs of implementation or of the impact a decision could make on industrial relations, nor can part-time working *per se* provide a defence to a claim. Employers will find it difficult to defend a case unless they use an analytical evaluation scheme. In *Bromley v Quick (1988)* the Court of Appeal ruled that a job evaluation system can only provide a defence if it is analytical in nature. The employer must demonstrate absence of sex bias in the job evaluation scheme, and jobs will be held to be covered by a job evaluation scheme only if they have been fully evaluated using the scheme's factors – slotting whole jobs against benchmark jobs is insufficient.

Other equal-value issues

Several related issues have been dealt with by case law.

Transparency – In what is usually referred to in an abbreviated form as the 'Danfoss' case, the European Court of Justice in 1989 ruled that:

> The Equal Pay Directive must be interpreted as meaning that when an undertaking applies a pay system which is characterised by a total lack of transparency, the burden of proof is on the employer to show that his [sic] pay practice is not discriminating where a female worker has established, by comparison with a relatively large number of employees, that the average pay of female workers is lower than that of male workers.

Number of comparators – In the case of *Pickstone v Freemans (1988)* the House of Lords ruled that females were not precluded from claiming equal pay for work of value equal with higher-paid men who performed different work just because there were a small number of men doing the same work as themselves.

The basis of comparison – The case of *Hayward v Cammell Laird (1988)* concerned Julie Hayward, who was a cook in her employer's canteen and who claimed equal pay with a joiner, a painter and an insulation engineer. Following an independent expert's report, the tribunal ruled that her work was of equal value to that of the comparators and should be paid at the same rate. Some of Hayward's terms and conditions of employment other than pay were more favourable than those of the comparators and the company argued that they should be taken into account to offset the difference in pay levels. However, the House of Lords ruled that the Act required a comparison of each term of the contract considered in isolation. Hayward was therefore entitled to the same rates of basic and overtime pay as the men, even though the other terms of her contract were more favourable.

Separate bargaining units – In *Enderby v Frenchay Health Authority (1993)* the European Court of Justice made another important ruling in this case relating to separate bargaining units, stating that: 'The fact that the rates of pay at issue are decided by collective bargaining processes conducted separately for the professional groups concerned without any discriminating effect within each group does not preclude a finding of *prima facie* discrimination where the results of these processes show that two groups with the same employer and the same trade union are treated differently.' Otherwise, it would be easy for employers to 'circumvent the principle of equal pay by using separate bargaining processes'.

Industrial tribunal procedures in equal-value cases

The procedure followed by a industrial tribunal starts with the receipt of the application setting out the applicant's case (IT1) and a Notice of Appearance Form (IT3) in which employers are asked whether they intend to contest the case and if so, their grounds for doing so. The tribunal may hold a pre-hearing assessment to discuss whether the case has substance or not, which may involve informal talks. A preliminary hearing may be held to determine jurisdiction – the entitlement of either party to bring or to contest the proceedings. The tribunal may ask for further particulars and the 'discovery' of relevant documents. During this period an ACAS Conciliation Officer attempts to achieve conciliation between the parties. If there is jurisdiction and conciliation fails at this stage, the proceedings continue as set out in the flow chart below (Figure 11.1).

Figure 11.1
PROCEDURE FOR ESTABLISHING EQUAL VALUE

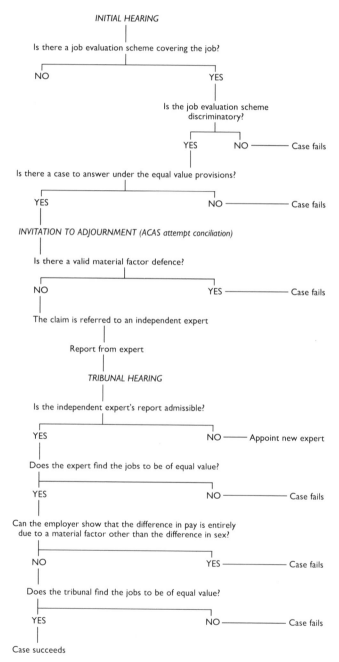

The role of the independent expert

The Industrial Tribunal (Rules of Procedure) Regulations require that an industrial tribunal, unless it is satisfied that there are no reasonable grounds for determining that the work in question is of equal value, must require an independent expert to prepare a report. This requirement stipulates that the expert must

☐ take account of all information supplied and representations that have a bearing on the question

☐ before reporting, send the parties a written summary of the information and invite representations

☐ include the representations in the report together with the conclusion reached on the case and the reason for that conclusion

☐ take no account of the difference in sex, and at all times act fairly.

Experts conduct their investigations by means of interviews, discussion and observation. *The Guide to Good Practice for Independent Experts* (ACAS, 1990) strongly recommends that experts should observe the whole work cycle for the jobs being compared, and if this is not possible, suggests that the expert must ensure that tasks are demonstrated or discussed in detail and illustrated on the spot. Independent experts only assess the demands made on the jobs under consideration; they have no remit to carry out investigations beyond the jobs specified in the requirement. They do not take into account the perceived value of the job (or the jobholder) to the organisation.

The Rules of Procedure state that any job evaluation system chosen by experts must be designed under factor headings (ie be analytical). Subject to this, experts can decide for themselves the system they want to use, depending on the circumstances of the case. The ACAS *Guide*, however, emphasises that there are two essential differences between conventional job evaluations and the task of independent experts:

☐ A conventional system covers a wide range of jobs whereas independent experts consider only a few jobs.

☐ Conventional analytical job evaluation is concerned with

relative value (ranking jobs and indicating the differences in value between them), whereas independent experts are concerned only with *comparative value* (establishing whether the jobs are equal in value or not).

The ACAS notes for guidance quote the Rules of Procedure and the Act's factor headings of effort, skill and decisions, and although stating that these are not prescriptive, recommends that, because aspects of skill and effort appear in most cases, they should be included. The notes also suggest that independent experts might use responsibility as a main factor, as was given considerable prominence by the Employment Appeal Tribunal in the case of *Eaton v Nuttall (1977)*. 'Decisions' could be used as a subfactor of 'responsibility'.

The guidance notes state that large-value number systems are not necessary for the restricted comparisons made by independent experts, but suggest that: 'Experts will usually have to allocate or imply a "number" value to each factor and subfactor assessment across factor and subfactor levels . . . It is possible for assessments to be regarded simply as "wins, draws or losses, and to aggregate these using, for example, number values of 2, 1 and 0 respectively".'

The ACAS guidance notes indicate, however, that such a system might be open to criticism because of its crudity, and state that independent experts have to steer a middle course between extremes, using systems that are neither cumbersome nor over-intricate. The notes suggest that a 'profile' type of system could be used with a relatively low number of levels; for example 'low', 'medium-low', 'medium high' and 'high'. To aggregate the results, number values of 1, 2, 3 and 4 may be allocated, and if further refinement were needed, each level could be further allocated to a 'plus' or a 'minus' subdivision that would double the possible number values.

The ACAS notes do not mention weighting the factors, presumably because any weighting could only be subjective and difficult to justify and, in any case, is superfluous in the limited comparisons made by experts. In practice, experts do not usually weight factors.

Examples of the evaluation factors and subfactors used by independent experts are given in Table 11.1 below.

Table 11.1

FACTORS USED BY INDEPENDENT EXPERTS

Bromley & others v Quick	Brown & Royale v Caerns & Brown	Hayward v Cammell Laird	Wells & others v Smales
Knowledge	Responsibility	Physical demands	Skills
Experience	– for other people's work	Environment	– manual
Judgement and	– for goods handled	Planning and decision-	– manipulative
decision-making	– for equipment used	making	dexterity
Contacts	– for safety (of self	Skill and knowledge	– mental demands
	and others)		– experience and
			– training
Physical effort	Effort	Responsibility	Responsibility
	– strength and stamina		– for materials or
	– mental demands		products
Consequence of errors	Skills and knowhow		– for plant and
	– experience and training		equipment
	– trade and product		Working conditions
	knowledge		– environmental
	– versatility		– other
	– judgement and initiative		Effort
			– physical
			– visual and mental

Job evaluation and equal value

The equal-value legislation clearly has important overall implications for job evaluation, and to help in the understanding of these implications the first part of this section analyses the differences between conventional approaches to job evaluation within organisations and the methods used by independent experts in equal-value cases. The succeeding parts of this section assess other general aspects of potential gender bias in job evaluation – namely the suggestion that job evaluation simply reinforces existing hierarchies and the degree to which gender bias is inevitable in organisations, with or without a formal, analytical job evaluation scheme. The next sections of this chapter consider the specific ways in which job evaluation can be discriminatory or non-discriminatory; and the chapter ends with some conclusions on the approaches organisations should use to ensure that job evaluation can minimise, if not eliminate, gender bias.

Implications of the legislation for job evaluation

The original legislation and subsequent case law clearly state that the existence of an analytical and non-discriminatory job evaluation scheme applied to all the parties between which comparisons can be made provides a good defence against equal-values claims. The question of what makes job evaluation schemes discriminatory or non-discriminatory is discussed in the next section of this chapter.

However, an organisation that has conducted extensive research into equal value issues, the Trade Union Research Unit, stated in 1987 that 'The existence or introduction of a traditional job evaluation scheme may actually militate against the achievement of equal value because of the differences between the conventional use of job evaluation within organisations and the assessment methods of independent experts in equal-value cases.'

Differences between conventional job evaluation and equal value assessments

The Trade Union Research Unit's paper mentioned above argues that while the job evaluation techniques used within organisations and the assessment methods used by Independent Experts are superficially the same, they are in fact very different. The differences put forward are:

- *Coverage* – A job evaluation scheme usually covers all the jobs in a negotiating or occupational group, whereas an 'equal-value' assessment normally covers only those jobs in dispute and their named comparator jobs.
- *The evaluators* – Job evaluation exercises within organisations are usually conducted by a panel, whereas in an equal-value assessment the evaluation is the responsibility of one person, the independent expert.
- *Factors* – Most modern job evaluation schemes are based on a limited number of factors and subfactors, but in an equal-value assessment the evaluator is duty bound to take into account all the significant features of the jobs under consideration, and therefore uses different plans, often with more factors and subfactors
- *Weighting* – Most analytical job evaluation schemes incorporate some form of factor weighting, whereas independent experts tend to avoid weighting their factors, possibly

to avoid the taint of discrimination that can be attached to a normally weighted factor plan.

☐ *Aims* – Traditional job evaluation has conventionally been used to rationalise and hence perpetuate the *status quo* within an organisation, whereas an equal-value exercise usually aims to change the relationships within a graded structure by demonstrating, for example, that some skills and responsibilities have historically been over- or under-valued in that structure.

Job evaluation as a reinforcer of existing hierarchies

The last assertion is the most controversial one – many organisations and management consultants would hotly deny it. But it is a view supported by other commentators. Quaid (1993) for example notes that 'Job evaluation tends to adopt those "values" that are already "important" and builds them into the process of evaluation . . . Job evaluation really serves to both reinforce and endorse an already existing hierarchy (or a newly desired one).' She noted from her research into the application of the Hay system of job evaluation in 'Atlantis' (a pseudonym for a Canadian province) that 'The Atlantis hierarchy remained . . . relatively stable in spite of the job evaluation process. Where there was change, it reflected more the belief systems of the actors involved than the powers of the job evaluation process to sort out "objectively" and "rationally" the relative worth of jobs.' McNally and Shimmin (1988) asserted on the basis of their research into 19 different organizations that in general the job evaluation objectives of these organizations were

> to tidy up a muddled situation, and to do this with minimal disruption. While understandable, this emphasis on stability evidently militated against the interests of equal pay . . . Job evaluation was used to simplify and regulate grade and pay structures, not to disrupt established status differentials . . . Most of the schemes examined in the study had been tailored to reproduce the *status quo* in the job grading. In effect, this meant that job evaluation had little or no potentiality for equality purposes.

More recently, Michael Rubinstein (1992) said that from the

management standpoint there is one overriding criterion for whether a particular job evaluation scheme is successful, and that criterion is acceptability. The results of the scheme must be acceptable to those covered by it and those responsible for its administration. It is hardly then surprising, he argued, that what is seen by the majority as acceptable or fair is usually that which has the result of establishing a rank order very similar to the existing pay structure.

It is certainly the case that any whole job ranking exercise based on 'felt fair' judgements is likely to do no more than reproduce the existing hierarchy. Indeed, from the point of view of equal pay, the felt fair principle tends to re-endorse managements' preconceptions if it is they who make the judgement on whether or not a rank order or grading is fair. And it is worth remembering that decisions on grade structures are often made by management alone *after* a joint management/employee panel has completed the job evaluation exercise.

Another factor that may lead to the perpetuation of the existing hierarchy is the selection of benchmark jobs. Traditional job evaluation practice requires that benchmark jobs should represent the various levels in the pay structure. In other words, as McNally and Shimmin (1984) point out,

> The original rank order of the jobs is reproduced by the re-affirmation of the status of these key posts. The remaining jobs are then grouped around the benchmark jobs and, with the exception of a small number which are regraded, the 'new' job hierarchy takes on an appearance which, to all intents and purposes, is identical to the old.

Perhaps this traditional approach is less common nowadays, but if it is followed trade unionists may suspect that, once selected as benchmarks, the jobs concerned will not be regraded as a result of the job evaluation exercise. This could be because employers would not want a 'knock-on effect' to disturb the grading and therefore the pay levels of non-benchmark jobs. Thus, it is argued, benchmarks will help to perpetuate the existing hierarchy and differentials.

Is gender bias in job evaluation inevitable?

Sue Hastings (1991) believes that 'there is no such thing as a non-discriminatory job evaluation scheme', but then goes on to say that it is possible to identify the obvious sources of discrimination and the associated risks. Arvey (1986) comments, 'Because many of the procedures involved in job evaluation are inherently subjective, these practices have been suspect for being biased and discriminatory against jobs held predominately by females'.

Gender bias can exist in the components of the scheme (the choice of factors and their weighting), and this is the discriminatory aspect of job evaluation given most attention by the Equal Opportunities Commission and trade unionists, possibly because some employers are introducing job evaluation schemes solely as a means of avoiding equal-value problems. As Sue Hastings (1991) comments: 'The present state of equal pay legislation is such that an employer introducing a job evaluation scheme covering all potential "equal-value" applicants and comparators is effectively protecting itself against "equal-value" claims'.

It should be remembered, however, that it is not only the scheme itself which can discriminate but also the way in which the scheme is applied. In other words, the *process* of job evaluation can be discriminatory as well as the system used.

Treiman and Hartmann (1981) asserted that sex stereotypes could possibly influence the nature of job evaluation procedures. Madigan and Hills (1988) note that market rates 'reflect the effects of historic discrimination against women in employment and pay position – any pay structure developed by reference to market rates may therefore be subject to gender bias'. They also state that 'the central issue in developing a job evaluation plan is one of determining whose values will be reflected in the plan'. If these values are tainted by the gender bias that still exists in many organisations, possibly under the surface, then the scheme and the way it is applied will discriminate.

Gender bias does exist in society, so it is reasonable to suppose that it can be present within the organisations in that society. As a management consultant said to McNally and

Shimmin (1988) of job evaluation, 'People are subjective, and therefore so is the technique', and subjective judgements in a climate where gender bias exists may well be discriminatory.

As Rubinstein (1992) emphasised, what is regarded as acceptable because it is fair and what is not sexually discriminatory are not the same:

> Since the work women do is undervalued because it is performed by women, the effect of traditional job evaluation which emphasises acceptability is merely to perpetuate the *status quo*. In such circumstances, job evaluation does not get rid of pay discrimination against women. All it does is to make pay discrimination more subtle, more covert, and more difficult to prove.

But gender bias in job evaluation is not inevitable. The impression we gained from some of the organisations we visited during our research was that efforts were being made to eliminate it, at least in the way in which the scheme was applied, although it is often the case that the design elements have been allowed to remain without sufficient scrutiny.

Achieving gender neutrality

The issues raised above suggest that if an organisation is determined to achieve gender neutrality and end discrimination, it should not be obsessive about equal-value law. It should instead concentrate on both the evaluation scheme it is developing and the processes it uses to implement the scheme. These processes go beyond merely establishing internal relativities – they extend to the key decisions made on grade structures and the relationship between internal rates of pay and market rates. The rest of this chapter examines the issues concerning discrimination in job evaluation, and what organisations can do to achieve gender neutrality.

Discrimination in job evaluation

Discrimination in job evaluation starts with the design of the scheme, and, as the Trade Union Research Unit (1987) noted,

> It is the Unit's view that most discrimination, and the most serious forms of discrimination because they are the most difficult to identify and the least easy to do anything about, occur

in the design of the scheme. The reason for this is simple. A job evaluation scheme will achieve the aims, broadly speaking, of those who design it. If those aims are directly discriminatory (to make sure that women's jobs remain at the bottom of the structure) or indirectly discriminatory (to replicate the existing hierarchy), then they will have been achieved through the scheme's structure.

The point is well made. Clearly, the first thing to do when attempting to eliminate discrimination is to look at the scheme itself. But, as noted earlier, the way in which the scheme is implemented can discriminate, especially when organisations have simply installed off-the-shelf schemes that appear to be non-discriminatory, and then proceed to allow grading and pay decisions to be made which continue to be gender-biased. Both these issues have to be considered.

How job evaluation schemes themselves can discriminate against women

Type of scheme
If the scheme is non-analytical (a whole job ranking or classification scheme), it may simply replicate existing views on job demands which may be biased against women.

Appropriateness
A scheme is only non-discriminatory if it takes account of the significant features of all the jobs it covers. Designed for a different type of organisation or area of work, a scheme may fail to do this. According to Sue Hastings (1989),

> The problem of inappropriate evaluation schemes may actually be a growing one as organisations, often encouraged by management consultants, try to introduce or extend schemes to cover all employees to increase their protection from equal-pay claims.

Choice of factors
The choice of factors alone can discriminate, as described by Hastings (1991):

1   *Omission* – Discrimination can result from the omission of factors such as those listed below while retaining factors such as physical strength which favour men. Factors frequently missed include:

  □ caring skills and responsibilities for patients, clients or customers, which in service industries are equivalent to the responsibilities for product usually included in job evaluation schemes designed for manufacturing operations

  □ human relations skills needed by those dealing directly with customers (internal and external) and clients; these skills are exercised by secretaries, receptionists, telephonists, sales assistants, and customer service staff dealing directly with customer orders, queries or complaints – all these jobs are generally, or at least frequently, carried out by women

  □ organisational skills and responsibilities where, as in many administrative, clerical and secretarial posts held by women, the work may involve the continuous re-ordering and re-prioritising of tasks to meet changing demands

  □ responsibility for product quality – the exclusion of this factor may discriminate against the women who often carry out finishing and packing work where a final check on quality is carried out.

2   *Duplication* – This takes place when a factor plan contains features of predominately male jobs which can be counted under more than one heading. These could include:

  □ judgemental factors – Sue Hastings quotes a scheme put forward by a management consultant in an equal-value case which included three overlapping features, each defined in similar terms: *evaluation and judgement* under a mental demands heading, *problem-solving* also under the mental demands heading and *decision-making* under a responsibility heading

  □ education, training, experience and knowledge and skills factors – education, training are alternative ways of achieving a particular level of knowledge and skill;

double counting takes place if any combination of education, training or experience factors are included as
well as skill and knowledge factors, and/or if education, training or experience is included as a separate
factor; a scheme that demands a considerable number
of years' experience could be discriminatory because it
ignores the fact that the careers of women may be
interrupted for means of child-care.

Elision – This occurs when a single factor is used to cover
two or more job features. It almost invariably leads to one
of the factors' being undervalued relative to the other(s).
For example, when a single physical effort factor is used
to cover both strength and stamina, it is probable that the
latter will be undervalued relative to the former. This
could result in discrimination against women's jobs.

Research conducted by Lorraine Paddison (1987) for the
London Equal Value Steering Group on white-collar evaluation in London local authorities identified the following over-
and under-rewarded work attributes:

Over-rewarded
  professional status
  managerial role
  position in the status hierarchy

Under-rewarded
  caring and other interpersonal skills – eg nursery nurses,
    people doing social work, and those caring for the elderly
  difficult or demanding contacts – eg housing benefits officers
  volume of work/pressures/deadlines – eg revenue officers
  stress – eg counter staff
  creativity, other than writing reports
  skills where there may not be recognised professional qual-
    ifications – eg race/women's advisers, posts with child-
    care responsibilities, caring for the elderly
  experience which may not be gained through work – eg
    experience in minority ethnic cultures
  where post-holders are required to manage services to
    people, rather than other council sections – eg luncheon
    club supervisor

language skills where there is not an associated qualification.

These under-valued job demands were found mainly in work performed by women.

Sins of commission and omission like those mentioned above can affect the fairness of any factor plan which aims, as it must do, to provide a non-biased means of assessing both relative and comparable worth.

Examples of discriminatory and non-discriminatory job factors provided by the Equal Opportunities Commission (1985) are given in Tables 11.2 and 11.3.

Table 11.2
EXAMPLE OF DISCRIMINATORY JOB FACTORS

Factors	Maintenance fitter	Company nurse
Skill		
Experience in job	10	1
Training	5	7
Responsibility		
For money	0	0
For equipment and machinery	8	3
For safety	3	6
For work done by others	3	0
Effort		
Lifting requirement	4	2
Strength required	7	2
Sustained physical effort	5	1
Conditions		
Physical environment	6	0
Working position	6	0
Hazards	7	0
TOTAL	64	22

Note: each factor is scored on a scale from 1 to 10 – for simplicity no weights have been applied.

Table 11.3
EXAMPLE OF NON-DISCRIMINATORY JOB FACTORS

Factors	Maintenance fitter	Company nurse
Basic knowledge	6	8
Complexity of task	6	7
Training	5	7
Responsibility for people	3	8
Responsibility for materials and equipment	8	5
Mental effort	5	6
Visual attention	6	6
Physical activity	8	5
Working conditions	6	1
TOTAL	53	54

Note: each factor is scored on a scale from 1 to 10 – for simplicity no weights have been applied.

The Equal Opportunities Commission's check-list, *Good Equal Opportunities Practice in Analytical Job Evaluation*, is given in Appendix G.

Number of factors

Conventional wisdom has dictated that the number of factors must be kept to a minimum to avoid duplication and complexity. It was, and still is, argued that the same results can be obtained with a smaller set of factors as with a larger.

The impact of equal value means that more factors may be needed than in a traditional scheme to cover all the significant features of both men's and women's jobs. The number of factors required depends on the number of jobs to be covered. A scheme for jobs of a similar structure or type needs a smaller number of factors than one covering a whole organisation. Sue Hastings suggests that six to twelve factors may be sufficient if a limited range of jobs has to be covered, while up to twenty may be necessary in a large organisation where a wide range of jobs, functions and services are to be catered for. Attempting to cover all the jobs in an organisation with a multiplicity of factors can, however, be difficult and confusing. There is a real danger of duplication, and the time taken to analyse and evaluate jobs increases considerably.

This problem is particularly acute in the National Health

Service and to solve it Sue Hastings (1992) has suggested an approach along the following lines:

☐ A central working party consisting of representatives from all occupational groups draws up a 'menu' of factors to represent all the significant features of the jobs to be covered.

☐ Core factors for, say, skill, knowledge and effort are selected to cover all occupations.

☐ Working parties for each occupational group then select the additional factors from the menu that are relevant to their own group.

☐ Levels of demand are identified from a sample of jobs, and each level is defined; the central working party co-ordinates the process to ensure that where factors overlap between groups the level definitions are written in the same way.

☐ Scoring and weighting systems for the core and the occupational group factors are agreed.

☐ The similar but distinct schemes for the different occupational groups are 'linked' by evaluating some 'key' job which could equally well be covered by more than one scheme by means of two or more relevant group schemes.

Sue Hastings admits that the above suggestions sound unwieldy, and would require careful planning and co-ordination. But she believes that it would eliminate some of the major difficulties inherent in trying to develop one scheme to cover all diverse Health Service groups, and could achieve more satisfactory and equally defensible results. Since this paper was written, Burnley Health Care Trust has developed a 'branching' evaluation scheme along these lines (as described in Chapter 10).

The arguments for having one scheme to ensure that there is a 'read-across' between different occupational groups or job families are very powerful, however, and from an equal-value point of view, the advantages gained from being able to cover all occupational groups with one scheme may outweigh the disadvantages. It is a matter of choice, but a 'linked' approach as described above is well worth considering in any organisation in which there are a number of distinctive occupational groups or job families.

Factor measurement

Particular care needs to be exercised with the definitions of levels for skills, knowledge and experience factors. Discrimination can be introduced if some sorts of qualifications are assumed to be of a higher level than others. This could produce an arbitrary hierarchy where, for example, the questionable assumption may be made that a formal qualification leading to a certain level of applied knowledge and skill is inherently better than the acquisition of the same level of knowledge and skills through some combination of education, training and experience.

The scoring system may also result in discrimination if the size of the steps simply reinforces the existing hierarchy, making it more difficult for women's jobs to be upgraded or found equal at the end of the exercise.

Factor weighting

Factor weighting is likely to be discriminating if it favours factors predominately related to male jobs (eg physical effort) *or* to women's jobs (eg manual dexterity). Some form of balance must be achieved between any factors that may favour either men or women. Weighting based on regression techniques linked to 'felt-fair' rankings may reinforce existing differentials and could thereby perpetuate discrimination.

Weighting can either be explicit (the variations between the maximum scores attached to different factors) or implicit (when some factors have more subfactors than others, or where there are different numbers of levels for each factor but each level carries the same number of points).

How the introduction and application of job evaluation can discriminate against women

Job evaluation processes

These could be discriminatory if the job evaluation panels are not fully representative of both men and women. A prejudiced evaluation could result if the sex of the jobholder is identified.

Job analysis and descriptions

Job analysis may not take account of all the features of both men's and women's jobs. As Blummrosen (1979) has stated, 'The value system and related perceptions of the job analyst influence what information is collected and therefore what is available in later stages of the process.'

Arvey (1986) suggests that gender bias can occur because the information collected is 'a hodge-podge of human capital as well as job content information'. Job evaluation procedures usually include both the supply or input elements of a job (ie the traditional human capital variables of education, training and experience which indicate what is needed to perform the job) with the demand (actual job content) and output elements of the job. If the supply elements are over-emphasised or distorted (eg requirements greater than truly necessary are indicated as essential for performing a job), women may find that their work is undervalued because their opportunities for training and their experience are likely to be less than those of men.

He also refers to the ways in which gender bias can exist in the job analysis phase of job evaluation:

☐ Job analysts may perceive and recall differential information, depending on whether the job involves 'women's work' or whether the work is carried out predominently by men.

☐ Job analysts may neglect information more related to women's work – for example, asking about working conditions that involve considerable physical exertion but neglecting aspects of work such as sitting still for long periods of time, visual strain, etc.

☐ Job analysis information may be pre-selected by questionnaires or job inventories which are in themselves biased.

Such risks can best be reduced by extensive training of job analysts in the system *and* in awareness of how gender bias occurs.

Drawing grade lines

As explained in Chapter 9, the process of drawing grade lines is largely judgemental. The Equal Opportunities Commission suggests that boundary lines should be drawn wherever there is a significant gap in the distribution of scores between job clusters.

This sounds like good advice, and follows the precepts of most standard texts on job evaluation. What the EOC fails to appreciate, however, is that scattergrams of points scores do not always arrange themselves with convenient gaps. It may be impossible to avoid boundary lines which dissect clusters of jobs, and there will inevitably be problems of deciding which jobs should fall on either side. The problem may be alleviated in a broad-banded system by the fact that there are not so many boundaries. In such systems it may therefore be easier to draw the lines where there are convenient gaps – although broad-banded structures may create other problems, as noted below.

Broad-banded structures

Broad-banded structures (see Chapter 9) can facilitate flexibility and reduce the problem of grade drift so often encountered with narrower-banded structures. But such structures may discriminate indirectly if they rely entirely on 'anchoring' zones by reference to market rates, and if they 'slot' jobs into bands by means of whole job comparisons. The former approach could be attacked from an equal-value point of view unless 'objectively justified' grounds can be produced, and this may not be easy. It would probably be insufficient to rely on published pay surveys or advertised rates. The latter approach can form the basis of an equal-value claim on the grounds that an analytical job evaluation scheme has not been used to grade the jobs.

Competence-based structures

If these are designed by reference to an analytical competence-based job evaluation scheme (ie one in which competence headings are used as factors), they are not discriminatory *per se*. Discrimination only exists if there is gender bias in the choice of the competence-based factors. A job family structure that uses competence levels to define the bands or levels within job families could, however, be regarded as discriminatory (see below).

Generic role definitions

The use of generic role definitions could discriminate if sufficient account is not taken of the particular characteristics of women's roles.

Job family structures

Whether or not job family structures are competence-based, there are three ways in which they might be found to be discriminatory:

☐ if the levels are defined as in a job classification scheme – ie evaluation is non-analytical, being conducted by slotting whole jobs into the job family levels

☐ if there is no 'read across' by means of an analytical evaluation process between job families

☐ if they are in effect 'market groups' containing jobs believed to have to be paid higher because of market forces than is indicated by the internal evaluation process – market rate differentials of this nature may need to be 'objectively justified'.

Job families have not yet been tested as such in an equal-value case, but the decision of the European Court of Justice in *Enderby v Frenchay Health Authority (1993)* indicates that any differences in average earnings between job families of different predominant gender would have to be objectively justified by the employer.

Computer-assisted job evaluation

Computer-assisted job evaluation systems could be held to be discriminatory if they are based on biased questionnaires or 'rules' in terms of factors, weightings, and the conversion of questionnaire responses to evaluation scores. These points should be checked for gender bias before the system is implemented (it may be more difficult to change it later). There is also the question of transparency – how much is revealed or *can* be revealed about what goes on inside the black box? Such systems have not yet been tested in an equal-value case.

Implementation of the pay structure

Following the creation of a new grade and pay structure by means of job evaluation and market pricing, employees may have to be regraded or placed in a radically re-designed grade structure.

It is generally accepted as good and fair practice not to reduce the pay of anyone whose job is overgraded following evaluation. In this situation, employees are normally 'personally protected' or 'red-circled' – in other words, their rate of pay is frozen until it falls within the proper grade following general increases to the pay brackets for grades. But to cut the costs of implementing the new structure, organisations may phase the increases required to undergraded employees to bring them to the level of pay appropriate to their new grade. This procedure, which is sometimes called 'green circling', could be held to be discriminatory if the preponderance of red-circled employees were men and most if not all of the employees whose pay increases were being phased were women. The practice of simply transferring employees into their new grade on their existing level of pay, even where the job evaluation has indicated that their jobs are worth more, could be regarded as discriminatory if this mainly affects women and they are still underpaid in comparison with men whose jobs have been evaluated at the same level.

Unbiased job evaluation processes

Research conducted by Ghobandian and White (1987) established that certain specific approaches to job evaluation are more likely to result in an unbiased process:

- ☐ a formal scheme
- ☐ an analytical scheme
- ☐ a high number of factors (to enable job comparisons to be made in greater detail)
- ☐ a high proportion of women covered by the scheme
- ☐ job evaluation as the sole determinant of pay – ie no variable rates within grades
- ☐ openness (transparency) in the shape of a formal communication programme on the aims and methods of job evaluation

□ the presence of female employees on job evaluation working parties and panels

□ trade union representatives as job analysts and as members of the steering committee and job evaluation panels.

It was also found that the larger the establishment the fairer the scheme, and that manual workers' schemes were less likely to be biased. The researchers did not explain the latter phenomenon, but it could arise because there is less emphasis on decision-making and related factors, and because clearer, and therefore less subject to bias, skill hierarchies exist.

What needs to be done

It has been suggested by Fouracre (1995) that 'Women's pay will undoubtedly be a major issue facing employers as the worst of the recession passes and the economy settles down, because trade unions will find it a useful platform for re-establishing bargaining strength.'

If, regrettably, an organisation simply wants to duck this problem and to avoid a successful equal-value claim (or should it be to 'evade' such a claim?), then all it *apparently* needs to do is to install an analytical scheme (preferably one of the well-known proprietary brands) and ensure that it is used to evaluate all the jobs. However, Michael Rubinstein (1992) has suggested that the use of proprietary schemes and the role of management consultants should be examined:

> In the UK, employers have been able to hide behind proprietary schemes, and such little experience as we have suggests that the courts will be very reluctant to find that an evaluation conducted by using a proprietary scheme is discriminatory because they think that it will mean invalidating the whole of a scheme that may be widely applied in many countries.

It can also be argued that the emphasis on the legalistic definition of equal value and the legal processes that take place before industrial tribunals and higher courts are distracting attention from the real issue. This is *comparable worth* – ie the need to determine fairly, without bias and consistently the comparative value of *all* the jobs within an organisation, whether carried out by women or by men. Of course gender bias exists, overtly (but not so often now) and covertly. And of course it needs to be eradicated. But eradication will only take place if the values of the organisation support it; an obsession about conforming to equal-value legislation is not enough.

It should also be remembered that, as expressed by Pritchard and Murlis (1992), 'We are faced with equal-value legislation which enshrines the perception of job evaluation and how it worked a decade or more ago . . . New processes and approaches to job evaluation are replacing the "set piece" implementation methodologies that were received wisdom in the 1970s.' The new process includes job family models, computer-assisted job evaluation and competence-based job evaluation.

Clearly, it is important when selecting or developing a new job evaluation scheme or revising an existing one to pay attention to all the factors referred to earlier in this chapter which can make such schemes discriminatory. There is, however, no question, as Fouracre and Wright (1986) noted, 'of any scheme being given a once-and-for-all clean bill of equal-value health'. And as Sue Hastings (1991) points out, there is no such thing as a model scheme that is automatically unbiased and fair to all those jobs within the organisation predominately undertaken by women, although, as reported in *Industrial Relations Review and Report* (1987 and 1989), some schemes have been designed explicitly to take into account the equal-value concepts of the legislation. These include the Local Authority Manual Workers' scheme and the schemes devised for production workers at United Biscuits and for non-manual workers at Save the Children Fund.

When developing, implementing and operating job evaluation, particular attention needs to be given not only to the design of the scheme itself but also to the way in which it is to be introduced and operated. The elements that make these processes discriminatory or non-discriminatory were also set out earlier in this chapter.

Some of the key issues that should be stressed in the development and implementation processes are:

☐ the design of a comprehensive and non-discriminatory factor plan

- the provision of 'read-across' mechanisms between different job families and occupational groups if they are not all covered by the same plan
- the development of comprehensive and unbiased questionnaires
- the provision of proper training in conducting job analyses and producing fair job descriptions which should include bias-awareness training
- the involvement of female as well as male employees in the development of the scheme, also trade union representatives when the organisation is unionised (involvement should extend to the choice of the scheme, the design of the factor plan, job analysis, the actual process of evaluation and the design of grade structures)
- the involvement of female as well as male employees (and trade union representatives) in the operation of the scheme through job evaluation panels or by some other joint process of evaluation in which employees and their representatives take part
- the creation of appeal processes using bodies with representatives from both management and employees
- the transparency of the whole scheme – its aims, methods of working and impact should be explained to all employees (not just the members of the working party or panel)
- great care over the selection and use of benchmark jobs so that they are fully representative of both men's and women's jobs, and so that the process does not simply reproduce the existing hierarchy

  equally great care over grade boundary decisions; the aim should be to avoid placing them between jobs that have been evaluated as virtually indistinguishable, bearing in mind that the problem will be most acute if grade boundaries are placed between traditionally male and female jobs (in any situation where such boundary problems exist – and they are almost inevitable – it is good practice to re-evaluate the jobs, possibly using a direct 'comparable worth' or equal-value approach which concentrates on the particular jobs)

□ the treatment of market rate comparisons with caution to ensure that differentials arising from market forces can be objectively justified

□ the training of job analysts and evaluators in how to avoid gender bias

□ great care over the implementation of the pay structure to ensure that female employees (indeed, any employees) are not disadvantaged by the methods used to adjust their pay following re-grading.

Further consideration is given to the selection, design, development, and operation of job evaluation schemes in the next four chapters.

PART 3

DEVELOPING, IMPLEMENTING AND MAINTAINING JOB EVALUATION

12

SELECTING THE APPROACH

Basic considerations

Where no job evaluation scheme exists, the first decision to make is whether or not a formal approach to job evaluation is needed, and if so, how much formality is required. If there is an existing scheme, it is desirable to review how well it is functioning.

The formal approach to job evaluation

The first point to bear in mind is that there is no choice about job evaluation. All organisations must make decisions on rates of pay, and these decisions are based on judgements about relative job values within the organisation or on market rate imperatives or perceptions. The choice is therefore not concerned with the need to evaluate jobs but with whether or not any type of formal evaluation is required at all, and the arguments for and against it are summarised below.

Many organisations, including a number of those covered by our survey, seem to be quite happy to do without formal job evaluation. Their organisational structure and methods of working, in their view, clearly indicate the relative values of roles without the need for a bureaucratic and, they feel, inflexible process of job evaluation. In some cases negotiations or custom and practice determine pay relativities, and they see no point in superimposing job evaluation. If asked about the danger of an equal-value claim they reply that they are quite satisfied that their pay structure is not discriminatory and that they are certainly not going to become obsessed by equal-value considerations. They may also feel that a formal process would be at odds with the culture of the organisation as manifested in its flexible and non-bureaucratic approach to managing its affairs.

Other organisations – the majority of those we contacted – believed that an orderly approach was essential in order to develop and maintain a logical, fair and manageable structure, and to minimise the risk of a successful equal-value claim.

In favour of formal job evaluation

A formal approach to job evaluation can provide:

- a basis for making fair, consistent, and defensible decisions about the relative and comparable worth of jobs
- agreed and understood methods and sets of criteria which can be used by all concerned and which represent the values of everyone in the organisation in relation to the factors to be taken into account when assessing job values
- a firm and well-understood basis for establishing pay levels and structures, and for managing relativities in organisations facing the challenge of handling diversity and operating flexibly in constantly changing conditions
- a means of fairly assessing the relative worth of the different types of occupations within organisations – managers, team leaders, team members, professional staff, knowledge workers, creative staff, people involved in selling and negotiating, those involved in caring for and dealing directly with people, administrators, support workers, etc.
- a basis for establishing comparable worth – eliminating gender bias in pay and grading decisions
- a means of avoiding equal-pay-for-work-of-equal-value claims and for providing a defence if such claims are made
- transparency in pay and grading decisions, which can help to ensure that all concerned feel that the system is fair
- a basis for devolving grading and pay decisions to line managers while still retaining the capacity to monitor the consistency of those decisions
- the data required to make valid comparisons with market rates.

Against formal job evaluation

The arguments that are sometimes used against formality are that job evaluation is

- unnecessary – 'we already know what rates to pay without such a system'
- inflexible
- bureaucratic
- costly, in time as well as money
- 'everyone is quite happy with the system as it is, so why bother?'

Making the choice

The choice is dependent on the organisation's culture, management style and methods of organising and conducting business. But even if the decision is against formality in the shape of a set-piece job evaluation scheme, it is undeniable that a systematic approach to assessing job values based on the considerations discussed in the first part of this book is desirable.

The arguments in favour of some degree of formality are very powerful, and it is perfectly possible to develop and use flexible methods of job evaluation which fit flexible firms and do not impose a costly and time-wasting system on the organisation. To follow this route, the areas for choice are discussed below.

At this stage an initial decision can be made on which jobs or occupations should be covered and how many schemes might be required. But final decisions should not be made without the further analysis of requirements and, preferably, discussions with employees.

Is it necessary to change the existing arrangements?

Job evaluation schemes can decay. They can be corrupted and subject to manipulation, and either create or fail to control grade drift (upgradings unjustified by an increase in the value of the job). They can become out-of-date, no longer relevant in a rapidly changing organisation. Organisational structures and processes, the composition of the workforce, or the values held by management and employees generally about what is important when assessing relative worth, could become very different from those existing when the scheme was originally introduced. The scheme may be perceived by those who run it and/or by those who are affected by it as inflexible, inappropriate, bureaucratic, and time-wasting.

Generally, people in the organisation may agree with the comment made by the IDS Top Pay Unit (1992): 'Laboriously compiled job definitions, often inflated or unusable for other purposes, and endless meetings of job evaluation panels and committees have given job evaluation a bad name.'

The questions to be answered when reviewing the operation of an existing job evaluation scheme are:

- Is it felt by management, employees and trade union representatives to operate fairly?
- To what extent are there perceived inequities in the ways in which jobs have been graded or paid?
- Is there any gender bias built into the scheme's factor plan or evidenced by the way it functions – the outcome of evaluations?
- Does the scheme provide an adequate defence against equal value claims?
- Is the scheme being manipulated?
- Does grade drift take place?
- Are the values expressed by the factors contained in the scheme appropriate and acceptable to all concerned?
- Can it respond adequately to the new role requirements emerging in the organisation – for example, increased flexibility, more project-teamwork, multiskilling?
- Is it appropriate for all the new occupations/jobs being created in the organisation?
- Is it relevant to the new structure of the organisation (eg delayered, emphasis on horizontal processes rather than vertical hierarchies)?
- Is the factor plan unsuitable (eg too many or too few factors, duplication, omissions, elision, imprecise definitions of factors or factor levels, inappropriate weightings)?
- Is the scheme over-complex and/or inflexible?
- Is it time-consuming and bureaucratic?
- Is the grade and pay structure produced by evaluation satisfactory from the point of view of the number and width

of grades, the existence of boundary problems, and diffi-culties in deciding on the correct grades or rate of pay for jobs?

☐ To what extent have job evaluation decisions been devolved to line managers in conjunction with individual members of their teams and, where appropriate, employee representatives?

☐ How well are job evaluation processes integrated with other reward and HR processes – for example, by the use of competences as factors, or the provision of information about roles for human resource planning, recruitment, per-formance management, training and continuous develop-ment purposes?

This audit could be carried out by the personnel function or, preferably, by an internal working party, which should not necessarily consist of members of existing evaluation panels. There is much to be said for getting external help with the audit, if only in the form of someone who can facilitate the working party's investigations.

It is unlikely that any job evaluation scheme that has been in operation for more than five years or so would stand up to this sort of audit in its entirety. There is always room for improvement by total replacement, rejigging the factor plan, or altering the various analytical, evaluation and grading processes used in applying the scheme. If the decision is to introduce an entirely new scheme or to radically revise the factor plan, the decisions required are summarised below and discussed in more detail in the remaining sections of this chapter. This leads to the introduction of a new scheme as described in Chapters 13 and 14. If, however, it is decided that only relatively minor changes should be made to the factor plan or to methods of operating the scheme, these could be decided internally in discussion with managers and other employees and employee representatives.

Formal job evaluation: areas for choice

There is plenty of choice when selecting a formal approach to job evaluation or replacing an existing scheme. The sequence of questions to answer is shown in Figure 12.1.

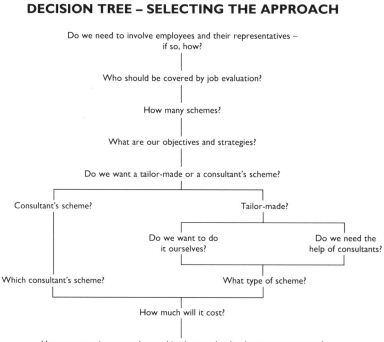

Figure 12.1
DECISION TREE – SELECTING THE APPROACH

The remaining sections of this chapter answer each of these questions in turn.

Should employees and their representatives be involved?

Some organisations see the whole process of valuing jobs as a management prerogative. They do not involve employees at all either in developing or in operating the scheme. Even line managers may be excluded from job evaluation decisions made behind locked doors in the personnel department.

Organisations which adopt this policy probably save a lot of time and money, and they may produce a result that is perfectly satisfactory from management's point of view. But what about the workers? It affects them too. Not involving them at all can deliver a clear message that this is an organisation which does not recognise that they have any interest in something that affects them deeply – ie their pay-packet. The outcome may be a fair and equitable pay structure, but it can be argued that fairness must not only be done, it must also be seen to be done. Transparency is important.

This approach may be adopted in organisations which operate entirely on an individual contract basis, and in these circumstances it might well be asserted that, as people take part in agreeing or even negotiating their own remuneration, there is no point in involving them collectively. The claim that individuals *are* involved and do influence their pay could be specious, but this is what many organisations do, as was established by our research.

Others may take the view that to go through the elaborate process of setting up a joint working party or job evaluation panel is time-consuming and unnecessary. All they need to do is to communicate to employees in general the basis upon which their jobs are graded and then rely on explaining grading and pay decisions individually.

This is probably not a tenable position when there is an active trade union in the organisation, for it will almost certainly want to be involved, if only to monitor equal-value implications. Even if the organisation is not unionised there is everything to be said for adopting a completely transparent approach. It is highly desirable to involve employees and their representatives (if any) at all stages of the decision-making process. Job evaluation can only be truly successful if it is owned by those who carry out and are affected by evaluations. They should be involved in assessing the need for the introduction of job evaluation, or the need to amend an existing scheme, and in decisions on which jobs and occupations the scheme should cover, and how many schemes are required. They should take part in defining objectives and criteria, and in selecting the type of scheme. They could even be involved in the selection of any consultants who are to install their own scheme, or help in the development of a tailor-made scheme. This may sound unusual, but such an approach helps to increase the acceptability of job evaluation – and of the consultants.

Employees and their representatives can participate as members of a job evaluation panel at later stages in the development process in designing or modifying a tailor-made scheme, customising a consultant's proprietary brand (so far as this is possible), conducting job analyses, preparing job descriptions or role definitions, and evaluating jobs. They may take part in discussions on the grade structure, but are much less frequently involved in grading decisions, and never in decisions on rates of pay for individuals, although rates of pay for jobs and pay scales may be negotiated with unions if they exist and have negotiating rights. Importantly, panel members can take part in communicating information about the scheme to their fellow employees. They can also be represented on the steering group which oversees the whole exercise. A further advantage of using panels is that they provide a forum for discussing any organisational issues that emerge from the job analyses.

But involvement can take place without using a formal job evaluation panel. At Burnley Health Care Trust, for example, job evaluation decisions are made with the help of their computerised system by individuals in conjunction with their managers – the individual's trade union representative also takes part. Panels are not used in a fully computerised evaluation system such as that operated by Norwich Union where the individual completes a job evaluation questionnaire that is converted through the computer software into a job evaluation score. But in these situations it is advisable, as in both the cases referred to above, to take great pains to communicate to employees how the process works and how it affects them. If there are formal consultation or negotiating processes, these channels should be used to discuss the arrangements and to communicate or agree the results.

Typically, however, as was evident from our research, organisations set up some form of working party or panel, and each of those we talked to who had done this was certain that it was the right policy from the point of view of obtaining consensus, understanding, and acceptance.

Who should be covered by job evaluation?

Having decided on who should be involved, the next decision to be made is on which jobs, occupational groups or levels in the organisation should be covered by job evaluation. Ideally everyone – except possibly board members and senior managers on individual contracts and terms and conditions of employment – should be included.

There are, however, many forms of organisation which contain a number of job families – clearly differentiated groups of occupations in which people work within a distinct function using a common range of knowledge, skills and competences at different levels. These job families might also comprise 'market groups', in which market rate levels are generally different from those in other occupational groups. Each job family could have its own sequence of defined levels or bands, but a general evaluation scheme might be used for 'read-across' purposes – ie to assess comparable worth between job families.

Consideration at this stage could also be given to the case for evaluating all occupations by reference to one set of core or generic factors, or the need to evaluate certain roles against additional factors relevant to their particular characteristics.

How many schemes?

Decisions on who should be covered lead naturally to the consideration of how many schemes are necessary. Preferably one scheme should be used for all occupations and levels, but this ideal may not be practicable where there is a very considerable range of occupational groups or a wide variety of job families. In these circumstances it may be impossible to avoid having separate schemes or job families. Wherever possible, however, an attempt should be made to link these schemes by having certain common factors or by overlapping evaluations as suggested by Sue Hastings.

Job evaluation objectives

It is essential at this stage to be clear about the objectives of the exercise before defining criteria for choice and deciding on what type of scheme to use. These objectives can form the basis for briefing employees generally, and for briefing consultants in order to develop terms of reference for an assignment.

Objectives could be defined along the following lines: to develop and implement a systematic and analytical process for evaluating jobs which will enable fair and consistent decisions to be made on their relative worth and provide a basis for the design and operation of a logical and equitable grade and pay structure and for managing relativities within that structure.

However, a measure of choice exists in defining objectives. You can adopt a reasonably comprehensive but bland definition such as that set out above. Or you can penetrate more deeply into the real purpose of job evaluation as an important aspect of reward, personnel and, ultimately, business strategy. This approach can be based on obtaining answers to four fundamental questions:

☐ What is our business strategy?
☐ What sort of personnel strategy do we need to support the business strategy?
☐ What sort of reward strategy do we need to support the business and the personnel strategies?
☐ What sort of strategy do we want to adopt for job evaluation as an integral part of our reward, personnel and business strategies?

At Triplex Safety Glass this approach was adopted recently by establishing overall pay and reward objectives:

☐ to develop a pay and reward structure that is capable of being applied to the whole of Triplex, underpins corporate values and business objectives, and facilitates the removal of any barriers preventing future growth of our business
☐ to recommend transition and implementation plans for moving from present reward arrangement to new proposals
☐ to ensure that proposals and plans are realistic and can be supported by the business financially and in principle
☐ to secure involvement/support of key influences in the business prior to the launch of new proposals.

This sort of definition provides a much better basis for ensuring that job evaluation plays its part in an integrated set of processes designed to further the objectives of the business.

At the Burnley Health Care Trust the job evaluation exercise sprang from the following key HR objective headings derived from the business plans:

☐ workforce flexibility and utilisation

- organisation and management structures
- employee relations
- job design – productivity and demarcation
- training needs – skill acquisition and professional development
- re-profiling – the skill and grade mix.

All these were formulated against the background of the move toward local pay determination in the NHS.

The objectives set at this stage should therefore not be limited to the narrow confines of developing a job evaluation scheme but placed in a context that emphasises the broader business and personnel issues which the various processes involved in job evaluation can help to address. They should also make it clear that the specific purposes underpinning the job evaluation exercise are to determine how people should be valued by the organisation and how they should be rewarded in accordance with their competence and contribution.

It is at this stage when formulating objectives that two of the key issues in job evaluation should be addressed: first, achieving flexibility, and secondly, achieving gender neutrality.

Achieving flexibility

Flexible firms need flexible job evaluation processes. The traditional approach to job evaluation treated it as a system that was based on rigid job descriptions. It was governed by the principles that people did not really count, it was only the job duties (as tightly defined) that mattered, and that the purpose of job evaluation was to reinforce existing hierarchies – the established pecking order and system of relativities.

This approach is clearly inappropriate in today's circumstances when, in the words of Pritchard and Murlis (1992) the pressure is 'to manage diversity rather than to control uniformity'. Role flexibility is an absolute requirement in flatter organisations in which considerable use is made of new technology and the emphasis is on projects, teamwork and horizontal processes rather than on command and control hierarchical structures in which individuals use a single skill or technique in a rigidly demarcated job.

The approaches that organisations may adopt to achieve greater flexibility are:

☐ to focus on roles rather than on jobs, stressing the need for people to work flexibly in carrying out roles in rapidly changing situations and as members of a multidisciplined or multiskilled team. The use of generic descriptions for such roles as project/process manager, team leader, team member, professional specialist adviser, and support worker, which emphasise the flexibility inherent in these occupations, can help. The roles of individual team members can be defined in terms of the contribution they are expected to make to the achievement of team objectives and the knowledge, skills and competences they need to play a full part in the team

☐ to avoid the use of over-detailed and restricting job descriptions and instead to rely on role definitions which focus on key result areas rather than on tasks and duties, emphasise the need for flexibility and continuous development, and spell out the core competences relating to the role

☐ to clarify individual roles by the agreement of objectives, relating both to work and to personal development

☐ to focus on people as well as jobs – to emphasise that people should be valued for the skills and competences they use to deliver results, rather than for their capacity to carry out the detailed tasks laid out in a traditional job description

☐ to incorporate flexibility as a factor in the job evaluation factor plan, thus demonstrating that it is one of the key values of the organisation and that flexibility will be rewarded

☐ to emphasise that people are valued not only as individuals but also as members of teams to which they contribute by working flexibly; teamwork as a value can be highlighted by incorporating it as a separate factor in the factor plan

☐ to introduce broad-banded pay structures in which it is recognised that progression is not simply a matter of climbing up the narrowly spaced rungs of a promotion ladder in a job hierarchy but is achieved by gaining and using additional skills and competences effectively in situations in which new demands are constantly being made on teams and their members

☐ where appropriate, to create job family structures in which progression through the bands depends largely on the ability of individuals to use higher levels of competence effectively in achieving project, team and individual objectives.

Achieving gender neutrality

Approaches to achieving gender neutrality were set out in Chapter 11. What is important to remember is that not only should the scheme itself (the factor plan) be free of gender bias, but so also should the processes used to identify and select benchmark jobs and to analyse, describe, evaluate and grade those jobs and the rest of the jobs in the organisation.

Job evaluation strategies

Before developing criteria for job evaluation it is necessary to consider how job evaluation strategies should be formulated to support reward, HR and business strategies. The ways in which this support can be provided include:

☐ providing a framework within which strategic decisions can be made about rewards

☐ focusing both on input factors that extend the skill base and increase levels of competence and on output factors concerned with contribution, influence and impact

☐ enabling the total reward system to be more responsive and supportive to organisational needs for flexibility, multi-skilling, teamwork, quality, customer service, etc.

☐ helping to eliminate gender bias and to promote equal opportunity

☐ helping with the management of diversity

☐ generating information on role requirements which can be used to improve organisational effectiveness and to provide a basis for continuous learning and employee development processes.

The requirements for job evaluation can be set out in the form of a process specification which should be drawn up on the basis of an analysis of the internal and external environment of the organisation.

Internal environment

The analysis of the internal environment should provide answers to the following questions:

Culture

What are our values about work – the particular characteristics of roles that we believe should influence decisions on relative worth?

To what extent can the prevailing management style in the organisation be described as autocratic or democratic?

Is the climate in the organisation one of mutual trust or is there open or underlying conflict between different interest groups?

To what extent could the organisation be described as having a 'command and control' culture?

Is there any need to change the culture – for example, to focus more on performance, quality and customer service, or to develop a more open (transparent) approach to managing the organisation?

Technology

What are the fundamental technical development, operational, administrative and information technology processes and systems used in the organisation?

To what extent is this a high-tech organisation, making the maximum use of new technology?

To what extent can the management and operational systems be described as bureaucratic, flexible, or innovative?

Structure

To what extent is the structure

hierarchical, with a number of layers?

flat, with the emphasis on process and teamworking?

flexible, involving constant changes in the composition of project teams and roles?

decentralised or devolved, involving the devolution of decision-making to business units or line managers?

Occupations and roles

Is there a multiplicity of occupations and roles in the organisation?

Are there wide variations in the demands made on people in those roles?

To what extent are roles in different parts of the organisation flexible or tightly defined?

Is the requirement for role flexibility increasing?

Employee relations

What is the climate of employee relations?

To what extent can job evaluation improve this climate?

How co-operative are trade unions and employee representatives likely to be in a job evaluation exercise?

How can the purpose of job evaluation and the methods proposed to introduce it best be communicated to all concerned?

External environment

An analysis of the external environment is concerned with such issues as

- the changes likely to occur to the organisation as a result of business, economic and political pressures
- the changes in the demands the organisation has to meet in order to achieve competitive advantage – for example, in the areas of innovation, quality and cost leadership
- the impact of market forces on rates of pay.

Criteria

The environmental analysis provides the foundation for the definition of the criteria for evaluating alternative approaches and specifying requirements. Clearly, the criteria vary from organisation to organisation depending on the objectives and strategies for job evaluation and the analysis of the internal and external environment. However, examples of possible criteria include:

- congruent with and aligned to organisational strategies, culture and values
- integrated with other HR processes

☐ structured
☐ analytical
☐ systematic
☐ people-oriented
☐ gender bias absent
☐ transparent
☐ accepted as fair and equitable
☐ defensible
☐ developed and operated with the involvement of all concerned
☐ flexible
☐ inexpensive to introduce and operate
☐ easily administered and maintained
☐ computerised, but user-friendly.

Process or system specification

The criteria can be used to develop a process or system specification that lays down what is required of the job evaluation process and that outlines the key features of whatever system is used for evaluating jobs.

The following is an example of a system specification produced by the Burnley Health Care Trust prior to introducing job evaluation:

1 transparency
2 developed in the NHS
3 expert software-based system
4 user-friendly
5 analytical – points rating system
6 gender neutral
7 trade union involvement
8 pay modelling facility
9 low development and maintenance costs
10 capable of adjustment to local circumstances – flexible.

Consultant's package or tailor-made scheme

The process/system specification provides the background against which the next decision can be made: whether to purchase a consultant's package or to develop a tailor-made scheme.

Why choose a consultant's package?

Our survey indicated that the majority of organisations (68 per cent) that went in for an analytical job evaluation scheme used a consultant's proprietary brand. The reasons given to us for this decision were that proprietary brands are:

☐ credible – they have been well tested and tried in a wide variety of organisations

☐ offered by consultants who should be experienced, good at facilitating working parties, expert at dealing with any problems that may arise, and who are convincing

☐ relatively easy to install – consultants have developed well-honed methods for introducing their scheme covering job analysis, questionnaires, the format of job descriptions, methods of evaluation, and methods of converting evaluation scores to gradings; if they wish, personnel specialists can take a back seat and let the consultants drive the installation programme

☐ equal-value claims-proof – consultants' schemes are usually analytical and, so far, none has been found to be discriminatory (although it is said that some unions are only waiting for the right opportunity to challenge one or other of them)

☐ convincing to employees when presented with the help of consultants expert in communicating the particular virtues of their scheme and how everyone in the organisation will benefit from it

☐ computerised to save installation and administration costs and time or either as part of the package or as an add-on

☐ frequently linked to a database of market rate comparisons – this can be a particularly powerful incentive to adopt a scheme which obtains data from organisations using the same analytical evaluation method, thus, it is claimed, ensuring that like is compared with like.

Not everyone accepts that it is desirable to use a proprietary brand. Candrilli and Armagast (1987), for example, assert that 'Many compensation consulting firms claim that they have one job-evaluation methodology that is appropriate for every organisation; this is simply not the case. The values that are important to a high-tech electronics organisation may not be the key factors in a low-tech manufacturing company; in like manner, the values appropriate for an insurance company may not be appropriate for a fast-food distribution company.' Alan Fowler (1992) suggests that 'the advantages of operating a scheme that is specific to the characteristics and values of the organisation can be considerable'. Craggs (1990) claims that in France organisations want a highly company-specific solution with a maximum of tailoring in system design.

The arguments often marshalled against using a proprietary brand are:

☐ The factors included in the scheme and the factor weighting (if any) might not be appropriate to the type of jobs to be evaluated within the organisation and the organisation's values on what should be rewarded. Factors which, as in some consultants' schemes, emphasise the number of people supervised and the size of budgets controlled, may be quite irrelevant in research, development and creative jobs, and the contribution of people doing this type of work could be undervalued. There is also the possibility that they may encourage empire-building, something that is totally inappropriate in today's leaner and flatter organisations.

☐ The schemes tend to be inflexible and bureaucratic.

☐ In spite of what the consultants say, the schemes can be manipulated by people determined to inflate job levels.

☐ No consultant's scheme has yet been developed which totally eliminates subjective and possibly prejudiced judgements about job values.

Management consultants may assert in reply to these criticisms respectively that:

☐ They are prepared to modify their factor plans and guidecharts (ie to customise their scheme) to fit particular organisations and their values. But they cannot go too far without abandoning their plans or charts. Moreover, if they operate a market rate comparison service based on job evaluation scores, the extent to which they can vary their plans must, presumably, be limited. Some consultants' schemes can be customised more readily than others, and consultants have developed modified versions of their schemes for particular sectors, for example NHS Health Care Trusts.

□ There is no need for their schemes to be run bureaucratically (except, presumably, in a bureaucratic organisation).

□ Manipulation of job descriptions and evaluations can be controlled through well-trained and experienced job evaluation panels, the members of which are familiar with the jobs and are encouraged to probe wherever a job description appears to be inflated. In any case, manipulation is possible in any job evaluation scheme, whether or not it is a consultant's proprietary brand.

□ No job evaluation scheme has ever been devised which totally eliminates subjective and prejudiced judgements, but at least a well-tried and tested consultant's scheme should be more successful in doing so than one developed from scratch.

Why develop a tailor-made scheme?

Although it sometimes seems that the consultants' proprietary brands totally dominate the job evaluation market, 32 per cent of the respondents to our survey used tailor-made schemes. Additionally, we identified through our research a number of impressive examples of bespoke schemes, including those developed by the Automobile Association, Burnley Health Care Trust, Thomas Cook, The National & Provincial Building Society, Pilkington Optronics, and Triplex Safety Glass. And in the public sector three major tailor-made national schemes have been developed recently, namely for the civil service, JESP (Job Evaluation for Senior Posts) and JEGS (Job Evaluation Grading Support), and for local authority manual workers, the Local Authority Conditions of Service Advisory Board's scheme.

The main advantage in developing a tailor-made scheme is that the factor plan can be specifically aligned to the values, occupations and roles within the organisation. It can be shaped to meet the strategic needs of the business in accordance with its technology, structure, core competences and culture. As stressed by Madigan and Hills (1988), 'The central issue in developing a job evaluation plan is one of determining whose values will be reflected in the plan.' Why, say those who advocate tailor-made schemes, should these values be ones imposed upon us by consultants, often incorporated into schemes developed 30 or 40 years ago when values within organisations about what should be rewarded were substantially different from those of today?

One reason for developing a tailor-made scheme in-house was provided by Alan Fowler (1992), who wrote that 'A major test of any scheme is its credibility within the workforce, and this may be enhanced by the knowledge that it has been designed by and for the organisation.'

The design and development of a tailor-made scheme can be a major exercise, however, and it should not be embarked upon without thinking very carefully about the amount of expertise required and the time and effort involved. As discussed later in this chapter, these considerations may make it advisable to enlist outside help from management consultants in developing a bespoke scheme.

Making the decision

A decision can be made only by weighing the pros and cons listed above in the light of the circumstances of an organization. A key factor may be the belief that a proprietary brand is most appropriate because of the reputation of the scheme, the expertise of the consultants from the firm that is offering the scheme, the ready availability of market rate data and, importantly, the perceived ease with which the scheme can be introduced. But do not assume that installing a proprietary brand will save much of your time or that of others involved in the process. Unless you are going to get the consultants to do all the analytical work and to carry out the evaluations (a highly undesirable practice – this is going to be your scheme, not theirs) you and other people will be heavily involved in the programme. Introducing job evaluation is always a time-consuming affair.

If your major concern is to have a scheme that fits the needs of your organisation, you may favour one that is tailor-made, with or without the help of consultants.

But you do not have to make a final choice at this stage. You can give further thought to the implications of developing your own scheme, possibly in discussion with consultants who will provide expert assistance, *and* study the offerings of two or three proprietary brand consultants before making up your mind. The next two sections of this chapter examine the criteria for choice between proprietary brands and whether to develop a tailor-made scheme yourself or with the help of consultants. Cost considerations are discussed later in the chapter.

Choosing a consultant's scheme

Summaries of the better-known consultants' proprietary brands are given in Appendix A. More details of these and other consultants' schemes are provided in the IRS (1994) publication *Job Evaluation in the 1990s* (Neathey, 1994). The points to be considered in making a choice are:

□ the reputation of the scheme and the consultants who offer it

□ the experience of the consultants in installing the scheme in similar organisations

□ the degree to which the factors included in the scheme appear to fit the requirements and values of the organisation

□ the extent to which the consultants can customise their scheme to fit the requirements of the organisation

□ gender neutrality (an absolute requirement)

□ the availability of reliable market rate data linked to the scheme

□ the likely acceptability of the scheme to employees and their representatives

□ the ease with which the scheme can be installed and operated

☐ the quality of the questionnaires, check-lists, and the briefing and supporting material provided by the consultants

☐ the availability of computerised systems to help in job analysis, job evaluation and scheme maintenance

☐ the ability of the consultants to train job analysts and evaluators

☐ the capacity of the consultants to provide advice and help with related reward and HR issues including the design of pay structures, pay modelling, performance management, competence analysis and profiling, and organisation development

☐ the time it would take to introduce the scheme

☐ the costs involved (always a consideration but not necessarily the first consideration).

The selection and use of consultants is discussed further in Chapter 14.

Developing a tailor-made scheme

As Alan Fowler (1992) has emphasised, 'Designing and validating an in-house scheme, including ensuring its freedom from discriminatory bias, is no task for an amateur.' It is, of course, possible to do it yourself with the help of the guidelines included in this book, the excellent Trade Union Research Unit technical note on developing a less discriminatory job evaluation scheme (Hastings, 1991), and the publications of Industrial Relations Services (IRS) and Incomes Data Services. The IRS publication *Job Evaluation in the 1990s* (Neathey, 1994) provides some useful job evaluation case-studies. It is also possible to do some benchmarking – finding out the 'best practices' adopted by similar organisations which have developed their own job evaluation schemes.

But you may well decide that you lack the expertise or the time to act as an 'internal consultant' in developing your own scheme. In this case you will need to seek outside help from a management consultant. Such help could mean anything from providing initial and intermittent fairly lightweight advice to being fully involved from start to finish in developing and launching a job evaluation scheme.

If you do want to go it alone, there is much to be said for using an external consultant to provide advice, encouragement and, possibly, warnings of potential pitfalls. It is useful to have a sounding-board for your ideas. Without this sort of guidance it could be difficult to guarantee a satisfactory result unless you and, ideally, one or two other people in the organisation, have had some experience in job evaluation, if only in operating a proprietary brand or some other established scheme.

If you have decided to develop an in-house scheme, with or without the help of consultants, you now need to decide what sort of scheme you want. You may have decided from the very start that you want a point-factor or competence-based scheme (or a combination of the two), but now is the time to review all the alternatives and settle on your final choice.

The type of scheme

The advantages and disadvantages of each of the main types of job evaluation schemes described in Chapters 3 to 7 are summarised in Table 12.1.

Choosing a method

The method you select depends, of course, on your particular needs as summarised in the objectives and criteria you have developed for the project. Examples of the choices that might be made according to circumstances include:

☐ Your organisation is fairly small but growing and operating flexibly in a highly competitive market, and you are not over-concerned with equal-value considerations. Your approach might be to start by ranking benchmark jobs, then develop a grade structure into which you slot the jobs, price the structure by reference to your own market intelligence and published data, and use an internal benchmarking process to slot jobs into the grades. This is an exercise you could quite easily undertake yourself. It would not protect you from equal-value claims and it may not be felt fair by employees unless they have been involved in the project.

☐ Your organisation is fairly large and is structured on a

Table 12.1
COMPARISON OF JOB EVALUATION SCHEMES

Scheme	Brief description	Advantages	Disadvantages
Non-analytical			
Job ranking	jobs are compared with one another and placed in rank order	□ simple □ quick	□ no defined standards □ not acceptable in equal-value cases
Paired-comparison ranking	whole jobs are ranked by the statistical method of paired-comparisons	□ easier to compare one job one job with another than having to make multi-comparisons	□ no defined standards □ not acceptable in equal-value cases □ only a limited number of jobs can be evaluated
Job classification	the characteristics of the grades in a structure are defined and jobs are slotted	□ standards for making grading decisions are provided □ quick and easy to use	□ cannot cope with complex jobs □ inflexible □ not acceptable in equal-value cases
Internal benchmarking	jobs are compared with internal benchmark jobs and slotted into the appropriate grade	□ simple □ quick □ in accord with 'natural' way of grading jobs	□ relies entirely on judgement □ benchmark comparisons may perpetuate existing inequalities □ not acceptable in equal-value cases
Analytical			
Factor comparison	benchmark jobs evaluated against common factors and the score is converted directly into monetary terms – remaining jobs slotted into pay scales by reference to benchmarks	□ analytical □ no need for level definitions □ directly prices the job	□ depends on selecting the 'right' benchmark jobs □ complex □ subjective judgement still required
Point-factor rating	jobs assessed in terms of the degree to which defined factors are present; points are allocated	□ defined standards provided to guide judgements □ credible – will probably be	□ complex □ spurious impression of scientific accuracy

		Advantages	Disadvantages
	for each factor according to the level at which this factor is present in the job; the points for each factor are added to give a total score	perceived as being fair and objective	☐ does not obviate the need for judgement
Competence-based job evaluation (factor plan type)	competences used as factor headings as in a point-factor scheme	☐ as for point-factor scheme additionally: – directs attention to people and their roles – can be integrated with other competence-based HR/reward processes	☐ as for point-factor scheme additionally: – depends on thorough competence analysis – competence profiles do not necessarily translate readily into evaluation factors – danger of rewarding the acquisition of competences rather than their effective use – not tested in an equal-value case

Others (quasi or non-analytical)

Competence-based job evaluation	levels in job families are defined in competence terms and people are slotted into bands in accordance with their level of competence	☐ recognises that progression may be within a job family on the basis of competence levels ☐ people-oriented ☐ can be integrated with other HR competence-based processes	☐ no 'read-across' between job families therefore dangers of inequities and inconsistencies ☐ danger of rewarding the acquisition of competences rather than their effective use ☐ may not be acceptable in an equal-value case
Market pricing	rates of pay and differentials are established on the basis of market rate comparisons	☐ in line with the realities of the marketplace ☐ quick and straightforward (if reliable data is available)	☐ market rate data not necessarily reliable ☐ relies on judgement ☐ probably unacceptable in equal-value cases

well-defined hierarchical basis. You are genuinely concerned with avoiding gender bias, not just evading an
equal-value case. Your approach might be to develop a
point-factor scheme taking particular care to avoid discrimination in the design of the factor-plan. You would
want to involve employees and, if you have unions, their
representatives. You may well want to obtain advice from
consultants in developing your scheme, and you would
almost certainly want to use computers.

☐ Your organisation has been delayered and following a business process re-engineering exercise is now functioning on
a process/project team basis. You would probably want to
operate a much more flexible approach to job evaluation
within a broad-banded structure. The emphasis would
therefore be on people and roles, and you may decide to
adopt a competence-based approach with generic roles. You
could position people in the bands in accordance with
their level of competence, their contribution, and the
market rate for their role. If you have already carried out a
programme of competence analysis to produce competence
frameworks you may well develop your own evaluation
process, although you might enlist the support of consultants to develop or customise computer software to help
you in operating the scheme.

☐ Your organisation is high-tech and is structured into project teams of scientists and development engineers who
work closely with manufacturing teams using computerised systems for planning, control and operation. You
may decide on a job family approach using competence definitions to identify levels of contribution in the job families and market pricing to fix rates of pay. You might still
retain some form of job evaluation (graduated factor comparison or point-factor rating) to provide for internal equity
between job families. Alternatively, you might allow competence levels and market pricing to determine relativities
within job families and only carry out some form of graduated factor comparison where you believe there is a need to
establish comparative worth. The factors used for this purpose could be derived from the core competences defined
for generic roles.

☐ Your organisation has a diverse range of professional, technical and administrative functions. You may decide that you want to use an analytical point-factor approach but that you may need separate schemes for the major occupational groups. They could be linked through core factors or overlapping evaluations.

Cost considerations

Your choice of the method to adopt has to take account of cost considerations. The main costs are considered below.

Opportunity costs

Opportunity costs arise out of the time you and other members of your organisation spend on job evaluation which could be used more profitably doing something else. This could be considerable – job evaluation, if done properly, is always a time-consuming exercise. There is therefore a major opportunity cost element in a job evaluation exercise, although it may not be normal practice in your organisation to calculate such costs.

Consultancy fees

The cost of consultants of course varies considerably depending on the extent to which they are used – for example, they may only provide general advice, they may be involved at various levels in the development and implementation of a tailor-made scheme, or they may install their own job evaluation package or computer software. Clearly the size of the project in terms of the number of benchmark and other jobs to be evaluated and the number of functions and sites to be covered directly influences the cost.

Consultancy fees vary considerably. A major firm of consultants may charge around £1,000 a day for a resident consultant, more for any overall advice, guidance or supervision provided by a partner or managing consultant. An independent consultant or member of a small firm may charge between £500 and £750 a day, occasionally more, sometimes less. It is easy to see, therefore, how the costs can mount up in a full exercise, even if the consultants are not spending much time on job analysis and actually evaluating jobs. In an organisation with about 200 employees in a range of managerial, professional, administrative and support jobs, a typical job evaluation programme conducted with the help of consultants might look like this:

	Steps	Consultant days
1	Preliminary discussions and analysis	2
2	Briefing and training job evaluation panel	1
3	Developing factor plan	2
4	Providing guidance and quality control on job analysis	3
5	Facilitating job evaluations and re-evaluations	4
6	Conducting market rate survey (database/desk research)	2
7	Preparing and discussing grade and pay structure proposals	2
8	Preparing briefing papers	1
9	Helping to brief employees	1
10	Producing final report and guidance notes on operating and maintaining job evaluation	2
	Total consultant days	20

Of course, more or less time could be spent on any of these stages depending on the depth of the study and the extent to which the organisation's own employees carry out the work of job analysis and evaluation. But this is a fairly typical timescale. It means that the cost of consultancy fees could be anything between £10,000 and £20,000. If your organisation is about this size, you could start by assuming £15,000 as an approximate average cost of consultancy fees and anticipate variations on either side of that figure depending on who you use and how you use them. It is obvious that in larger and more complex organisations the costs could be considerable.

The information collected during our study suggested that costs could be broadly within the ranges set out in Table 12.2, depending on the size of the organisation and whether the assignment is to install a package or help to design a tailor-made scheme. Licence fees of up to £10,000 or so may be charged for any computer software packages.

Table 12.2
APPROXIMATE COSTS OF USING CONSULTANTS
(in thousands of pounds)

Small (fewer than 250 employees)		Medium (250–1000 employees)		Large (more than 1,000 employees)	
package	*tailor-made*	*package*	*tailor-made*	*package*	*tailor-made*
5–10	10–20	20–30	30–40	40–60	60–120

It should, however, be re-emphasised that these figures are merely indicative: costs can vary considerably and can be reduced by increasing the amount of work carried out by members of the organisation (with the guidance of the consultants).

Costs of implementation

A full job evaluation exercise always generates implementation costs. These arise because those who are placed in higher grades have to be paid more, whereas those whose jobs have been downgraded cannot be paid less and the jobholders are therefore 'red circled'. As a rule of thumb, increases to the payroll are seldom less than 3 per cent and could be much higher. For example, an organisation with fixed incremental scales would probably have to guarantee that not only would employees retain their current rate of pay but that they would also be allowed to continue earning the fixed increments they would have expected to be awarded in their old grade.

Organisations that cannot afford (or believe they cannot afford) the full costs of implementation may phase increases over two or three years (not more). This may be achieved by transferring employees across to their new grades at their existing rate of pay and allowing them to progress upwards through the grade by performance-related or fixed increments. This clearly reduces the immediate costs although eventually payroll costs will increase. But it may have detrimental effects on employee relations, and the practice of phasing increases could be regarded as discriminatory if it applied mainly to female employees while men tended to be red-circled.

It is essential to estimate costs as realistically as possible at the outset so that that there are no surprises when it comes to implementation.

13

IMPLEMENTING A TAILOR–MADE

JOB EVALUATION SCHEME

This chapter provides guidelines on setting up and running a programme designed to develop and implement a tailor-made job evaluation scheme. It concentrates on the most popular form of conventional job evaluation – ie point-factor rating – but reference is also made at the end of the chapter to competence-based and job family approaches. It is assumed that decisions will already have been made as described in Chapter 12 on the need for job evaluation, the type of scheme, the extent to which outside help is required, and the role of the job evaluation panel. The chapter is of special interest to those who want to introduce job evaluation in the role of an internal consultant on an entirely do-it-yourself basis, or to those who seek outside help as discussed in Chapter 14.

The job evaluation programme
The job evaluation programme can be conducted following the stages shown in Figure 13.1 according to decisions made on the method of approach.

Project planning

Responsibility for the project
The first step should be to clarify who has the overall responsibility for the project and who is going to be involved in each stage, either carrying out the work or facilitating a working party or evaluation panel. A common approach is to have a steering committee to oversee the whole project, and a working party or job evaluation panel to carry out the detailed work.

Figure 13.1
JOB EVALUATION PROGRAMME

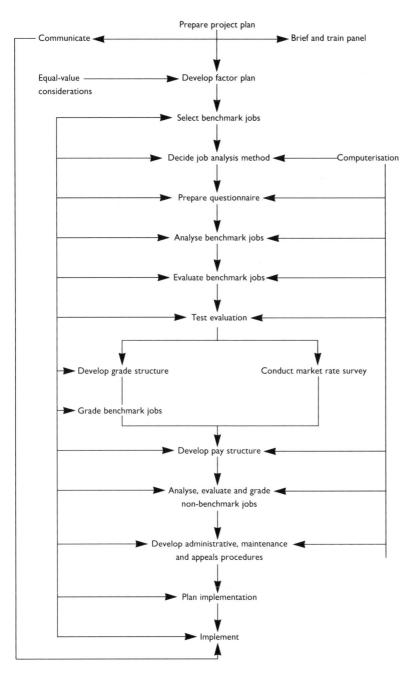

Although the overall control of the project might be carried out by a steering committee, a project director should be appointed from within the organisation to direct the project in detail, monitoring progress, providing for quality assurance, coordinating the activities of job evaluation panels, carrying out consistency checks, ensuring that the cost budget is not exceeded, dealing with problems as they arise and, if they are used, ensuring that consultants deliver. This is an important, demanding, and time-consuming role. It is often carried out by the head of personnel or the head of a pay and benefits (remuneration) function, if one exists. But there is no reason it should not be a line manager.

If consultants are involved in a large-scale exercise, they will appoint a project manager, but she or he should be accountable to the project director for deliverables, quality, keeping to the timetable, and not exceeding the cost budget.

The project plan

The project plan should set out

- the stages of the project
- the deliverables at each stage
- the completion date for each stage
- the milestones at which the progress of the project are to be reviewed formally
- who is responsible, individually or jointly, for each stage and the overall management of the project – this will cover the roles of the steering committee, project director, the job evaluation panel and its chairperson, and the role of facilitator, if one is used (either an internal or external consultant).

Timetable

The timetable should be based on realistic estimates not only of the time that is likely to be spent on each activity but also the elapsed time, taking into account the intervals required between meetings, and the time to conduct job analyses and evaluations. The rules of thumb that can be used to estimate times are:

☐ *Job analysis* – Between half a day and a whole day is required to carry out a job analysis and prepare a job description, allowing for some interval in gaining agreement to the description (this time can be considerably shortened by the use of computers to record and summarise answers to questionnaires).

☐ *Job evaluation* – A job evaluation panel may take between 30 minutes and an hour initially to evaluate a benchmark job, but will speed up as it becomes familiar with the factor plan and more used to interpreting the level descriptions and relating information about the job to them. It is probably advisable to plan for about five to six jobs to be evaluated during the first day's meeting, which can later be increased to seven to eight. Job evaluation panels can run out of steam if they try to do too much in one sitting. The result may be that superficial evaluations are made and consensus is too readily reached. Ideally, the panel should meet only for a half a day or at most a short day (eg 10 am to 4 pm). This time could also be reduced if the evaluation is carried out with the help of a computer, and possibly without the use of a panel at all, involving only the jobholder, the manager, a specialist job evaluator and, possibly, a trade union representative.

☐ *Market rate surveys* – If a special survey is being conducted, it may be necessary to allow about four weeks between inviting organisations to take part and getting their replies. It can take longer.

Taking as an example the programme referred to in Chapter 12 for an organisation with about 200 employees and 25 benchmark jobs the timetable could look like this:

Stage	Days	Elapsed time (weeks)
1 Preliminary discussions and analysis	3	2
2 Briefing and training job evaluation panel	1	1
3 Developing factor plan	2	2
4 Developing questionnaire and training analysts	2	1
5 Conducting job analysis	10	5
6 Evaluating jobs	6	3
7 Conducting market rate survey	3	2*

8	Preparing a grade and pay structure	2	2
9	Analysing and evaluating remaining jobs	5	4
10	Grading remaining jobs	2	1
11	Preparing administrative and appeal procedures and implementation plan	1	1
12	Preparing briefing notes and briefing employees	3	1
		40 days	25 weeks

* start during stage 6

Some of the elapsed time periods could be shortened but it may be difficult to compress an exercise involving panel meetings and full analyses and evaluation below an elapsed time of three to four months or so in an organisation this size, although computerisation helps. The length of time does not increase in direct proportion with the number of jobs to be covered, but in large and complex organisations job evaluation programmes can easily last nine months or more.

For project planning and control purposes, a programme such as that outlined above could be reproduced on a bar chart, as illustrated in Figure 13.2.

Steering committee

A steering committee is desirable to control the project overall. It might consist of at least one representative of top management, the head of personnel, and a representative of line management. An employee representative is sometimes also included. If consultants are being used, they could be co-opted on to the steering committee as required, but they would not normally be full members – the steering committee will, after all, be monitoring their performance in conducting the assignment.

The terms of reference for a steering committee could be defined as follows: to plan and coordinate the implementation of job evaluation to meet the objectives set for the exercise to the satisfaction of all concerned and within the agreed project timetable and cost budget.

The steering committee would probably review proposals on grade and pay structures but its remit may be confined to making recommendations on these matters to the board – it

Figure 13.2
JOB EVALUATION PROGRAMME

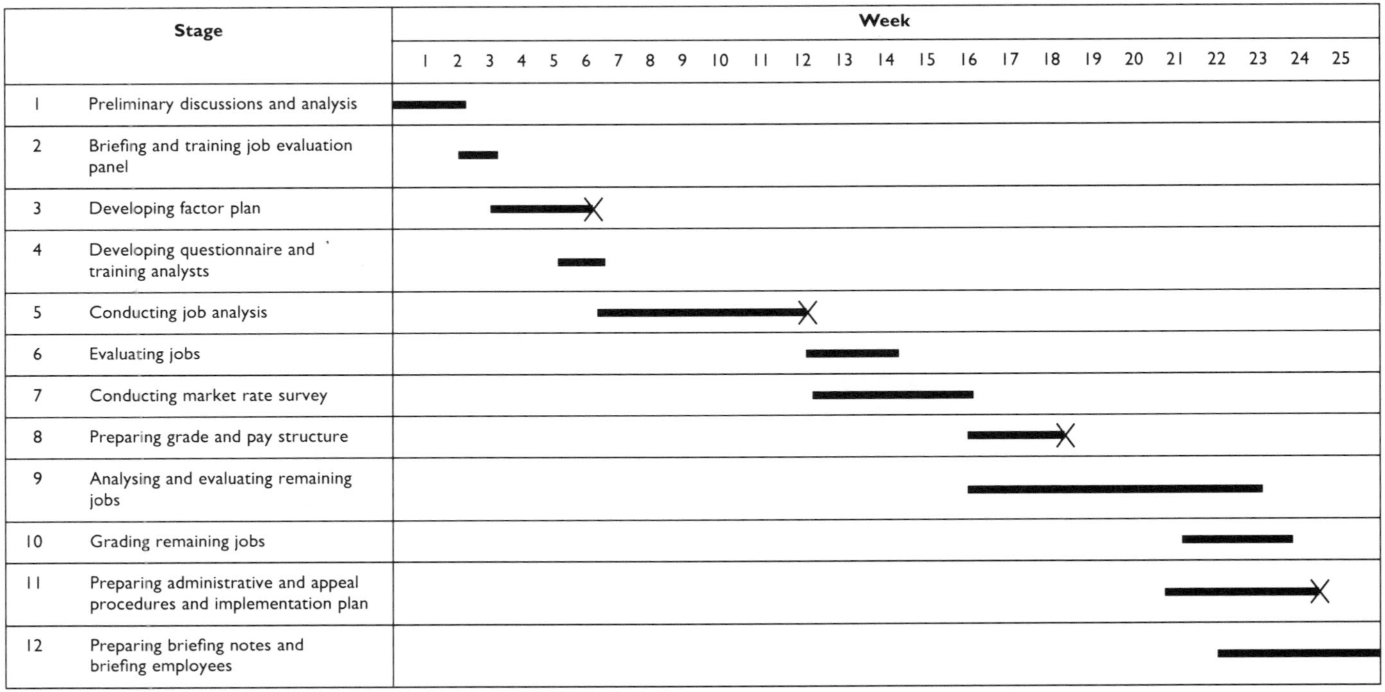

Stage		Week
		1 2 3 4 5 6 7 8 9 10 11 12 13 14 15 16 17 18 19 20 21 22 23 24 25
1	Preliminary discussions and analysis	
2	Briefing and training job evaluation panel	
3	Developing factor plan	
4	Developing questionnaire and training analysts	
5	Conducting job analysis	
6	Evaluating jobs	
7	Conducting market rate survey	
8	Preparing grade and pay structure	
9	Analysing and evaluating remaining jobs	
10	Grading remaining jobs	
11	Preparing administrative and appeal procedures and implementation plan	
12	Preparing briefing notes and briefing employees	

X = main milestone meetings

might not be empowered to make final decisions. Steering committees are there to control the project; they do not normally get involved in individual grading and pay decisions.

Job evaluation panel

Job evaluation panels are the key vehicles for obtaining involvement and consensus in developing and implementing job evaluation. The arguments for and against setting up panels were discussed in Chapter 12.

If a decision has been made to set up a panel, its members should include representatives of line managers, professional, technical and administrative staff, and employees in manufacturing and distribution functions. Women should be properly represented on the panel to counteract any tendencies to gender bias and to ensure that the particular characteristics of any work carried out predominantly by women are given full consideration. Union representatives should also be included in a unionised organisation.

The panel could be given the responsibility for developing, testing and, as necessary, modifying the factor plan as well as for selecting benchmark jobs, analysing and evaluating jobs and developing a grade structure. It would not normally be involved in making decisions on pay ranges or scales, and it would certainly have nothing to do with individual rates of pay.

So far as possible, the panel members should collectively be reasonably familiar with a representative sample of the jobs they will be analysing and evaluating. This may not be possible in large and complex organisations, and it may therefore be necessary in these circumstances to set up sub-panels to cover particular functions, occupational groups or job families. The membership of these sub-panels should always include at least one representative of the main panel who might act as chairperson/facilitator. Consistency between panels could be achieved by overlapping evaluations (different panels evaluating the same jobs) and overlapping membership. The main panel could carry out consistency checks under the auspices of the steering committee to whom it would be responsible.

A line manager may be appointed chairperson of the panel(s)

but some unionised organisations have successfully appointed a union representative joint chairperson. Personnel specialists should preferably not chair panels, on the grounds that if they do, job evaluation may be regarded as *their* scheme rather than one owned by line managers and other employees.

Personnel specialists can however play an important role in training panel members and facilitating panel meetings. But the role of the facilitator as described later in this chapter is a key one, and there are advantages in getting an independent adviser to carry it out. Chairpersons can, of course, also act as facilitators as long as they have the required skills.

Panels should not be too large – they can become unwieldy, and the more people who are involved the more difficult it will be to achieve consensus. Neither should panels be too small – this would mean that the collective knowledge of panel members about jobs in the organisation would be limited. Somewhere between five and eight members is probably best.

The terms of reference for a job evaluation panel could be:

- □ to develop and test a factor plan
- □ to select benchmark jobs
- □ to analyse and evaluate benchmark jobs
- □ to advise on the grade structure and the grading of benchmark jobs (but the panel would not be authorised to make decisions on the structure and gradings which would be referred to the steering committee).

Job evaluation panels are normally only concerned with internal relativities. Decisions on pay scales and individual rates of pay are usually made by management, although if there are trade unions, rates of pay and scales may be negotiated.

Communicating with employees

The evaluation process should be as transparent as possible. Employees should be informed at this stage that the evaluation exercise is going to take place and why. They can be given broad details of how the programme will be conducted, and told that the steering group and job evaluation panel have been set up to develop and implement the scheme. The terms of reference for these bodies might be summarised and information given on any outside help that may be enlisted to carry out the exercise. A well-thought-out question-and-answer document has been found helpful by some organisations.

It should be emphasised that the project is concentrating on internal relativities in order to develop a more rational and equitable grade structure. As far as possible any expectations that it will result in pay increases all round – or any pay increases at all – should be disabused. If this is not made clear now there may be trouble later. Few organisations which conduct a job evaluation exercise have ever been able completely to suppress expectations of pay increases, but they can at least damp them down at the start of the exercise. At the same time, it should be pointed out that no one's pay will be reduced as a result of the project.

Briefing and training the job evaluation panel

The panel should be briefed carefully on the objectives of the exercise and their terms of reference. Their role in developing the factor plan, selecting benchmark jobs, analysing and evaluating jobs, and advising on the grade structure should be explained.

It should be emphasised that panel members must do their best to be open-minded about their judgements. They should be asked to leave their preconceived notions of relative values behind them when they enter the room in which the evaluations take place. But this is a counsel of perfection. It is almost impossible for people to evaluate a job without already having some views on where it fits in the hierarchy. It is the role, therefore, of the facilitator to ensure that as far as possible members of the panel focus on the facts and do not rely on pre-formed subjective opinions.

Background notes could usefully be issued explaining in general the purpose and methods of job evaluation. Initial training could also be given on methods of job analysis and the basis upon which the relative value of jobs can be determined. It should be stressed that they will not be involved in appraising the performance of individuals or in fixing individual rates of pay. At this stage a preliminary briefing should be given on the need to achieve gender neutrality. More detailed briefings could be given at appropriate stages in the programme on how to avoid gender bias in conducting job analyses and evaluations.

Developing a factor plan

General considerations

General considerations to take into account when developing a factor plan were discussed in Chapter 5, and specific approaches required to achieve gender neutrality were described in Chapter 11. But to summarise, the key points to be remembered when designing a factor plan are:

☐ The plan should reflect the values of the organisation on what it believes are the most important considerations determining the relative worth of jobs.

☐ The factors should be appropriate to the jobs being covered, taking into account the range of work carried out in the organisation generally and, in particular, the characteristics of women's work (which have often been treated as being invisible in traditional factor plans).

☐ There should be no duplications or omissions in the factors and no double counting (ie more than one factor measuring the same characteristics).

☐ The factors should be defined as clearly as possible – broadly enough to cover all the work, but not so vaguely as to leave too much room for interpretation.

☐ Factor levels should be defined in a way that captures significant differences in the nature of the work carried out, clarifies those differences step by step, and focuses on what the work actually entails at each level.

☐ The weighting should be based on reasonable and tested assumptions about the relative significance of the factors, and it should not discriminate against women or men – it may be decided to avoid arbitrary weighting decisions by selecting factors assumed to be of equal value although, in a sense, this is also an arbitrary decision.

Identifying factors

The panel should be given as much freedom as possible to identify those factors they believe to be important in line with the parameters listed above, and on the understanding that too many factors make the scheme unwieldy and may lead to duplication.

The process of identifying factors can be started by a brainstorming exercise set up by the facilitator under normal brainstorming rules – ie instant ideas, anything goes, no second thoughts, no comments on other people's contributions. The panel members can be briefed to think about jobs they know and what distinguishes them from one another in terms of their comparable value: 'What makes you think that one job may be worth more, the same, or less than another?'

The job of the facilitator is then to encourage members of the panel to distil their original list under a number of headings, eliminating overlaps and duplications and any headings which, on reflection, are inappropriate (but in no circumstances should the facilitator allow the discussion to develop in any direction which forces panel members to defend their initial ideas). It is better to leave an inappropriate heading in at this stage than to force it out. The list of factors must be the panel's list of factors, not the facilitator's.

The next stage is to discuss the distilled headings in order to reach broad agreement on how they might be defined. It is advisable not to get the panel as a whole to draft the definitions (drafting by committee is always a time-wasting and often a frustrating experience). It is better for the facilitator to record the panel's ideas on a flip chart and go away to prepare draft definitions for their consideration at another meeting.

When the definitions have been agreed, level definitions can be produced. Each factor should be taken in turn and the panel asked to consider by reference to actual jobs the different levels at which that factor can apply. Some initial guidance should be given on how the factor levels might be distinguished, but as much freedom as possible should be allowed to members of the panel to come up with their own ideas. Again the facilitator should note their suggestions and go away to produce draft level definitions for discussion and, subject to any amendments, agreement at the next meeting. At the end of this part of the exercise a draft factor plan should have been produced. This should include factor and level definitions, but weightings and level scores should be determined later in the light of experience in evaluating the benchmark jobs.

The panel should be informed at this stage that the draft factor plan is to be used as the basis for analysing and evaluating the benchmark jobs. It should be emphasised, however, that the plan can (and probably will) be amended in the light of the experience gained in applying it to those jobs.

They should also be informed that they will be asked later to weight the factors – ie assess their relative importance on the assumption that some are more significant than others in determining job values. They can be told that it would be premature to weight the factors now because it is almost certain that they will want to amend the plan during the course of the exercise after they have put it to the test on actual jobs.

Clearly this process places a heavy load of responsibility on the facilitator, who will have ideas about the 'best' plan which in no circumstances should be divulged. But the facilitator must ensure that the criteria for a good plan, as described in Chapters 5 and 11 and summarised earlier in this chapter, are met. In the experience of the writer in developing a number of factor plans in this manner, a considerable degree of skill has to be exercised in helping panel members to recognise for themselves the validity of the ground rules and how their ideas might be improved by applying them. In this situation it is all too easy to cross the dividing-line between facilitation and manipulation. If the panel feels it is being manipulated, all is lost – and quite rightly so.

Selecting benchmark jobs

Benchmark jobs provide the reference-points for making comparisons, bearing in mind that job evaluation is essentially a comparative process. Benchmarks are the representative jobs that enable standards to be developed and refined for making judgements about comparative worth. They form the datum points that are the basis of the framework within which other jobs are evaluated. Benchmarks will consist of the key jobs at different levels and in different functions of the organisation, and need to be selected whenever the total number of jobs is too large for them all to be compared with one another (as a rule of thumb this may be the case when there are 40 jobs or more, although it could be less if there are wide variations between a smaller number of jobs). Normally between 15 per cent and 30 per cent of the total number of jobs may be selected, depending on the complexity of the organisation, although some jobs may be carried out by a number of people and this percentage is therefore likely to be less than the total numbers employed. It is not usually necessary to select benchmark jobs if a job family is being developed, as described at the end of this chapter.

Benchmark jobs are used to test the analysis and evaluation procedures, and produce the information required for the initial design of the grade structure. They can then serve as reference points within the structure when other jobs are evaluated. The analysis and evaluation of the benchmark jobs helps to refine the factor plan and breathes life into factor and factor level definitions which can later be illustrated by reference to benchmark evaluations.

The criteria for selecting benchmarks are that they should

☐ represent the entire range of jobs according to level and function and the extent to which jobholders are predominantly male or female

☐ be well-recognised jobs with which the members of the job evaluation panel between them are familiar

☐ be reasonably stable – ie they are unlikely to change much in content (although this presents difficulties in a rapidly changing organisation)

☐ be clearly and exactly defined with regard to skills, responsibilities and requirements

☐ stand out clearly from other jobs so that they can be easily identified

☐ include at least some jobs which can form the basis for external comparisons.

Benchmark jobs are needed in any job evaluation exercise that covers a fairly diverse range of jobs at different levels. But there are dangers in their use. Evaluators should try to avoid making pre-judgements on how the benchmarks should be graded against one another. If they are allowed, or allow themselves, to make such assumptions the evaluation process will do no more than reproduce the existing hierarchy. It would be a worthless exercise. Benchmark jobs can serve as valid reference points only when they have been evaluated without any preconceptions about their relative worth. And although they do assist in establishing the comparative worth of other jobs, a change in the content of the benchmark job leading to regrading does not invalidate the original evaluation of those jobs.

Deciding role analysis methods and preparing a questionnaire

Role analysis methods have to be devised as described in Chapter 8 to provide information about roles in terms of the agreed factors which will enable evaluations consistently to assign the level at which the factor is present in the roles under review.

Analysing and evaluating benchmark jobs

Depending on the decisions made at the previous stages, the analysis of benchmark jobs can be carried out by means of interviews and/or questionnaires, or the process can be entirely computerised as described on pages 162–73.

Evaluation: the aim

The aim is to achieve consensus about evaluation amongst panel members, but consensus should only be achieved through the thorough discussion of any issues raised by panel members on any differences between their evaluations. Compromise agreements should be avoided as far as possible, and individuals should be encouraged to give free expression to their views.

Role of the facilitator

When carrying out evaluations, the role of the facilitator is to assist in the process of making judgements and to ensure that as far as possible thorough and objective discussions take place. The facilitator should not take any responsibility for making decisions that emerge from the panel.

Deciding on the order of jobs to be evaluated

If the panel is going to carry out evaluations without computer assistance, as is still usually the case, the chairperson or facilitator should select, or discuss with the panel, the order in which the benchmark jobs are to be evaluated. It is best to start with jobs that most, if not all, the panel members are reasonably familiar with. This means that they will not immediately be confronted with serious problems of understanding the job content, or of translating that understanding into judgements about factor levels by reference to the draft factor and level definitions in the factor plan.

In the first batch of three or four jobs it may be desirable to include one that might be expected to come out with a low evaluation, one that could be expected to come out high, and one or two middling ones. The panel can then become familiar with the different levels of the factor plan and be in a better position to make amendments to the plan in the light of experience.

Care must be taken, however, to ensure that in selecting a range of jobs to be evaluated at different levels the panel is not encouraged to make prior judgements on evaluations. This problem can be alleviated by getting the chairperson or the facilitator to make the selections rather than the panel. This militates against the principle of giving the maximum amount of freedom to the panel to make its own judgements, but could be justified as a practical expedient designed to achieve fairer and more objective evaluations in the longer term.

The initial evaluations of selected benchmark jobs are used to pilot-test the factor plan, which should be amended in the light of any problems experienced in interpreting and using the factor and level definitions. The modified plan can then be used to evaluate the remaining benchmark jobs. The plan should be finalised when all those jobs have been evaluated. The weightings and factor level scores can then be determined and tested.

If there is only one panel, it may be desirable as a matter of convenience to select departments or functions and work through all the jobs in that area. This would mean that panel members could immerse themselves in similar tasks, jargon and relationships without disrupting their concentration by having to deal with major changes in job content. But it will be necessary at a later stage for the panel to review all their evaluations on a read-across basis to assess the comparable worth of jobs in different functions, and they may need to modify their original evaluations after they have made these comparisons. It is important in a job evaluation exercise to make both horizontal (or diagonal) and vertical comparisons.

If there are separate sub-panels covering different functions, they should also start with more familiar jobs at different levels in the same way as the main panel. In this case, however, the sub-panels would not be developing the factor plan, although they can propose any improvements they think are necessary to the main panel.

Ground rules for evaluation
The panel should be reminded of the ground rules they should follow in evaluating the jobs. In essence these refer to a check-list of tasks:

1   Evaluate the role requirements and the demands on those who carry them out, but do not be influenced by the performance of the person(s) in the role.
2   Recognise that some roles have been built around the particular skills and competences of the people who carry them out, but concentrate on what these people actually do and the attributes they need rather than their personalities.
3   Consider what the role holder is normally responsible for doing; do not allow what might occur very occasionally to over-influence the evaluation. At the same time, recognise that many roles now require a considerable degree of flexibility, and this should be taken into account as a 'normal' demand on people in the role.
4   Consider the role requirements and demands in terms of what a fully competent individual may be expected to do;

avoid focusing on what outstanding performers do on the one hand, or what people are capable of doing before they have completed an orientation and induction period. Do not allow your knowledge of individuals and their levels of performance to sway your judgement.

5   Assess each factor independently of the others – remember that this is an analytical process, which means that each element of the job – ie the factors – must be considered separately prior to making an overall judgement.

6   Do not allow any preconceived notions of the value of the job or the work carried out to sway your judgement on the level of each factor – forget the present grade or rate of pay both when evaluating each factor separately and when looking at the overall profile of the job as expressed in the factor levels assigned to it.

7   Ensure that every aspect of the role is covered – do not attach undue significance to any one characteristic.

8   Be aware of the danger of gender bias; do not allow your judgement to be affected by unsupported assumptions about the relative value of women's and men's work.

9   Use judgement in selecting the factor level closer than any of the others to describing the incidence of that factor in the role. The fit may not be exact because factor level definitions can never be written with enough precision to guarantee that this happens all the time. But remember that these definitions become more useful as the panel increases its understanding of the meaning of the words by interpreting how they apply to the benchmark jobs at different levels.

10 Consider the relative value or comparable worth of the job within the organisation; do not take any account of the current or anticipated market value of the role.

The chairperson or facilitator should ensure that these guidelines are thoroughly discussed by the panel so that they are understood and accepted in full. The panel can then proceed to take the steps listed below.

Evaluation steps
1   Panel members independently read the role definition and

analysis of the job, taking up with the analyst (who should be present even if he or she is not a member of the panel) any queries on matters of fact. These can also be discussed between members of the panel. If the panel members feel that the analysis and description are inadequate, they can request a further analysis to fill in gaps or to provide answers to specific questions. Alternatively, they may co-opt someone who has direct knowledge of the job to attend a panel meeting and answer queries.

2   The panel members independently evaluate the job by reference to the factor and level definitions in the factor plan. Because the weighting (if any) and the factor scales should not yet have been determined, panel members should only indicate the level for each factor. They should not be encouraged to give a plus or minus to their ratings, for such fine distinctions cannot be made with any validity with reference to the necessarily generalised factor definitions (although many people prefer to make such fine distinctions and it may be difficult to dissuade them). The facilitator should not commit himself or herself to an evaluation at this stage.

3   Each of the panel members records a judgement on a form (such as the one illustrated in Table 13.1) together with any explanatory comments he or she may wish to make.

4   The facilitator reproduces all the individual ratings on a flip chart. Starting with the more significant deviations, the panel members are asked to explain their reasoning. It is essential that facilitators manage this part of the process with great care. No panel member should be forced onto the defensive or feel threatened by critical comments. Facilitators should ask other panel members for their views, but the focus should always be on matters of fact, not opinion. Any views must be substantiated with reference to the evidence, and the facilitator may have to step in to ask probing questions about the factual basis for the views expressed, but only as a last resort. Where necessary, facilitators can suggest that the panel re-examines the factor or level definition very carefully to make sure it is fully understood or to note any ambiguities that may have served to cloud their judgement. Such

ambiguities should be noted for future reference when amending the draft factor plan. As the panel gains experience its members, possibly helped by the facilitator, will be able to refer to previous evaluations that will clarify the definitions.

5   The process described above continues for the three or four jobs being used to pilot-test the scheme. When their evaluation has been completed the panel can pause and consider any changes that it would like to make to the factor plan. If these are significant, it may be necessary to re-evaluate the pilot-scheme jobs. To be absolutely certain that a substantially revised factor plan is appropriate and usable, it may be necessary to test it again before producing a final version for the rest of the evaluations. Even this version may benefit from fine-tuning. No factor plan should be regarded as sacrosanct during the benchmark job evaluations. But it should not be amended once these evaluations have been completed.

6   The remaining benchmark jobs are evaluated in the same way by the main panel and/or any sub-panels.

7   The main job evaluation panel then scrutinises the completed evaluations of all the benchmark jobs. Even if the process has not been fully computerised, they can usefully be loaded into a computer to form the database for future evaluations. The panel can assess the factor level gradings across all the benchmarks to identify any inconsistencies or what appear to be out-of-the-ordinary judgements (this process is sometimes called 'sore-thumbing'). The panel can then re-evaluate the jobs concerned in order to reach agreement on ironing out the inconsistencies.

8   The panel then discusses the need for weighting the factors as defined for the final version of the factor plan. If it decides that it is necessary to weight the factors, it carries on along the lines described in Chapter 5. The next step, whether or not the factors are weighted is to decide on the points scales for each of the factors. This is a crucial but essentially judgemental and iterative process which continues until the panel feels that the weightings (if any) and scales are appropriate.

Table 13.1
JOB EVALUATION RECORD FORM

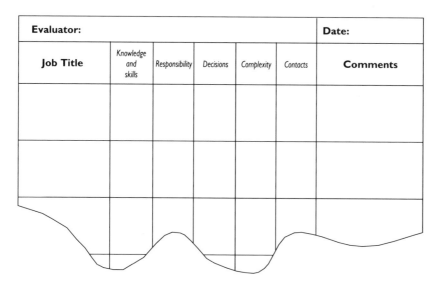

Evaluator:						Date:
Job Title	Knowledge and skills	Responsibility	Decisions	Complexity	Contacts	**Comments**

Test evaluations

The weighting exercise referred to above leads directly to a review of the overall results of the benchmark job evaluations as expressed in the points scores for each job. The jobs can be listed in rank order according to their scores and the panel members have to assess whether this order and the points differentials between jobs are reasonable. But what does 'reasonable' mean in this context? The answer to that question is that a rank order is reasonable if the panel believes it is reasonable; in other words, it is 'felt-fair'. And there's the rub. We are back in the realms of subjective judgement in spite of all the hard analytical work that has taken place to date.

It is possible to make this judgement somewhat less subjective by using the paired-comparisons technique as described in Chapter 3 to rank the benchmark jobs. If the rank order is different, the panel can re-examine the evaluations or the weighting plan (especially the latter) until they are brought into line. But who is to say that the paired-comparison rank order is better than the order produced by points rating? Paired-comparisons are non-analytical and they may therefore be less reliable. They should not be allowed to replace the judgements made by means of the analytical scheme. All they can do is to highlight areas of potential concern. Once these have been identified and dealt with, the paired-comparison rank order should be forgotten.

Clearly, it is at this stage that a point-factor job evaluation is in danger of doing no more than reproduce the existing hierarchy, and this is what many equal-value commentators (as quoted in Chapter 11) accuse it of doing. The only way to avoid this trap is to ensure that the panel concentrates, as far as possible, on the facts – the evidence produced by the analysis and evaluation processes that they have been considering. If panel members do this, their 'felt-fair' judgements should be based on this factual analysis rather than on preconceived notions of the 'correct' rank order. If there is still any reasonable doubt on comparable worth, then the jobs in question should be re-evaluated before the decisions on benchmark job scores and the factor weighting plan are confirmed. The rest of the exercise can then go ahead as described below.

Developing a grade structure

Methods of developing a grade structure following the evaluation were described in Chapter 9 and need not be repeated here. It is, however, worth reiterating that this is a highly judgemental process. It would be very convenient if there were neat clusters of evaluated jobs at regular intervals with substantial gaps in scores between them. If that were the case, boundaries could be drawn so as to avoid placing jobs for which the evaluation scores are close together on either side of the dividing line. But life is not like that. In practice, judgemental decisions have to be made on where the lines can be drawn in a way that minimises boundary problems. Jobs graded on either side of the line may have to be scrutinised with special care and, possibly, re-evaluated to ensure that the grading decision can be justified. The existence of potential boundary disputes is one good reason for not having a narrow-banded structure. In a broad-banded structure it is easier to draw lines that leave reasonably large gaps between the jobs immediately on either side of them.

Grading benchmark jobs

Each grade in the structure is defined in points terms, and any benchmark job with a points score within the grade bracket is allocated to that grade. This means that the wider the grade, the wider the differential between the points scores for jobs in that grade, and this could be difficult to justify unless a broad-banded structure (as described in Chapter 9) is adopted.

By definition, however, a job grade means that all jobs within that grade are paid within the same pay range. At this stage, therefore, the job evaluation score is no longer significant in a graded structure except as an indication of the grade into which the job is to be placed. In other words 'points do not equal pounds', and this has to be made clear to all concerned.

This means that if individuals are aware of their scores (which in a transparent system they should be), those with scores at the higher end of the bracket may appeal against their grading. A multiplicity of such appeals can too easily lead to unjustified upgradings (grade drift) which could rapidly destroy the integrity of the pay system and the job evaluation processes that support it. All the more reason, therefore, for taking particular care over drawing grade boundaries.

Points may, however, be related to pounds in an individual job range system in which each job has its own pay range and where rates of pay may be determined by a formula which incorporates a sum based on the points score. Such structures are sometimes adopted for more senior jobs. Individual job ranges may be incorporated within a broad-banded structure where the pay brackets could be 'anchored' to market rates.

Acceptability

The degree to which grading decisions in a graded structure are acceptable is usually based on such judgemental criteria as:

☐ the gradings are consistent with the way in which the organisation functions and is managed

- [ ] the jobs are perceived to be similar in level
- [ ] the roles have common features in terms of content, skill, and competence requirements
- [ ] the jobs are interchangeable
- [ ] the jobs are graded in accordance with a 'natural' ladder of levels of responsibility and competence
- [ ] there is a natural and obvious allocation of key jobs to the various grades around which other jobs are perceived to 'cluster'.

These judgements are likely to be subjective, but the fact that the gradings have been based on a structured and systematic process of analytical job evaluation should make it more likely that the structure is felt to be fair.

Surveying market rates

Market rate surveys are usually conducted by the personnel function, possibly with outside help but not involving a job evaluation panel, although in negotiations trade union representatives may challenge the data if they have not taken part in obtaining it. (Methods of conducting surveys were described in Chapter 9.)

Designing pay structures

Methods of designing pay structures were also described in Chapter 9. It is particularly important at this stage to cost the implications of the alternative structures that might be developed. These consist of the cost of bringing the rate of pay of employees who have been upgraded up to the new pay point or range for their new grade. Computer pay-modelling software can be used to develop projected costs of alternative structures before a final decision is made.

Evaluating non-benchmark jobs

Non-benchmark jobs are sometimes slotted into the structure by a process of internal benchmarking. This can lead to inequitable decisions if the process is not based on the results of thorough role analysis. From an equal-value point of view, it is preferable to deal with non-benchmark jobs in exactly the same way as the benchmark jobs. Individuals may feel aggrieved if they realise that they have simply been slotted into the structure without any consideration given to the characteristics of their particular roles.

But this difficulty may be avoided by the use of generic role descriptions as long as they cover – albeit broadly, and with an emphasis on flexibility – the whole range of responsibilities and competences relating to any person who carries out the role. The generic definitions should cover the essential nature of the role which determines its place in a grade and pay structure. Individual differences can be addressed through agreements on objectives and standards relating to the specific role. Achieving or surpassing these objectives and standards could be rewarded by some method of paying for performance (performance-related pay, achievement bonuses, sustained high performance bonuses, etc.).

Developing procedures

There may be circumstances in which the administration of job evaluation is entirely handled by the personnel function. But there is much to be said for involving other people – line managers and employee representatives. Job evaluation will be much more acceptable, and therefore effective, if it is regarded as *their* scheme.

If a job evaluation panel has developed the scheme, it can become the body that maintains it. The panel can then act as the guardian of the scheme's integrity. It can carry out this role by ensuring that job analyses and evaluations are conducted thoroughly, that no one is allowed to manipulate the wording of role definitions or the process of evaluation in order to enable unjustified upgradings to take place, and that evaluations are consistent across occupational and functional boundaries. The panel should ensure that equal-value considerations are given constant attention so that gender bias is eliminated and jobs of comparable worth are paid equally. It should be responsible for evaluating new jobs and re-evaluating jobs in which the responsibilities have changed. The panel should not, however, hear appeals because it would thus be considering appeals, against its own decisions.

The role of the personnel function should be to service the panel, providing information, conducting analyses, facilitating meetings, and auditing evaluations to ensure that they are consistent. It could also be responsible for training new panel members and providing refresher training for existing members.

The procedures to be administered by the panel – or the personnel function if a panel is not used – are:

□ the general processes and methods used to analyse and evaluate jobs

□ the arrangements for evaluating and grading new jobs, including how the analysis should be conducted and what supporting information is required to explain the context within which the new role is to be carried out

□ the arrangements for re-evaluating existing jobs; these should spell out how the case for re-evaluation should be put together (ie what information is required and who prepares it), how the role analysis is to take place, and who is to make the final decisions on the evaluation and regrading

□ the arrangements for hearing appeals, which could be made along the lines described below.

Job evaluation appeals

Job evaluation appeals are against decisions made by the job evaluation panel and, as mentioned above, they should be heard by another body. Such a body could consist of three or four people, including a senior line manager and, possibly, an employees' representative. The appeal committee should be attended by a member of the personnel department but that person might not necessarily take part in making the final decision on the appeal.

The appeal committee should call for supporting evidence from the appellant, and ask the job evaluation panel to provide a rationale for its original decision. If necessary, it could ask for the panel (or whoever carried out the original evaluation) to re-analyse and re-evaluate the job. The appeal committee should not carry out evaluations itself, although its members should be entirely familiar with the job evaluation processes and how grading decisions are made.

There may be situations when it would be preferable for the re-evaluation to be carried out quite separately by a trained analyst and evaluator who is not a member of the standing job evaluation panel but who is fully conversant with the job evaluation scheme. This could be a member of the personnel department, but any conclusions reached by that person could take the form only of recommendations to the appeal committee, who might still wish to get the reactions of the panel before reaching a conclusion. In really tricky cases where there are major equal-value implications, the views of an independent consultant or other qualified individual could be sought. He or she would, in a sense, be playing a similar role to that of an independent expert in an industrial tribunal equal-value case.

The procedure for hearing appeals should not in turn be responsible for setting up an elaborate system of higher 'appeal courts'. If an individual is dissatisfied with the appeal committee's decision, he or she could take it up through the normal grievance procedure.

Planning implementation

The implementation plan should cover

☐ the general communication to all employees about the outcome of the job evaluation exercise

☐ decisions on how employees who are over- or under-graded as a result of evaluation should be dealt with (see below)

☐ how individual employees should be informed of the effect of the evaluation on their grading and pay, if it affects them at all.

Dealing with over- and under-graded employees

The decisions on over- or under-graded employees are critical. If this part of the exercise is mishandled, the result could be serious demotivation and disaffection. The usual practice is to 'red circle' those employees who are now over-graded – ie to maintain their pay at its present level until it falls within the new pay bracket or scale for the grade after any general increase to pay scales.

The situation may also arise in an organisation with a pay spine or a fixed increment progression system that freezing employees' pay at the current level could prevent their progressing to the level contractually provided for by the present scale. In such cases the organisation may have to allow pay to progress to the contracted level. In effect, employees in this situation would be on a red-circled or 'personal to jobholders' scale.

Employees who are undergraded should be placed within the pay bracket or scale for their new grade. The costs of doing this should have been estimated when earlier decisions were made on gradings and the pay structure, and adjustments may have been made to the gradings and scales to minimise these costs. But if it is felt that the additional payroll costs cannot be sustained all at once, a decision may have to be made to phase increases over two, or at most three, years. The possibility that this might happen should have been explained at the outset of the exercise by some sentence along the lines of: 'Employees who are placed on a new grade with a higher pay bracket or scale as a result of the exercise will have their pay increased to bring them up to the minimum of the new scale but – if such increases are considerable, they may be phased over a period of two to three years'.

Phasing increases causes dissatisfaction. The organisation should avoid doing so unless it truly cannot afford a once-and-for-all increase. Ideally, the costs should have been anticipated and budgeted for. But there may be more readjustments than were anticipated, even if care was taken to minimise them when devising the pay structure and grading jobs.

Trade unions may object to this procedure, which can be justified on the grounds of affordability but may be less defensible from an equal-value point of view if it is mainly men who are red circled and women whose increases are phased.

A further problem may arise concerning where individuals should be placed in their new scale. To save cost they may be moved to the minimum rate or simply transferred across at their present rate of pay. But it could be argued that this is inequitable. They may have progressed within their present bracket to a higher level through merit, competence or experience. Why, they or their union representatives may well ask, should they therefore not be placed in the same position in the new scale to recognise the extra contribution they are making through their merit, competences, etc.? Why should new recruits to the grade be paid exactly the same, in spite of their lack of experience? They would have a point. The only answer is that of affordability, and that may be arguable. This potential problem has to be anticipated and a policy worked out on how to avoid it, or, if it is unavoidable, on how to manage the situation.

Project management

A job evaluation programme can be lengthy and complex. It can involve a lot of people in many different roles. It is essential therefore to have a project plan as described at the beginning of the chapter – this sets out the deliverables at each stage, timing and responsibilities. It is particularly important to designate in advance the 'milestones' of the project – the key steps that must be taken by a certain time. At milestone meetings the steering committee reviews progress to date and confirms the future project plan. It can initiate corrective action and approve any changes to the plan. The project director should not, however, rely on the milestone meetings. He or she should continually monitor progress so that immediate action can be taken.

Competence-based job evaluation

The programme for developing and introducing a competence-based point-factor job evaluation scheme could broadly follow the stages described above. The difference is that either the system starts from the basis of existing competence frameworks which provide an indication of the competence-based factor headings, or, if the exercise is going to involve developing competence frameworks from scratch, special studies may be required to produce competence profiles. This could be done by workshops as described in Chapter 8, and the members of those workshops could be formed into job evaluation panels. Alternatively, a panel could be set up that would devise the competence frameworks and carry on from there to develop and apply a job evaluation scheme.

Job family structures

If it is thought that a job family structure is appropriate (such structures are described in Chapter 6), an approach different from that set out earlier in this chapter would be required. There is no point in having an organisation-wide job evaluation panel to carry out the full exercise. It would, however, be desirable to involve a representative group of employees from different levels in the job family in defining the competence clusters required at each level, and the criteria for deciding how individuals are to be assigned to a competence level or band within the job family.

A separate exercise has to be carried out to provide the 'read-across' between job families. This can be done by setting up a project team with its members drawn from the main job families. This team could agree on the form of job evaluation to be used and take part in any cross-evaluations.

PART 4

JOB EVALUATION
TODAY

14

INTRODUCING JOB EVALUATION WITH THE HELP OF CONSULTANTS

Management consultants can help with job evaluation in two ways: either assisting with the introduction of a tailor-made job evaluation scheme or installing their own proprietary brand. The pros and cons of using consultants were discussed in Chapter 12, which also contained a checklist of the criteria to be used when selecting a proprietary brand. This chapter concentrates on the approaches which can be adopted to select and make the best use of consultants in either of the two ways mentioned above.

How much help do you require?
If you simply want consultants to help you develop or revise a tailor-made scheme, you should at this stage consider the extent to which you want them to be involved, which could vary.

Light involvement
Consultants could be quite lightly involved, asked simply to feed you with ideas and act as a sounding board during the course of your project. They could also be asked to comment on your initial conclusions.

Moderate involvement
At a higher level of involvement, consultants could be used to brief and train members of job evaluation panels on role analysis and job evaluation techniques. They could also facilitate panel meetings, providing members with suggestions

on alternative approaches, helping to prepare factor plans, and guiding them during their first job evaluation sessions. The consultants could monitor the quality of role analyses and definitions, and review the outcome of evaluations. Their advice could be sought on the grade structure, market rate surveys, and methods of communication and implementation.

Fairly heavy involvement

The consultants could be more heavily involved, doing everything described above, especially facilitating meetings, but also providing more direct assistance and advice with some or all of the following activities:

- [ ] playing a fuller part in devising a tailor-made factor plan in conjunction with the panel – providing examples, drafting factor and factor level definitions, and possibly using multiple regression techniques to determine factor weightings
- [ ] devising job analysis questionnaires
- [ ] conducting market rate surveys
- [ ] preparing recommendations on grade and pay structures (possibly using computer modelling techniques)
- [ ] advising on the computerisation of job evaluation generally
- [ ] preparing briefs and job evaluation manuals
- [ ] advising on administration and maintenance procedures.

Heavy involvement

The consultants carry out all the above work but are involved also in analysing benchmark jobs and take the lead in preparing the factor plan (which may be based largely on one they have used successfully elsewhere). They may play a major part in evaluations and pay structure design decisions. Very occasionally, consultants may be asked to go even further and carry out all the analyses and evaluations themselves, but this is undesirable unless the circumstances are exceptional – eg when a remuneration committee or board of trustees wants the consultants to carry out a confidential evaluation of senior staff.

This analysis should help in the choice of consultants and can serve as a basis for discussions with them about how they can help. You need not decide finally at this stage, but it is desirable to have some preliminary views on the degree to which you want consultants to be involved.

Selecting consultants

It is always advisable to select consultants from a field of three or four potential firms or individuals (not more) unless you are absolutely certain from direct experience that a particular firm, individual or proprietary brand is exactly what you need. Even so, it could still be useful to test your assumptions by seeing one or two other firms or individuals.

Who you approach in the first place depends on what you want them to do. If you are convinced that you want a proprietary brand, approach two or three of the consultants listed in Appendix A. If you want a tailor-made scheme, the same consultants would no doubt be happy to oblige, or at least offer to customise their own brand. But there are some large firms who specialise in helping clients to develop their own scheme. Coopers & Lybrand is a good example. Then there are many small firms and independent consultants who offer help. The Institute of Personnel and Development has 300 such firms or individuals on its consultant's register. Again, identify three or four of these firms – say, one larger one, a medium-sized firm, and one or two independent operators – and arrange for them to prepare a proposal for you. Remember that the large firms charge more but may have a wider range of experience and better back-up services, including a data-bank of market rates for comparison purposes. At this stage you could still have an open mind about whether to use a proprietary brand or to develop a tailor-made scheme in-house, in which case you might invite both proprietary brand and non-proprietary brand consultants to submit a proposal. The selection process then consists of the following stages: briefing, reviewing proposals, interviewing the consultants, and taking up references.

Briefing

Your brief to the consultants – which should be in writing and preferably supplemented by an initial meeting – should set out the background (the circumstances in which you are seeking help), the objectives, and your interim terms of reference (these may be amended later in discussion with the consultants). You should request a written proposal in which the consultants set out their proposed programme of work, the 'deliverables' they would offer, their experience in this type of assignment, an indication of exactly who would carry out the work (with supporting CVs), and details of training and costs. If you have prepared a process specification (as you should have done – see Chapter 12), you might issue it at this stage. But there is something to be said for keeping this to yourself as it will be interesting to use it as a check-list to assess from the consultants' proposal and presentation the extent to which they really understand and can meet your requirements. If, however, you have any particular needs – eg deadlines for completing the project or the use of computers – these should be mentioned in your brief.

It is not necessary to spell out in detail at this stage the help you might require. It is always useful to allow the consultants some scope to develop their own ideas – they could be well worth listening to, and you do not necessarily want to put them into a straitjacket. The quality of the ideas they produce in their proposal may also give you some indication of the likely quality of their contribution.

Consultants' proposals

The written proposals submitted by the consultants should be compared in terms of their quality, relative costs and timing. They ought to be studied carefully to decide what questions should be put to them at the presentation.

Presentation

The consultants should be asked to present their proposals to a selection panel. The presentations should be made by the consultant(s) who will conduct the assignment. They should be briefed to keep their presentations fairly short (10 to 15 minutes). Allow a further 30 minutes or so for questions and discussion.

Selection

The selection panel might comprise one or two line managers and the head of personnel. If, however, the evaluation exercise is to be carried out by a job evaluation panel, it is desirable to include other representatives of the panel on the selection team. This could consist of, say, three people, a line manager, an employee's representative, and the head of personnel. They would submit their recommendations to the full panel and then the steering committee for approval.

Each consultant should be asked to give their presentation and then reply to questions from the selection panel. The panel members should agree in advance on the questions they are going to ask; these could be about methodology, deliverables, timing and the relevant experience of the firm and of the consultants who will actually carry out the assignment.

The relative merits of the consultants could be assessed by the selection panel against the following criteria:

☐ the overall quality of proposal and presentation
☐ the degree to which the consultants demonstrate that they understand your real needs (it would be particularly interesting if they show insight into problems which you had not identified)
☐ the extent to which their approach and promised deliverables meet your objectives and specification
☐ the credibility and appropriateness of the methodology they propose to use
☐ the relevant experience of the consultancy firm in dealing with similar organisations and providing the range of services required in this situation
☐ the relevant experience and the quality of the consultant(s) who will be assigned to the project – it is particularly important to find out what experience they have had in developing factor plans and questionnaires, job analysis, facilitating job evaluation panels, using computerised systems, conducting pay surveys, and designing grade and pay structures

□ the degree to which the consultancy firm's approach and, indeed, the consultant's, will 'fit' the organisation's culture and management style – in the last analysis, the panel has to be satisfied that its members and any other people taking part in the project will be able to work with the consultants

□ the timing of the proposed programme – is it realistic? and will it meet the required deadlines?

□ the costs of the consultant's fees *and* expenses.

Cost is a consideration, but it should not override the other criteria – with consultants, as with most other services, the cheapest is not necessarily the best. The panel has first to satisfy itself that the consultants meet the other criteria, especially those concerned with reputation, deliverables, methodology, the quality of their team, and the degree to which they fit. Cost considerations should take priority only in the unlikely event of other things being equal.

References
If you do not know the consultants well, or if you have not been given a strong recommendation, it is always worth while taking up one or two references.

Making the best use of consultants
To make the best use of consultants it is necessary:

□ to agree explicit terms of reference which cover deliverables, the timetable, and costs

□ to review the proposed project plan to ensure that it is likely to meet the objectives and the deadlines

□ to ask for regular progress reports and check these against the project plan

□ to hold regular 'milestone' meetings at pre-arranged points in the project programme which coincide with the completion of the project stage and the start of the next stage

□ to scrutinise thoroughly any proposals made by the consultants to ensure that they are relevant to the project objectives, realistic, and can be implemented with the

agreement of those concerned and within the cost budget
- if the programme seems to be drifting or the deliverables have not been produced on time, to step in quickly to ensure that corrective action is taken.

15

IMPLEMENTING AND

MAINTAINING JOB EVALUATION

The job evaluation programme itself may go well, but problems can arise when it comes to implementation. Following implementation, job evaluation schemes easily become out-of-date or deteriorate unless careful attention is paid to them.

Implementation

Job evaluation programmes can turn sour during or after implementation for any of the following reasons:

☐ Employees do not understand how their jobs have been evaluated and how this has produced the grade and pay structure.

☐ Employees' expectations about increases in pay following the exercise have been disappointed.

☐ Grading and/or pay decisions are felt to be unfair or inequitable (including where people have been positioned on the new scales).

These reactions can arise all too easily unless they are anticipated. Overall, the approach should be to make the whole exercise as transparent as possible, briefing employees initially on why and how it will take place and informing them collectively and individually of the results as they affect the organisation generally and themselves in particular. It is important to explain why decisions have been made, and to spell out the policy guidelines which have provided the basis for those decisions. It would be a tragic irony if a programme which started off with high aims of delivering an equitable pay structure ended up by being perceived as producing fundamentally inequitable results. And this *can* happen unless great care is taken.

Line managers and team leaders must also feel that they 'own' the process in association with the members of their teams. It is therefore important to keep them informed of the scheme's development and brief them thoroughly on their own roles in it.

Transparency and acceptability are increased by the use of a job evaluation panel to develop the scheme and to undertake evaluations. The latter may be carried out by a computerised process, although in such cases it is essential to involve the line manager, the employee and, as appropriate, the employee's representative jointly in the process. In effect, they would form a job evaluation panel which could be facilitated by a job evaluation specialist from the personnel department.

It is, however, unwise to rely on a job evaluation panel to guarantee the acceptability of the project, especially if – as is commonly the case – it is not involved in vital decisions concerning gradings and pay. In the writer's experience such panels can take on a life of their own. What often happens is that, with the help of a good facilitator, they go through the group dynamics processes of forming, storming, norming and performing. Panel members may perform very effectively as a well-knit group, but as such they can become increasingly remote from the outside world. It is essential, therefore, that steps are taken to ensure that they keep in touch with their colleagues and constituents, reporting on progress, testing ideas, and obtaining feedback.

The panel can issue progress reports to employees from time to time, and it may be desirable to use a form of team briefing system, with the involvement of panel members, to communicate outcomes to employees generally. Panel members can individually and jointly make presentations and lead discussions in briefing sessions and focus groups. At Triplex Safety Glass trade union representatives on the panel made presentations to senior management and other groups on what the panel had achieved. This approach certainly increased a feeling of ownership all round as well as being an effective means of communication.

The launch of the new evaluation process should be carefully planned. Briefing packs should be made available to line managers, team leaders and employee representatives, and should include visual aids (OHP foils) as well as written material. A list of typical questions and answers may be provided, and the list could be amended in the light of experience.

A letter to every employee, with a booklet explaining the scheme, can be used to supplement briefing sessions. Individual employees should also be seen by their managers or team leaders to explain how the new process and structure affects them. The managers/team leaders should be briefed carefully on how they explain decisions and how they should reply to any queries.

It should also be conveyed to employees in group or individual briefings and in leaflets that they have the right to appeal against grading or pay decisions arising from the evaluation exercise.

Evolutionary pressures

Job evaluation schemes can easily become out-of-date. They need to evolve as the organisation evolves. Form follows function in job evaluation as in organisation structures. In other words, the method of job evaluation and the factor plan flow from organisational requirements and processes, and must be changed as they change. Job evaluation is futile unless it supports and is integrated with other organisational processes. It cannot be allowed to lead a separate existence; nor, for example, can it be allowed to support rigid bureaucratic hierarchies in a process-based, project orientated and flexible organisation.

The core values of organisations also change, and the values built into evaluation schemes must be brought into line with the new values to support – indeed, promote – them. It is therefore essential to review the relevance of a job evaluation scheme at least every five, preferably every three, years. It will be even more necessary to rethink job evaluation processes after a major organisational change (for example, a business process re-engineering exercise) or before embarking on a culture change programme. It should be remembered that job evaluation processes themselves can act as agents for change by underpinning new values or focusing on the competences required by individuals and teams within the context of the business strategies, core competences and critical success factors of the organisation.

The ultimate objective should be to reinforce the part job evaluation can play in the creation of added value and the enhancement of competitive advantage. Job evaluation programmes always have to be justified in terms of how they contribute to organisational effectiveness, remembering that the main differentiator between successful and less successful organisations is the quality of the people they employ. The reward strategies and processes of the business, of which job evaluation is an integral part, make a major contribution to ensuring that high quality people are attracted to the organisation, remain with it, and contribute to the best of their ability. That is why it is vital to ensure that these reward and job evaluation processes are aligned to the continually developing business and people strategies of the organisation.

Maintenance

Job evaluation schemes decay. This seems to be almost inevitable, perhaps because no one involved in job evaluation can be infallible or completely objective all the time. And there are always pressures for upgrading from both individuals and their managers which may be supported by enhanced job descriptions and tendentious arguments, often phrased in the language of the factor plan to indicate that the job is operating at, say, level four rather than level three. The shopfloor employees in one organisation we came across had produced their own blue book on how to prepare job analyses and phrase job descriptions to support a request for upgrading. The booklet highlighted the phrases from the factor plan (a proprietary brand) that could be used to substantiate claims.

It is interesting to note that in the experience of many personnel people who are involved in job evaluation it is often line managers who are the most vociferous and tendentious in putting forward claims for upgrading. Whether they think this is something they must do to help their people, or whether, more cynically, they are doing it to curry favour or enhance their own status, is not always clear. One personnel director told us that the biggest problem he had ever met in handling an appeal was one caused by his own personnel manager who was pushing hard – without any real justification – to get one of his specialists upgraded.

Preventive maintenance

Job evaluation schemes can be manipulated (whatever those who promote their proprietary brands may say) and they can be corrupted. Inconsistent evaluations are made, gender bias creeps in, and grade drift occurs. Preventive maintenance is therefore required through periodical audits of evaluations and gradings and, on a sample basis, the re-evaluation of jobs to check on the validity of the original evaluation or to establish whether changes mean that the evaluation needs to be amended.

Consistency checks

Consistency checks should be made periodically by means of cross-evaluations and by analysing the outcomes of any new evaluations compared with the benchmarks. Not too much reliance should be placed on the benchmarks as the anchors for the job evaluation and grading process. Benchmark jobs can change just like any other job, and need therefore to be re-evaluated or even replaced by new benchmarks. A re-evaluation or replacement of a benchmark for this reason should not be allowed to affect adversely the evaluation of non-benchmark jobs that have remained unchanged. Any evaluation, once made, should stand on its own merits, irrespective of what happens to the benchmark job with which it was originally compared.

16

WHAT IS HAPPENING IN JOB

EVALUATION TODAY –

THE RESEARCH FINDINGS

Job evaluation is changing. That much was obvious to us before we undertook to produce this book. But what forms the changes are taking, and why, were more difficult to ascertain. As part of the data gathering process for the book we therefore decided that a survey would be the most appropriate way to collect up-to-date information about the practice of job evaluation in the UK. A survey questionnaire was developed and sent to approximately 1,000 organisations. The questionnaire was designed to find out whether or not people are using formal job evaluation techniques, what kind of problems they are experiencing, how these are being overcome, and what their future intentions are.

Surveys are only a guide to what is actually happening in the big wide world. However, this one confirmed that job evaluation is indeed changing, and that many organisations are experiencing various difficulties with existing arrangements used to describe and value jobs. It also demonstrates that the trends are far from clear and that a myriad new approaches are being tried out.

In all 316 organisations responded to the questionnaire which gave us a response rate of 33 per cent. Twenty-four per cent of respondents are from the public sector, 33 per cent from the private manufacturing sector, 36 per cent from the private service or voluntary sector, and 7 per cent describe themselves as belonging to another sector.

The survey sample was originally chosen to reflect a range of economic groups and organisational sizes. Of all our respondents, 59 per cent describe an organisation employing more than 500 people, 32 per cent employing between 100 and 499 people, 8 per cent employing between 50 and 99 people, and 1 per cent employing less than 50 people. We are, therefore, confident that the survey results give a reasonable spread of answers from all levels and sections of industry, giving us a reasonably accurate picture of what is actually happening to job evaluation. The breakdown in use of job evaluation is given in Figure 16.1.

Figure 16.1
USE OF JOB EVALUATION

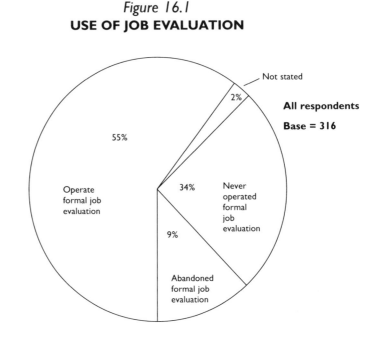

Use of job evaluation

More than half, 55 per cent, of all our respondents operate a formal job evaluation scheme. This figure rises to 66 per cent in the public sector, and compares to 52 per cent in the private sector and 55 per cent among those respondents describing themselves as operating in another economic sector.

Those respondents who do not make use of formal job evaluation schemes are highly likely to use managerial judgement to decide pay rates and relativities; 41 per cent say this is the means by which they decide pay for all staff. However, 36 per cent make use of market rates, 26 per cent use competencies or skills to decide rates of pay, 14 per cent use pay statistics, 12 per cent trade union negotiations, 6 per cent individual negotiation, and 6 per cent some other means to decide the pay rates of all staff. Generally manual workers are less likely to have their pay decided by market rates, individual negotiation and pay statistics and, not surprisingly, more likely to have pay determined by trade union negotiations. A number of respondents said they are looking at skills and competencies as a way of determining the pay of manual workers – a trend that seems to be affecting all levels of employee to some degree.

Of the 45 per cent of all respondents who do not currently operate a formal job evaluation scheme, 22 per cent have plans to implement such a scheme in the future. This group gives a variety of reasons for the need they perceive for more formal ways of describing and evaluating jobs. These include ensuring consistency in pay rates and promoting fairness and equal opportunities. Respondents who are planning to implement formal job evaluation arrangements are most likely to be considering a customised scheme, 61 per cent saying that it is their preferred option. Only 19 per cent of this group thought it likely they would opt for a proprietary brand scheme.

The majority of respondents without formal job evaluation arrangements had never operated such a scheme, and only 20 per cent say their organisation has any past experience of formal job evaluation.

Types of job evaluation used

Sixty-eight per cent of all respondents who use formal job evaluation techniques use a proprietary brand scheme. By far the most popular of these schemes is the Hay guide chart which is employed by 78 per cent of respondents using a proprietary brand scheme to evaluate at least some of their jobs. Twenty-eight per cent of all respondents using a proprietary brand scheme are using the Hay Guide Chart to evaluate all the jobs in their organisations, and 46 per cent use the scheme to evaluate the jobs at managerial level. Figures 16.2 and 16.3 give the breakdowns for respondents making use of the most well known proprietary brands.

Figure 16.2
PROPRIETARY BRAND SCHEMES
N = 79 (68% respondents with formal job evaluation)

Scheme	% of respondents employing a proprietary brand scheme using this scheme for all or some jobs
Hay Guide Chart – Profile Method	78
Watson Wyatt – EPC	5
Towers Perrin WJQ	5
PE Points & Direct Consensus Method	4
Institute of Office Administration	3
KPMG Equate	2
PA Consultancy	2
Price Waterhouse Profile Method	2
Other	14

Base = 118

The respondents who do not make use of a proprietary brand scheme say they are most likely to use points-factor rating or job classification to decide pay rates (see Figure 16.4).

Only 34 per cent of all respondents with a formal job evaluation scheme say they have had to adjust their scheme to meet their organisation's specific requirements. There was very little difference between the incidence of adjustment reported by respondents from the public and private sectors. Adjustments are made for a variety of reasons, such as the introduction of performance related pay, the need for more flexibility, or because of extension of the scheme to a wider number and type of staff or a change in the workforce profile.

Figure 16.3

PROPRIETARY BRAND SCHEMES

N = 79 (68% respondents with formal job evaluation)

Scheme	% of respondents with a proprietary brand scheme using scheme to evaluate all jobs	% respondents using scheme for managerial employees only	% respondents using scheme for Admin./Clerical employees only	% respondents using scheme for technical/professional employees only	% respondents using scheme for manual employees only
Hay Guide Chart – Profile Method	28	46	27	32	–
Watson Wyatt – EPC	4	–	–	–	–
Towers Perrin – WJQ	4	2	1	–	–
PE International	2	3	3	3	–
Institute of Office Administration	–	–	3	–	–
KPMG Scheme	2	–	–	–	–
PA Consulting	–	–	2	2	–
Price Waterhouse Profile Methods	–	–	–	–	2
Other	2	3	6	5	6

Figure 16.4
NON-PROPRIETARY BRAND SCHEMES

Process	% of respondents with formal job evaluation but no proprietary brand scheme using process
Points-factor rating	29
Job classification	21
Factor comparison	11
Competencies	9
Skills	3

Base = 51

Implementation of job evaluation

The majority of respondents (64 per cent) said they had introduced their job evaluation scheme more than three years previously. Seventy-one per cent at that time used consultants to help them in the introduction of job evaluation; 63 per cent consulted with union or employee representatives about job evaluation arrangements. Only 13 per cent operated computerised schemes.

Operation of job evaluation

Sixty-five per cent of all the respondents replying to the questionnaire who operate a formal job evaluation scheme indicated that they are reasonably well satisfied with their existing job evaluation arrangements. Only 4 per cent of such respondents say they are totally dissatisfied with their scheme although 21 per cent express some measure of dissatisfaction. Again there was a wide variety of reasons for this dissatisfaction, and these were explored in greater depth in follow-up interviews along with the reasons for satisfaction with existing job evaluation arrangements. However, the survey results indicate a slightly higher level of satisfaction with job evaluation in the private sector as opposed to the public sector (see Figure 16.5).

Figure 16.5
SATISFACTION WITH EXISTING JOB EVALUATION ARRANGEMENTS

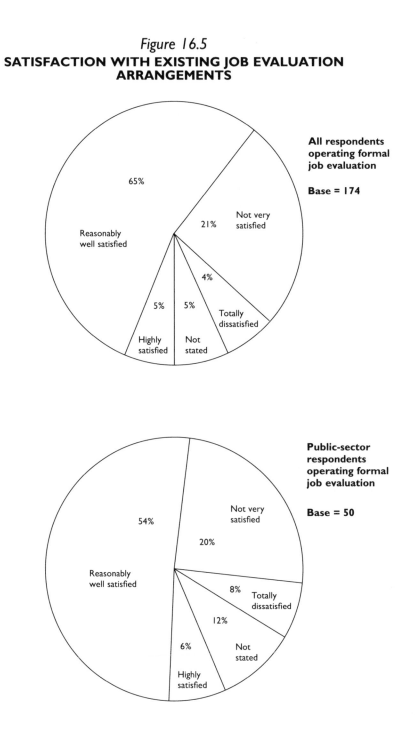

Figure 16.5 cont.

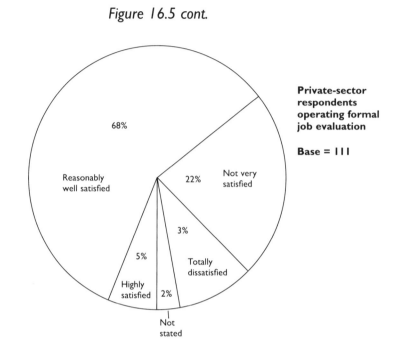

Although relatively few respondents have made changes to their formal job evaluation arrangements in the past, 42 per cent have plans to do so in the future. As Figure 16.6 demonstrates, this percentage is slightly higher in the public sector. Again reasons for such changes vary from necessity because of a merger of two organisations to a quest for more flexibility, from a re-structuring programme to a move towards performance-based pay.

Planned changes to job evaluation or pay structures

Pay structures

Most of the responding organisations operate a graded pay structure. It is evident, however, that some operate more than one pay system for different categories of staff. For example although 64 per cent of all the respondents operating formal job evaluation arrangements use grades, only 30 per cent use them to cover all jobs. Figure 16.7 shows the use of different types of pay structure.

Figure 16.6
PLANNED CHANGES TO JOB EVALUATION OR PAY STRUCTURES

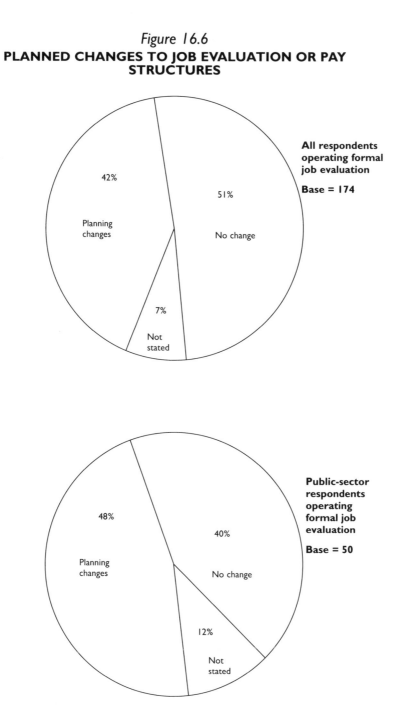

Figure 16.6 cont.

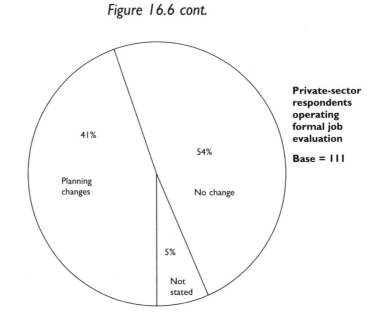

Private-sector respondents operating formal job evaluation

Base = 111

Figure 16.7
TYPE OF PAY STRUCTURE USED BY RESPONDENTS USING FORMAL JOB EVALUATION

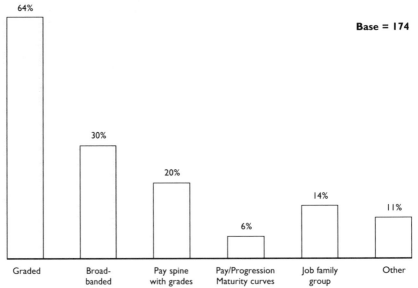

Base = 174

Conclusions

The results of this survey indicate that there is a great deal of activity and thought taking place around job evaluation. But there are no apparent strong trends away from formal arrangements and it appears that even when dissatisfied with existing job evaluation arrangements organisations are reluctant to throw them out altogether.

Most organisations were looking for ways to cope with change more generally within the organisation. In particular, the drive for flexibility was a key issue driving changes to job evaluation arrangements. Moves in the public sector towards local pay determination and performance management seem to be having a significant influence in the way in which jobs are being described and evaluated.

Most of the criticisms levelled against traditional forms of job evaluation centre around inflexibility and an inability to cope with knowledge workers, teamworking or flatter structures. Some organisations also mentioned cultural problems, indicating that a job evaluation system perpetuated a culture of hierarchy in which additional work equates with promotion, whereas they needed more flexibility to encourage people to broaden their range of skills and responsibilities within their existing jobs.

Finally, it is apparent that a significant number of organisations are implementing formal job evaluation for the first time or tightening up their existing arrangements. This seems to indicate that formal arrangements for job evaluation are far from dead in UK organisations. Certainly, despite the drive for increased flexibility and the removal of artificial restrictions on the roles on individuals in the workplace, the survey results demonstrate that the majority of organisations are still a long way from taking the leap of faith that is required to abandon job evaluation.

17

JOB EVALUATION IN ACTION

This chapter reviews the information about job evaluation in action that we obtained from the 31 organisations we visited during our research. The issues we explored were

□ methods of introduction
□ methods of operation
□ the benefits perceived by organisations to arise from their job evaluation practices
□ the problems organisations are meeting
□ impact on pay structures
□ approaches to the achievement of flexibility and the increased emphasis on lateral development in flatter organisations
□ job evaluation as part of an integrated approach to human resource management and organisation development
□ job evaluation for manual workers
□ future intentions – many of the organisations we visited were going through the process of reconsidering their approach to job evaluation.

Methods of introduction

Aylesbury Vale Community Health Care NHS Trust
At this NHS Trust a proprietary brand of job evaluation was used for some time for administrative and clerical staff, but managers felt that the scheme had been corrupted.

The Trust is now using KPMG's MEDEQUATE health-care system. The main reason for the selection of this system was that it was developed in the NHS and is computer-based.

The intention is to create a pay structure following job evaluation into which all staff are placed, except medical staff and executive level managers who will be have a separate structure. The Trust wants to move away from the automatic increment culture of the NHS to progression payments based on competence.

There is no job evaluation panel and no intention to set one up. Analysts trained by KPMG evaluate jobs in conjunction with the jobholder which is then verified by the manager. The computer system carries out the evaluation, thus avoiding the inconsistency and potential bias of a panel. Sixty benchmark jobs have been analysed (there are about 1,100 employees), but the intention is to continue with the evaluation of all other discrete jobs. This may lead to separate evaluations of jobs which the jobholders perceive as being different although they may in fact be the same, because the Trust believes that the system should be felt fair by everyone concerned. Implementation will be viewed in the context of the national situation. Some NHS staff do not want to leave the Whitley system, and some would prefer separate pay systems reflecting their differing professions and occupations.

Cancer Research Campaign

The development of the Cancer Research Campaign's job evaluation scheme was carried out by a working party with the help of consultants from William M. Mercer. The first part of the exercise was to draw up a list of factors in a brainstorming process based on the overriding question: 'What are the things you believe matter most in this organisation?' This produced an initial list of some 55 to 60 factors which was first refined to about 25 factors and, finally, after a pilot-scheme exercise with about 50 benchmark posts (out of a total number of 420 staff) reduced to 13. As personnel manager Ralph McKee pointed out, this was difficult because of the diversity of jobs in the organisation. The consultants then produced factor and level definitions, and the final version of the job analysis questionnaire was sent for approval by the working party. This asked employees to select the level in each factor which applied to their job. (An extract from the questionnaire is given in Appendix D.) All employees other than the 206 charity shop managers came to headquarters to complete the questionnaire in groups, Ralph McKee and the external consultants remaining on hand to give guidance. The completed questionnaires were then checked by line managers, who agreed any changes they thought necessary with the employee concerned.

The working party gave each factor a weighting, giving precedence to skills and knowledge. Next came effort, responsibility and finally, working conditions. Although it was fairly straightforward to rank jobs according to points scores reflecting these factor weightings, the working party found it more difficult to determine cut-off points between the nine new grades they had devised. As the director of finance Adrian Randall said to *Personnel Management Plus* (May 1993),

> There were about 500 to 600 points between the lowest and highest scores and we were looking at ranges of 50 points per grade. We did quite a few re-evaluations of jobs just below or just above the line. We didn't want to have the sort of situation where if the span was, say, 200–250 points, someone with 249 points and someone with 250 points and someone else with 250 points would be in the same grade while someone with 251 points would be in a different grade. So we tried to make sure that the top person in each grade was about 10 points away from the person at the bottom of the next grade.

Like all charities, Cancer Research Campaign recruits in a variety of job markets. To establish market rates, it was therefore necessary to look at salaries paid by organisations outside the voluntary sector as well as charities of similar size. Account had also to be taken of existing pay scales before arriving at the going rate for each job which indicated the mid-point on each salary scale. Most employees found that their existing salaries fell within the new scales for their jobs. They were moved up to the scale point nearest to their existing salaries which meant an increase of 1 to 2 per cent. Those whose current salaries were below the bottom point on their new grade were also moved up, in some cases receiving pay rises of as much as 10 to 12 per cent. A handful of employees, however, found that because their jobs had been overgraded under the old system, they would not be receiving any salary increase for the time being, although their existing salaries were protected.

The whole exercise took about six months to complete.

NAAFI

NAAFI, the supply organisation for the armed services, employs about 8,000 staff world-wide. A new job evaluation scheme was introduced in 1994 to reduce 'the plethora of job grades', generally simplify pay structures, and facilitate internal and external comparisons of rates of pay. The system chosen was the Hay Guide Chart-Profile Method.

Senior company trade union representatives and external regional officers were involved with the project from the start. As Dougie Pullen, the head of personnel told us: 'The only problem was getting the unions to talk to one another.' But he strongly recommends that they should be brought in at the initiation of the project. The steering group agreed on the composition of the job evaluation panels and nominated a squad of panellists to be appointed to particular panels. Someone who knew the job was always a member of each panel but if they were too close to the job they did not participate in the evaluation process but provided the panel with a proper understanding of the job. Continuity was provided by having the same chairman for all panels, and consistency was achieved by getting panels to re-evaluate jobs already evaluated by other panels.

Norwich Union

Norwich Union went to great lengths in communicating to staff through team managers and leaders the details of the design and development of their new job evaluation system. A briefing document was produced which explained why the old system was being changed and the need to

□ introduce a more efficient, consistent and structured process of evaluation

□ update the criteria used for measuring jobs, 'ensuring that they reflect the values of Norwich Union today and tomorrow'

□ clarify the role of job evaluation, emphasising that 'job size' is only one determinant of pay, and that the other measures are the individual employees' performance, the market rate for the job, and the company's performance.

The briefing document outlined the proposed approach, set out the project objectives, described the project structure and process, and defined the role of line managers and the communication and training programme. It also provided managers with a set of questions and answers, and a summary of job evaluation terms.

Methods of operating

The Automobile Association

The AA has a four-tier broad-banded (66 per cent) structure for its 800 managerial posts. This was introduced by the group personnel director Peter Stemp in 1994. The evaluation method associated with this structure replaces an over-complicated competence-based system which had in turn replaced an over-mechanistic and degraded analytical job evaluation scheme. The approach combines the use of tiering criteria and core benchmark jobs. It is therefore a combination of the job classification and internal benchmarking methods. An example of a tier definition is given in Appendix E.

In order for a position to move to a tier from a staff grade or into a different tier, the *Essential Guide* to the Performance Management and Reward System states that one of two things must have occurred:

□ *reorganisation* – where a completely new job is created or a job is eliminated and the responsibilities have been divided among existing jobs; or

□ *role change* – where a job has materially grown (or diminished) and this is reflected in the formal description of the role; such changes may have evolved slowly over time or they may been more immediately noticeable – normally, incremental changes in the role, temporary responsibilities, and superior performance of the incumbent are not 'role changes' which can lead to a tier move.

A proposal for a tier move requires the submission of a business case which includes an organisation chart, a current role definition and an explanation of how or why the role has changed. This includes the impact on other jobs (peers, managers and subordinates) and a summary of how the job meets the tier criteria (including comparisons with suitable bench-marks). The business case approach ensures that the job is not reviewed in isolation, and that the impact of changes in one job on other jobs is considered.

Peter Stemp believes that this approach is a robust way of allocating jobs to tiers. It is based on operating level and job grouping, not job evaluation in the traditional sense. It is seen as part of an integrated approach to performance management and reward which is based on clearly established common standards in accordance with the following principles:

- □ every position has a current, written job definition
- □ everyone has an annual statement of personal objectives to be achieved or results required
- □ all roles are allocated to a tier level that is an objective reflection of job size
- □ the competence of each person is formally reviewed at least annually
- □ the overall performance of each individual is reviewed twice a year
- □ salaries are determined on the basis of individual perfor-mance, taking into account the external market and the AA's ability to pay.

It was stressed by Peter Stemp, however, that the AA paid for 'delivered performance', not just for competence develop-ment.

Norwich Union

Norwich Union introduced the Watson Wyatt Multicomp computerised system of job evaluation in 1992 to replace a manual factor-based system. The Watson Wyatt questionnaire and software were customised for Norwich Union. The ques-tionnaire covers knowledge dimensions specific to Norwich Union and includes questions relating to expertise, physical skills, human relations skills, guidance available, complexity, physical demands, and impact. The questionnaire is 27 pages long and provides the full basis for the evaluation process. Data from the questionnaire is loaded onto lap-top computers and job analysts can provide an immediate response to their 'customers'. This enables the latter to obtain an in-depth view of the evaluation process. There are currently more than 5,000 jobs on the database relevant to just over 10,000 staff.

Perceived benefits

The provision of a framework for rational decision-making about rates of pay was mentioned by many of our contacts. One public sector manager said that they wanted to get away from a situation in which 'we think of a salary and then pin it on a spine'.

At *Norwich Union* their job evaluation scheme (based on Watson Wyatt Multicomp) is regarded as a logical and easily understood system that reflects the values of the organisation and copes well with knowledge workers.

Yellow Pages Sales Limited believe that the main benefit they have obtained from their scheme (a development of the Hay system) is that it has enabled the company to respond quickly to changes in the marketplace.

At *Cancer Research Campaign*, the computerised job evaluation scheme introduced in 1992 provides a logical and easily administered basis for grading jobs in a simplified salary structure. It provides a rationale for pay and grading decisions which replaces the approach previously adopted by managers who tended to say: 'I think I need to recruit a new ... I think the grade will be ...', and that was it.

The head of personnel at *NAAFI*, Dougie Pullen, said that job evaluation had 'at last provided a sound base on which we can align our salaries with the outside world'. He commented that it 'turned our perception of job values upside down – people who are responsible for putting pennies in the 'till are now seen as having bigger jobs than those who support their activities in a head office environment. A change in company culture is the result.'

Problems

The shopfloor workers at a large engineering firm we contacted had produced their own guidance notes on 'how to win points and influence gradings' for the proprietary brand recently installed in their company. In a charity with its own tailor-made evaluation scheme managers and employees compose their submissions by reproducing phrases from the factor plan definitions of the level above the present rating. The personnel manager in this case is required to adjudicate on these often fictionalised submissions, which puts her in an impossibly invidious position.

The London office of an international bank had a points based system that had been customised for them by management consultants. Managers disliked the system, however, because of its emphasis on factors which they considered to be irrelevant in their departments and it was abandoned. As a result, decisions on pay are based on market rates, the individual's ability to adapt to change, and the opinion of line managers. The disadvantage of this unstructured, albeit flexible, approach is that there is no back-up to answer people who challenge their grading. Having moved from a highly structured to a highly fluid situation, they now want to put some structure back.

At *Granada Television*, the Hay system of evaluation is held by some managers to be time-consuming and too mechanistic for their culture. Their creative people do not accept that they are doing a job in isolation. They are not status conscious and are uncomfortable with the concept that one job should be more highly scored than another. Few people have clearly defined areas of responsibility and much of the planning and decision-making is achieved collaboratively in groups. A people-based approach was felt to be more appropriate.

In the *ICL Group*, four different methods have been used to evaluate jobs in their UK operations. All are traditional points schemes customised for the company. The problem is that employees have tended to focus on getting more points and promotions in order to obtain more pay. People see the structure in hierarchical terms within which they progress upwards. There is no real value in lateral moves. However, the systems enabled them to control payroll costs, and they did work well in the past when the structure of the organisation changed less often and jobs were more rigidly controlled.

In the marketing division of an international group, the standard Hay system is at present being used for 14 grades. But there have been problems in applying the system. It is felt that the grading criteria are too broad and that people play the system to get their jobs upgraded by writing their job description in a way that will achieve a higher level. A further weakness of the system is felt to be the emphasis it places on jobs and job status rather than what needs to be done. This does not fit with the organisational culture the organisation is trying to build. However, the intention is to develop a new approach with the help of Hay.

At the *Scottish Provident Group*, Andy Chalmers, group personnel planning manager, says that their present traditional job classification has helped to reinforce a static culture. It focuses the attention of staff on career development through upgrading, and people tend 'to fix their job descriptions through semantics'. In other words, they enhance them. In his view, many line managers like traditional hierarchical grading and advancement structures (and the traditional job evaluation methods that support them) because they are easy to manage. But, he asked, 'Should they be managing grades or should they be managing people?' He also pointed out that organisations 'can no longer be static – if they don't change and really compete, they will no longer be in business'. The implication was that they cannot therefore afford to perpetuate traditional personnel practices which inhibit change and flexibility.

Flexibility and lateral development

ICL is moving rapidly towards an environment in which there are no standard jobs and everyone will be working more flexibly. Clive Wright, Manager, Corporate Remuneration, believes that in this new situation it is necessary when evaluating jobs to focus on the role and how it might develop and when valuing roles to emphasise the degree to which they have broadened. It is hoped that the new approach to job evaluation that is being developed will encourage people to improve their skills and capabilities, and to think laterally about their careers. The company should be able to move people sideways more easily by matching people to jobs and emphasising the value attached to broadening of experience.

A financial services company we visited has a flat organisation represented by only five levels. It therefore has a broad-banded structure. The requirement is for considerable operational flexibility, and this means that an equally flexible approach is adopted to job grading. Consideration was given to some form of analytical job evaluation, but research indicated that the conventional methods available were too rigid, too time-consuming and too bureaucratic. The company is growing rapidly and there is plenty of scope for individuals to grow with it. But staff are not status-conscious and have no perception that the only way to get on is to be promoted.

Jobs are slotted into the structure by means of a process of internal benchmarking using whole job comparisons based on job descriptions setting out key result areas, preferred behaviours and skill requirements (see example in Appendix E). But account is also taken of market value, and particular weight is attached to customer contact. The personnel manager said that this flexible approach worked well and was accepted by staff because of the culture of trust that had been built up in this relatively new organisation. It was, however, believed that as the organisation grew in size a more analytical approach to job evaluation might be necessary, but it would have to operate flexibly.

Norwich Union introduced the Watson Wyatt Multicomp computerised system of job evaluation in 1992 to replace a manual factor-based system. A key aim of the scheme is to help the organisation to manage greater operational flexibility and rapid change. The Norwich Union Group has undergone extensive reorganisation. The structure is now much flatter represented by ten operational levels rather than 18, and where appropriate, work is organised around multiskilled self-managed teams. It is recognised that as a result of the flatter organisation the fundamental processes for staff development and advancement have changed. It is necessary for all concerned to understand how individuals can develop laterally, and how advancement may well take place by a series of sideways moves. 'Grade-hopping' as a result of the traditional hierarchical approach has been replaced by the new processes. But changing the perceptions of staff that 'grade means pay' is a slow process, and Norwich Union is developing understanding among its staff that job evaluation should be seen primarily as a management tool that serves to underpin the total reward system.

At *Scottish Provident Group* Andy Chalmers informed us that consideration was being given to introducing new processes of valuing jobs to replace the existing system. No decisions had yet been made, but the approach is likely to be market and competence-based. A key question is 'does the work come to the job or does it come to the competences possessed by the person in the job or the team?' Andy Chalmers firmly believes that the latter should be the case. The emphasis is now on establishing what individuals are capable of doing, on ensuring that they have the competences required to do it, and on valuing and rewarding them accordingly. He thinks that organisations have to find ways of rewarding people without giving them the wrong signals about their career moves. He accepts, however, that 'work produces its own hierarchy', and that no evaluation scheme can ignore those areas of organisations in which hierarchy is inevitable.

Integration

One of the most important – and encouraging – messages delivered by our research was the extent to which a number of organisations saw job evaluation as an integral part of an overall approach to human resource management, and not as a separate entity. Moreover, in some of the organisations we visited the approach to job evaluation has flowed from a fundamental review of the organisation and human resource management practices, often arising from the introduction of new technology and/or a business process re-engineering exercise. This applied in *Pilkington Optronics*, where the introduction of computer integrated manufacturing (CIM), coupled with a comprehensive re-engineering project focused attention on competence analysis and mapping and was the driving force behind the development of a competence-based evaluation scheme.

At *Bass Taverns* (see below) and *The National & Provincial Building Society* (see Chapter 6), the approach to job evaluation followed major organisational change and process re-engineering programmes. Other integrated approaches developed or projected in *ICL* and *Yellow Pages* are described later in this section.

Bass Taverns is conducting a massive change programme linked to an all-embracing business process re-engineering exercise. As described by Gordon Steven, Project Coordinator for the Change Team, the change programme is driven by the belief that 'Taverns must be responsive and customer-focused if it is to meet the challenge of market trends.' The basic analysis revealed three core processes – 'operate pubs, develop pubs, manage cash' – and the whole business was redesigned around the successful delivery of these processes. The aim was to move from hierarchy to team, function to process, supervisor to coach, defensive to productive, and boss to customer.

The emphasis is on process with the maximum use of teams. For example, one team is now responsible for all stages of the new acquisition and development process which had previously been split between a number of functions. The new continual and seamless process for acquisition and development is delivering impressive improvements in performance that are rewarded appropriately by team bonuses.

The impact of this programme on the grade and pay structure was to reduce the previous 12 management grades to 4 bands covering, respectively, group resource, divisional resource, management resource, and professional resource. Although these bands are still defined in Hay points terms, they are sufficiently broad to eliminate the necessity for continual evaluations or re-evaluations. The objective is to build as much flexibility as possible into the system, and there are no rigid pay limits to the bands. A professional who is making a very considerable contribution could be paid more than anyone in the next band above. Individual pay is related to competence ('demonstrable behaviour') team performance, company performance and market rates.

At *ICL*, the plans are to develop a much more integrated approach to pay determination in which role evaluation in job families will interrelate with individual career development plans – all employees will have ownership of their own plan. This is in line with the belief expressed by Andrew Mayo (director of human resource development, ICL Group) in learning organisation theory. Role evaluation is therefore seen as part of a learning culture.

Yellow Pages Sales Limited would like to link job evaluation with competences both to match jobs and to judge performance. The competences have already been identified and embedded in learning and development plans.

Impact on grading

In almost every organisation we visited, the result of their job evaluation exercise was a reduction in the number of grades. And those who were contemplating the introduction of a new approach generally envisaged a considerable reduction in the number of grades. *Cancer Research Campaign* reduced the number of their grades from 27 to 9 and *NAAFI* reduced the considerable number of grades contained in their many different pay structures to a limited number of bands in one unified pay structure. Broad-banding has been introduced in a number of organisations we visited, including the *Automobile Association, Bass Taverns* and the *National & Provincial Building Society.*

Job evaluation for manual workers

Job evaluation schemes for manual workers, if they exist at all, tend to be traditional points or factor comparison techniques. Although skill-based pay is, in effect, a form of job evaluation. One of the key issues is equal pay for work of equal value and this was certainly a major concern of the trade unionists we met. The approaches adopted by a number of the organisations we contacted are described below.

British Waterways

British Waterways has six wages grades for its 1,000 canal workers. Workers move up through the grades subject to achieving and delivering the levels of competence defined for each grade. They can progress on the basis of delivered competence through the first four grades, but would normally have to wait for jobs to become vacant in grades five and six.

An engineering company

This manufacturer operates a multiskilled cell system of work on the shopfloor. All team members have to acquire a set of six core competences to qualify for the maximum rate of pay – there is only one rate for operators. They are then encouraged to acquire other competences to allow them to be interchangeable between cells or to be promoted to team leader.

Local Government Management Board job evaluation scheme for manual workers

The scheme for local government manual workers was developed in conjunction with the recognised trade unions with the objective of meeting equal value requirements. The factor plan which was devised after a prolonged development programme: 'the largest of its kind ever conducted' (*Industrial Relations Review and Report, 1987*) is shown in Table 17.1.

Prestige Group

The Prestige Group does not have a formal job evaluation system for its factory floor workers. During 1991–92 negotiations with the trade union resulted in a reduction of the previous 12 rates of pay to four straight day-rates for production operators, operator/adjusters, setters, and skilled toolroom craft workers (a decayed payment-by-results scheme was abandoned). The jobs to which these grades apply are defined and full flexibility was achieved through the negotiations.

Toshiba

Like other Japanese manufacturing companies, Toshiba does not have a formal system of job evaluation. In the operational area there are seven grades related to skills. Levels of pay in these grades are related to local rates. There are no job descriptions as such. All they have is a simple set of statements about what people are expected to do, which are used for recruitment purposes. Consideration is being given to introducing job evaluation for engineers and other specialist staff, but this would not extend to manual workers in operational areas.

Figure 17.1

LOCAL GOVERNMENT MANAGEMENT BOARD JOB EVALUATION SCHEME FOR MANUAL WORKERS – FACTOR PLAN

Factor	Evaluation level					Factor weighting
	1	*2*	*3*	*4*	*5*	
Skill	36	72	108	306	360	36%
Responsibility for people	12	30	90	120		
Responsibility for resources	12	30	90	120		36%
Responsibility for supervision	6	12	54	108	120	
Initiative	6	18	36	60		6%
Mental effort	8	24	48	80		8%
Physical conditions	8	24	48	80		8%
Working conditions	6	18	36	60		6%

Intentions

At a pharmaceutical company we visited, a new pay structure is being developed in the sales and marketing division to replace the existing job family structure which is regarded as having been too inflexible – inhibiting horizontal moves between job families. The proposed structure will be broad-banded – six bands covering the whole organisation. Jobs will be grouped into bands according to their Hay scores, but the main criterion for drawing the boundary lines will be the Hay 'know how' factor.

The emphasis is on continuous development, and the pay project is closely linked to this philosophy. Progression within the bands will be related to competence development and demonstrated flexible and adaptive behaviour. The aim is to encourage people to grow and take on new responsibilities, and to reward them accordingly. The basic philosophy underpinning this approach is that: 'You need to reward the right things to get the right message across about what is important.'

The bands are defined in fairly general terms. Competency profiles are also being developed for each band. The basic rate of pay for a competent individual in a role is aligned to the upper quartile market rate for that role. Currently, because of the importance attached to continuous development, bonuses up to the point when individuals reach the upper quartile reference point will be related to the acquisition of competences. Above that point they will be linked to the achievement of objectives. Pay decisions will continue to be devolved to line managers, who will make them by reference to the generic role definitions and competency profiles and to the achievement of agreed work and personal development objectives. It is proposed to abolish all performance ratings.

At *ICL*, the plan is to replace the current job evaluation arrangements with around 15 job families (eg marketing, production, finance, personnel). Each of these will contain two, three, or four job levels, and at each level they will analyse the knowledge, skills, experience, attitudes and outputs required. Pay progression will be related to three measures: individual objectives, appraisals, and personal development plans.

At *Index Limited* (a subsidiary of Littlewoods), Mike Hayes, the head of HR, wants to create a more flexible system that would recognise individual competence. But he also recognises the need to introduce greater consistency through an analytical approach which would reduce the risk of equal-value claims.

The *International Wool Secretariat* has used the Hay system since the 1970s. An update was badly needed, and with the help of Hay a world-wide re-evaluation of 50 benchmark jobs has just been completed. Louise Williams, the Personnel Manager would now like to introduce a broad-banded system to provide more flexibility.

An international marketing organisation is proposing to replace its present job evaluation system and develop a grade structure of 6 rather than 14 grades. With the help of Hay Management Consultants the intention is to identify job families on the basis of contribution to the company's success and the competences necessary to do a particular task. For example, marketing might be a job family containing jobs ranging from department head to clerical assistant. All would require some knowledge of marketing but in different degrees, and some would require specific cross-functional competences. The job family criteria would be agreed with significant input from the department concerned. An individual's grade would be decided on the basis of the role to be performed and the competences brought to that role by the individual. Evaluation would be carried out only to link grades to market rates. Job descriptions might still be used, but only for recruitment purposes.

Thames Valley University is replacing an out-of-date non-academic staff job evaluation scheme which failed to control grade drift with a system of grade definitions based on the following factors: knowledge, skills and experience; level of autonomy; judgement and decision-making; contacts; work complexity; and supervision and management. The system built around the analysis of 50 benchmark jobs conducted by outside consultants. The plan is to implement the scheme by training about 30 people to form job evaluation panels. The panels will consist of a staff representative, a management representative and a personnel representative. They will draw up the job purpose for each job and recommend a grade. It is proposed to replace the existing 13 non-academic grades with 5 (possibly 6) fairly broad grades aligned to 'pay points' based on the national scales.

As John Thompson, then director of personnel, told us: 'An essential element of the scheme will be that people are encouraged to become more flexible about the kind of tasks they are willing to undertake.' He hopes that the scheme will not only help employees look at their jobs in a more flexible way but will also create a better understanding of the relationship between accountability and the way people are paid. The scheme has still to be negotiated with UNISON, who recognise the need for a new approach.

18

CONCLUSIONS – THE

FUTURE OF JOB EVALUATION

Conclusions from the research

The conclusions from our research are that:

1   Job evaluation is not dead, not even dying; it continues to flourish because organisations dislike chaos and job evaluation at least brings some semblance of order and equity to the process of pay determination. But our research did reveal that some organisations were establishing the relative value of roles quite effectively without the use of bureaucratic job evaluation systems.

2   Traditional rigid, bureaucratic and hierarchical approaches to job evaluation, which purport to be objective, scientific and totally rational and which represent job evaluation as a system that can deliver the 'right answer' are inappropriate and are generally recognised as such.

3   Organisations which have de-layered and are team-, process- and project-based, are eliminating artificial restrictions. This is prompting them to seek means of valuing jobs that are more compatible with the need for operational and role flexibility. In some case such organisations are no longer using conventional job evaluation processes.

4   There is no one system or process of job evaluation that works equally well in all organisations; every business must develop its own processes which fit its particular culture, values, organisation, technology, administrative systems and management style.

5   Job evaluation processes – including a factor plan, if one exists – must reflect and support the values of the organisation. They should deliver clear messages to all employees to the effect that: 'This is what we believe to be

important about what people do at work; these are the factors that determine the basis upon which you are valued and rewarded; this is what we expect from you – and this is what we will do for you in return.'

6   The factors upon which organisations base their valuations of work and people have to measure the right things; they should not simply conform to the rigidly defined requirements of jobs. Instead, they should refer to the competences people need to deliver higher levels of performance, and the ability continually to develop skills and adapt to new demands in their roles. But it is important to ensure that the factors in the plan cover all the significant characteristics of the jobs covered by the scheme.

7   Competence-based job evaluation can form a valuable part of an integrated approach to competence-based personnel management. The evidence from our research reveals that this is frequently being achieved by introducing new competence-related factors to an existing points-factor scheme (and/or replacing existing factors). These factors are often related to generic competence frameworks. Alternatively, new factor plans are being developed which are wholly competence-based. However, there is still a risk that such schemes could suffer from the same drawbacks as traditional factor plans. This approach to valuing jobs will not necessarily in itself provide the answer to all the inherent problems of conventional job evaluation (discussed in the first part of this book). But some organisations are going even further by abandoning traditional formal job evaluation methods altogether and instituting more flexible and people-oriented processes that relate pay to individual competence and contribution within a broad-banded pay structure.

8   Although there is a considerable amount of interest in competence-based pay, many of the people we talked to emphasised that any method of valuing jobs or roles must measure outputs (results and contribution) as well as inputs (competence levels).

9   Business process re-engineering exercises and the de-layering of organisations may dictate the need to introduce more flex-

ible grade and pay structures (for example, broad-banding). But organisations cannot simply say, in effect, 'Down with structure' and leave a vacuum. Structures have to be replaced with processes that provide guidance on how individuals are to be paid and to progress within the broad bands in which they have been placed.

10 Job evaluation methodology itself has to be flexible and constantly under review. For example, job evaluations can be carried out by individuals together with their managers using computerised methods without requiring elaborate job descriptions and time-consuming meetings of job evaluation panels.

11 Job evaluation has to be regarded as a dynamic and evolutionary process. It cannot stand still. It must be continually reviewed and modified as required in line with changes to organisational structures, processes, technologies and values, and with the new demands such changes make on people.

12 Job evaluation is no longer a separate entity – a personnel technique. It has to be developed and managed as an integral part of the people management processes of the organisation.

13 In practice, job evaluation is increasingly being integrated with other people management processes, such as continuous development, career management, succession planning, and performance management.

14 Last, but by no means least: those concerned with valuing jobs, whether or not they are using formal methods, must be constantly aware of the need to achieve and maintain gender neutrality.

The way forward

Our research identified the following trends:

1 A continuing increase in the degree to which job evaluation is expected to function flexibly. This does not mean abandoning analytical processes such as point-factor rating, but it does require that they should be applied with discretion as indicators of relativities and comparable

worth rather than seen as the ultimate arbiters of the precise value of a job.

2   An increasing emphasis on the need to evaluate people *as well as* jobs (not *instead of* jobs – the two cannot be separated). The focus will be on the overall role that people play as the basis for determining relative worth. Account will be taken of the context in which the role is carried out (team membership and interpersonal relationships generally), the flexibility required of role-holders, the knowledge, skills and competences they need to perform the role effectively, and their capacity to extend their capabilities and adapt to new demands. Particular importance will be placed on measuring outcomes as well as inputs.

3   Traditional factor lists will be abandoned or at least modified. As necessary, they will be extended to cover all the characteristics that indicate the value of a role as opposed to a group of tasks. These include:

   □ roles in which flexibility and adaptability are major considerations
   □ the demands made on people in caring roles or on those who are constantly interrelating with customers, clients and members of the public
   □ roles with special requirements such as interpersonal skills or creative abilities
   □ roles in which there are particular pressures arising from the need to achieve exacting targets, meet deadlines, manage complexity, or re-prioritise work, etc.

4   Competence-based job evaluation processes will increase in popularity, but they are more likely to enhance traditional forms of job evaluation than completely to replace them.

5   It will be generally recognised that people should be valued both in terms of their competence *and* their contribution. But competence-related approaches can certainly link job evaluation more closely with other key personnel processes, such as those concerned with human resource planning, recruitment, performance management and continuous development.

6   Market forces will continue to exert a major influence on pay levels, especially in less stable conditions where job markets are more fragmented and fluid and people are looking elsewhere for ways to further their careers.

7   Awareness of the need to achieve gender neutrality – both in the job evaluation scheme itself and the way it is operated – will increase, but managements will not necessarily be so obsessed about equal value as to impose unnecessarily complex and inflexible analytical evaluation schemes on the organisation.

8   Computer-assisted job evaluation will become the norm in all large applications.

9   For job evaluation purposes, traditional methods of job analysis will be replaced in many organisations by computerised methods of processing the answers to job analysis questionnaires.

10 In line with trends in best practice, elaborate and restrictive job descriptions will be superseded by role definitions, often generic, which set out the core competences relevant to those roles and provide the foundation for agreeing individual objectives and formulating personal development plans.

11 Whatever method of job evaluation is adopted, no development will be undertaken without assessing the extent to which it will add value rather than create work. A value-added approach means that schemes will not be introduced or updated without considering the impact they will make on the motivation, commitment and performance of people and therefore on the results obtained by the organisation.

12 Job evaluation will be increasingly seen as an integral part of the overall reward and human resource management processes of the organisation. The pressure will be to ensure that any methods used to assess the relative worth of jobs reflect the core values and culture of the organisation and further the achievement of its strategic objectives.

APPENDICES

Appendix A:

PROPRIETARY JOB EVALUATION SCHEMES

Management consultant schemes

This appendix summarises the main points of the following commonly used management consultants job evaluation schemes:

Hay Management Consultants
52 Grosvenor Gardens, London SW1W OAU
Tel No: 0171 730 0833
Fax No: 0171 730 8193
Contact: Derek Pritchard
Scheme: Hay Guide Chart-Profile Method

Watson Wyatt
21 Tothill Street, London SW1H 9LL
Tel No: 0171 222 8033
Fax No: 0171 222 9182
Contact: Clare Muhiudeen
Schemes:
1. Employee Points Factor Comparison (EPFC)
2. European Factor Plan (EFP)
3. Computerised Job Evaluation – 'HR Edge'
4. Competence-based job evaluation

KPMG Management Consulting
8 Salisbury Square, London EC4Y 8BB
Tel No: 0171 311 8000
Fax No: 0171 311 8274
Contact: David R. Clifford/Jane Bryan
Schemes: Equate/Medequate

Towers Perrin
Castlewood House, 77–91 New Oxford Street, London WC1A 1PX
Tel No: 0171 379 4411
Fax No: 0171 379 7478
Contact: Ann Cummins/Duncan Brown

PA Consulting Group
123 Buckingham Palace Road, London SW1W 9SR
Tel No: 0171 730 9000
Fax No: 0171 333 5452
Contact: Clare Roberts
Scheme: PA Basic Job Evaluation Scheme

PE Consulting, Human Resource Practice
Park House, Wick Road, Egham, Surrey
Tel No: 01784 434411
Contact: David Turton
Schemes:
1. The Pay Points System
2. The Factor Plan Approach
3. The Direct Consensus Method

Price Waterhouse
Southwark Towers, 32 London Bridge Street, London SE1 9SY
Tel No: 0171 939 3000
Fax No: 0171 378 0647
Contact: David Thomas
Scheme: Price Waterhouse Profile Methodology

Saville and Holdsworth Ltd
3AC Court, High Street, Thames Ditton, Surrey KT7 OSR
Tel No: 0181 398 4170
Fax No: 0181 398 9544
Contact: Richard Rogers
Scheme: The Saville and Holdsworth Job Evaluation Method

HR Computing/LogoSoft™ in conjunction with the Institute of
Administrative Management (IAM)
Brearley House, Lymington Road,Christchurch, Dorset BH23 5ET
Tel No: 01425 279144
Fax No: 01425 271524
Contact: Warwick Temple
Schemes: The IAM Computerised Job Evaluation Scheme

The Hay Guide Chart-Profile Method

The Hay Guide Chart-Profile Method of Job Evaluation is claimed to
be the most widely used single job evaluation method in the world,
used by more than 7,000 profit and non-profit organisations in some
40 countries. It is used to evaluate all types and levels of jobs in both
the public and private sectors.

Initially conceived in the early 1950s, it had its roots in factor comparison methods in which Edward N Hay was a pioneer. It was designed to combine the sound conceptual basis of factor comparison with the ease of use of points-factor rating approaches. The method, its factors and their definitions, and the way it is used have evolved over many years of application to literally millions of jobs of every kind. Although the basic nature of the method has been stable for many years – an important feature in enabling intercompany comparisons and valid pay market data – the language in which the factors are expressed is frequently tailored to suit the particular language, values and emphasis of the organisation using it.

Description of method

The method is based on the concept that

- any job or role in whatever organisational context exists to provide some contribution or output to the organisation (its accountability)
- achievement of accountability demands an input of knowledge, skill and experience (the knowhow)
- to turn knowhow into results, it must be used to solve the problems that arise in the job (the problem-solving).

Any role can thus be characterised in terms of its knowhow, problem-solving and accountability and the method is based upon these three factors. To refine the evaluation, each factor is considered in terms of two or three elements.

Knowhow
    technical/procedural/professional knowledge and skill
    planning, organising and managerial skills
    human relations skills.

Problem-solving
    thinking environment
    thinking challenge.

Accountability
    freedom to act
    magnitude – the scale of events on which the job has its main impact
    impact – the directness of impact on the chosen magnitude.

A guide chart is used for each of the three factors, containing descriptive scales for each element and a numbering pattern based on a 15 per cent step difference, which is an important building block in making comparisons between jobs. Job size is the sum of the results from the three factors. In addition, an explicit judgement is made about the balance between the factors in each job – the profile – which provides a valuable consistency check.

Application of the method

The method can be applied by a wide range of processes, both manual and computer-assisted. The process needs to be designed to suit the particular requirements of the organisation, and Hay consultants work with each client to design and implement the most appropriate process. Specific features affecting the process design include:

- ☐ the way work is defined (eg as fixed jobs or flexible roles)
- ☐ the type, range and number of jobs involved
- ☐ the resources and time available for the process
- ☐ the need for participation/involvement, and for consistency with other HR processes
- ☐ the way in which the results are to be used – eg to develop a conventional grade structure, or to underpin a flexible competency-linked job family approach
- ☐ whether the process is centralised or decentralised.

In practice, many processes used fall into the following broad categories:

- ☐ evaluation by panel (participative or otherwise) using written job descriptions; benchmarks may be used to set standards
- ☐ evaluation by HR specialists (or consultants) for review with managers
- ☐ computer-assisted processes using *HRXpert* software, in which job information is provided on a multiple-choice questionnaire and the algorithm developed from benchmark judgements made by conventional approaches
- ☐ use of the method to underpin classification processes, in which a framework is evaluated, then individual jobs allocated to the levels
- ☐ use of the method to underpin job family models, in which a framework of competency-linked levels is evaluated and individual people/roles allocated to the levels.

Translating outcomes into job grades/pay scales

Hay say they have no standard approach to developing grades or pay structures based on the results of evaluation – these must be designed to suit the requirements of the organisation. Job evaluation, they argue, is only one component in developing pay strategy and policy, and Hay consultants work with clients to design pay arrangements to suit their particular needs. An illustrative range of pay arrangements using the Hay method would include:

☐ individual pay scales for each job based on unique job sizes

☐ grades (each with a pay scale) based on clustering groups of jobs of similar size: grades may be narrow (and many in number) or wider (and fewer), depending on how much job size differentiation is appropriate; recent years have seen a trend to fewer, wider grades

☐ broad bands calibrated using the method

☐ use of the method to calibrate job family approaches, in which pay is based on assessment of individual skill, competency and contribution, and JE is used to calibrate levels within and between families.

Hay say that an important feature of their method is that, because of its widespread use and its consistent numbering pattern, it can be used to make valid pay market comparisons. Hay's comprehensive worldwide pay and benefits surveys and databases use Hay job size as the basis of comparisons which, they say, avoid the ambiguities of more simplistic approaches. Hay claim their method thus combines the unique capability to satisfy, in a single process, the internal need for job evaluation with the means of accessing comprehensive external market data.

Using the scheme with computers

HRXpert is an integrated Windows-based software tool that allows the control and analysis of job evaluation by Hay Guide methods, tailor-made questionnaires, direct job comparisons and other new approaches to work comparison. It has the flexibility to link the job evaluation questionnaire to competency-based approaches to job and person assessment using Hay McBer methods, allowing a natural link to candidate selection, performance management and employee development requirements. Hay say that computer assistance in work comparison need not necessarily be off-the-shelf but can be designed to the client's specification, expressing the organisation's values and asking relevant questions to fully explore the requirements of the role. The questions asked provide the input to evaluating the job through pragmatic statistical techniques and direct cross-reference to Hay factors. The process puts greater emphasis on the structured job analysis but provides the evaluation as an output. Hay say the tailored approach can maintain the important link to the common language of Hay points, which can then be seamlessly linked into salary surveys, remuneration management and modelling tools available within the *HRXpert* suite of software modules.

Hay claim the system is designed to be fully compatible with Client–Server requirements and utilising industry standard software, databases and networking requirements, *HRXpert* pulls together the needs of the Human Resource Executive into an integrated software.

Special features

The following claims are made by Hay for their method:

☐ The sound conceptual basis of the method and the fundamental nature of the factors give it an inherent flexibility which enables it to respond to the profound changes now taking place in organisations. It deals equally well with the flexible roles emerging in today's environment as with more conventionally defined and structured jobs.

☐ It can be applied to any kind of job at any level, and hence can be used top-to-bottom throughout an organisation, which is important in supporting a move to integrated employment conditions and the breaking down of barriers between traditional job groupings. Because it makes no organisational assumptions, it can be used in any organisational context.

☐ Being an analytical method, with non-discriminatory factors, it can be used to support the achievement of equal pay for work of equal value, and is supported by a comprehensive Equal Value Code of Practice.

☐ The nature of the factors, and the step-difference principle on which the numbering pattern is based, make the method a powerful tool for organisational analysis and work design. Well-established processes exist for using the results of the method for these purposes.

☐ As described above, it is not restricted to any particular application process, way of defining roles, or approach to pay management. It can thus be used as a component in designing the most appropriate pay and grading structures and processes to meet an organisation's specific and often changing needs.

Hay remuneration database

The Hay job evaluation method is used as the basis for Hay's extensive remuneration database. Hay claim that by calibrating all remuneration data against this common job size measure, valid like-for-like comparisons can be made. In the UK, Hay's database contains information from over 1,000 organisations, with data on over a quarter of a million jobs, representative of a population of over 2.5 million jobholders. Worldwide, similar databases are maintained in 45 countries, enabling easy and consistent access to data on international remuneration practices.

Data is held not just on base pay but also on variable pay practices (bonuses and incentives) and non-cash benefits, enabling full analysis of all components of the total remuneration package. Data is updated on a monthly basis. Survey reports are published on a regular basis. These include:

☐ the main *Hay Compensation Report* (HCR), published quarterly, providing data, analysis and comment on remuneration practices and trends for the economy as a whole and for the broad industrial and service sector and the finance sector

☐ the annual *Hay Boardroom Remuneration Guide*, covering all aspects of executive remuneration

☐ the annual *Benefits Survey*, covering detailed analysis of all aspects of benefits practices

☐ a wide range of regularly updated reports focusing on specific sectors (eg retail pharmaceuticals); on particular functions (eg engineers, accountants); or on particular geographies (eg London and office staff in the south-east).

In addition to these regular reports Hay offer specific analyses or cuts of the database, made to focus on particular areas. Because all data is coded by job size, industry sector, function and geography, highly specific analyses can be made for any combination of these factors.

Watson Wyatt schemes

Watson Wyatt provide a spectrum of approaches to job evaluation. Flexibility is provided not only in terms of the methodology applied – proprietary or tailor-made – but also in terms of the process of evaluation – traditional panels to computerised job evaluation. The different methods and processes are described below.

EPFC (Employee Points Factor Comparison)

Watson Wyatt claim that EPFC is suitable for all jobs across all organisations because it is designed around factors common to all ie knowledge and skills. It is probably least suited to sizing very large jobs in complex organisations and better used in medium to small organisations especially for middle-level to junior jobs.

History and development

The scheme was developed in 1978–79 by Wyatt Harris Graham. Watson Wyatt describe it as the product of a search for a method that was quantifiable, that avoided the problem encountered in some factor schemes of scoring jobs twice on the same factor, and yet that arrived at an integrated evaluation of jobs at all levels. Because such a scheme would provide an acceptable framework for the collection of comparative pay information, Watson Wyatt devised the EPFC as a necessary preliminary to the establishment of their Remuneration Data Service (RDS). At that stage the scheme was not primarily intended for use by companies as a method of in-house job evaluation. Company in-house adoption of the scheme came at the request of individual participants and is not a condition of membership of the RDS. The EPFC approach is essentially a factor-based points rating scheme which superficially, because of the use of detailed scoring charts, resembles elements of the Guide Chart-Profile Method.

Basis of the scheme

The EPFC is based on the premise that since jobs cannot be carried out without people, why not measure them by reference to human characteristics? It is therefore based on a detailed analysis of two dimensions, knowledge and skills.

Knowledge
The axes on the chart for measuring knowledge are education and experience. The education breakdown measures the jobholders' knowledge gained from formal education or training. The experience analysis measures the knowledge and skills that cannot be gained by formal means but which are essential.

Skills
The axes for the chart measuring skills are mental aptitude, human relations and physical skills. The mental aptitude elements define the range of mental skills required, and start from simple observance of limited rules governing basic tasks through various levels of analysis, decision-making and original thought. The human rela-

tions breakdowns define the levels of social skill required for effective job performance. Physical skills are scored against three levels from no special skills to highly developed skills. A section of the skills chart is illustrated below. The full chart contains size degrees for human relations and seven degrees for mental aptitude. The chart is more complex than the knowledge chart because it has to represent three factors rather than just two.

EDUCATION	I. Experience is limited to basic exposure to the routines to life. Little or no previous business or commercial experience required.			II. Jobs requiring work related experience to gain limited but specialised knowledge of machinery, processes, procedures and and work routines.			III. Jobs requiring experience of a range of business procedures, specialised experience of complex industrial machinery or processes, or technical sufficiency in a specialised subject.		
A. Jobs requiring minimum formal education or general work training.	23	27	32	32	38	44	44	52	61
	27	32	38	38	44	52	52	61	72
	32	38	44	44	52	61	61	72	85
B. Jobs requiring either general schooling in a range of subjects, probably to 'O' level GCE standard, or specific training in one specialist subject or skill.	32	38	44	44	52	61	61	72	85
	38	44	52	52	61	72	72	85	100
	44	52	61	61	72	85	85	100	115
C. Jobs requiring a craft apprenticeship, City and Guilds, qualification or ONC	44	52	61	61	72	85	85	100	115
	52	61	72	72	85	100	100	115	132
	61	72	85	85	100	115	115	132	152
D. Jobs which require either: general schooling in a wide range of subjects, probably to 'A' level GCE standard, or specialist training eg City and Guilds technical qualifications or HNC.	61	72	85	85	100	115	115	132	152
	72	85	100	100	115	132	132	152	175
	85	100	115	115	132	152	152	175	201

For the purposes of comparison with the RDS, the scheme divides into levels or grades from 1 (eg cleaner/janitor) to 24 (eg international chief executive). Company structures vary from this pattern but are carefully cross-checked by Watson Wyatt for the purposes of salary comparisons on the databank.

The evaluation process

Watson Wyatt recommends that evaluations are based wherever possible on up-to-date job descriptions, although it is recognised that

MENTAL APTITUDE	PHYSI-CAL SKILLS	I. No more than ordinary courtesy required.			II. Jobs requiring the serving of others, perhaps in answering queries from the public, explaining instructions, supervising a team on routine work or in circumstances requiring tact and diplomacy.			III. Understanding and serving people is important for supervising a small team on technical work or a larger team on routine work, explaining complex technical material or organising others outside the establishment.		
A. Simple repetitive duties requiring no special mental skills. Job limits are defined by regulations and procedures and continuously available direction.	1	61	72	85	85	100	115	115	132	152
	2	85	100	115	115	132	152	152	175	201
	3	115	132	152	152	175	201	201	231	266
B. Routine duties requiring mental or visual concen-tration, attention to detail or simple analysis. Judgements are uninvolved and based upon standard instructions and procedures with readily available direction.	1	85	100	115	115	132	152	152	175	201
	2	115	132	152	152	175	201	291	231	266
	3	152	175	201	201	231	266	266	306	352
C. Jobs requiring mental alertness and concentration for controlling machinery or making judgements within well defined procedures and precedents, and with readily available advice.	1	115	132	152	152	175	201	201	231	266
	2	152	175	201	201	231	266	266	306	352
	3	201	231	266	266	306	352	352	405	465

the design of these has in each case to be consistent with the needs, goals and culture of the organisation. Jobs should be evaluated where practicable by panels of four to six members (although larger groups may be necessary where wider representation is required) including representatives from different areas of the organisation. All evaluation decisions should be recorded formally together with written justification of the score allotted to each job. Within this framework it is understood and accepted that no two organisations will want their job evaluation systems to be implemented in the same way, and Watson Wyatt's approach is appropriately flexible. Watson Wyatt prefer to use the method most suitable to an organisation's culture. They insist, however, that good records are the key to a fully supported job evaluation programme, and full notes of both job details and the evaluations are kept as part of the programme.

Method of application

The EPFC method can be applied in two ways: either through a traditional panel process for benchmark and future evaluations, or by using a computerised system.

To use *the traditional panel process*, Watson Wyatt recommend establishing panels that represent the range of jobs being evaluated. Where appropriate, a mix of staff and management representation is suggested. Watson Wyatt work with organisations to train panel members in the interpretation of the charts and the scoring methodology. The level of consulting support varies, depending on an organisation's requirements, but at a minimum Watson Wyatt will train the panel, and work with the panel at the beginning and at the end ('sore-thumbing') of the process.

In its *computerised approach*, Watson Wyatt offer organisations the option of computerising the scoring method established during the benchmark stage. Using multiple regression techniques, a mathematical relationship is established between the benchmark evaluation and the job information – ie emulating the panel's work.These equations are then coded into a software package such that all non-benchmark evaluations are generated by entering questionnaire data into the system and scoring both the EPFC factors and total points. The advantage of such an approach is that there is no on-going requirement to involve job evaluation panels and the software allows for sophisticated reporting facilities.

The computerised approach requires job information collected via a closed-response questionnaire. Watson Wyatt provides a standard questionnaire designed around the EPFC factors which can be tailored by each organisation. Traditional methods allow for more flexibility in terms of open-ended *v* closed-response questionnaires. Watson Wyatt do recommend the use of more structured questionnaires to improve the quality of information collected and the openness and transparency of the process. They advise that information is collected through discussions with jobholders, managers and trained facilitators.

Grading

Watson Wyatt will work closely with the personnel function to develop an appropriate grading structure. This process includes consideration of

□ natural point breaks
□ clustering of skill types
□ career ladders
□ equal value criteria.

The number of grades established varies between organisations and for companies who are opting for fewer grades. Watson Wyatt will provide guidance on the management within these grades in terms of pay levels and pay progression.

Pay scales

Although the EPFC methodology acts as the historical underpin of the Remuneration Database, Watson Wyatt does not recommend a direct matching between the points score generated through the evaluation process and the market grade, due to potential differences in internal relativities and external market values. A separate matching process is conducted using generic capsule descriptions to match individual jobs to the database.

Watson Wyatt have available a computerised salary management system that provides organisations with a sophisticated tool to design and cost pay structures using combinations of market data, job grade and current pay. The software has the facility to store and analyse multiple sources of market data.

European Factorplan

The European Factorplan is appropriate for all jobs and organisations. Watson Wyatt developed the European Factorplan in 1990 to support the requirement of organisations to be able to size jobs across borders. In particular it was developed to provide a job sizing methodology for Watson Wyatt's European database of market data, operated from Brussels.

Brief description of the scheme

The European Factorplan consists of eight factors:-

□ functional knowledge
□ business expertise

- □ interpersonal skills
- □ complexity
- □ responsibility for resources
- □ nature of impact
- □ area of impact
- □ physical demands (optional).

Each factor has a single scale and has defined level descriptions. Watson Wyatt believe the scheme is particularly suited to measuring jobs with different territorial responsibilities because there is no use of direct financial measures.

Each factor is preweighted. However, organisations are given the opportunity to review these factor weights, should they wish to do so.

Watson Wyatt describe the EFP system as providing more flexibility to an organisation than a proprietary scheme (like EPFC) without having to design a factorplan from scratch. As well as altering the weightings, organisations have the facility to review the factor levels, both in terms of number of levels and the terminology used.

Application of the scheme
The EFP methodology can be applied in two ways: using traditional evaluation panels or a computerised approach.

Watson Wyatt will work with organisations to implement the EFP method using *evaluation panels*. In the same way as using the EPFC approach, Watson Wyatt will train panels in the interpretation of the factors and level descriptions. If appropriate, Watson Wyatt will work closely with the panel(s) throughout the benchmark process or take a more advisory role in the early or later stages.

Alternatively, the EFP can be introduced using a *computerised methodology*. Watson Wyatt provide a standard questionnaire which can be tailored to reflect any changes in the standard factorplan. The questionnaire is pre-weighted either to reflect Watson Wyatt's standard factor weights or the values of the organisation and is built into a software package. Jobs are evaluated by entering questionnaire data into the software system. This generates both a weighted job score and series of checks and balances to test the appropriateness of the information.

Watson Wyatt provide a structured questionnaire to support either the panel or the computerised process. They recommend that any amendments made to the questionnaire should be tested in the organisation before implementation. Consultants will work with organisations to test for ease of use and understanding among the job population. Watson Wyatt suggest that the ideal process for data collection is a tripartite process involving jobholder, manager and trained facilitator. They say they work closely with companies during this stage because consistent interpretation of the questionnaire is critical to accurate results.

Translation of outcomes into job grades/pay scales

Watson Wyatt will work with companies in the same way as with EPFC to translate outcomes into job grades where required. Similarly, in common with EPFC, the EFP system can be set up within a salary management process allowing for the design of pay scales using appropriate market data.

Tailor-made job evaluation – Multicomp™

Watson Wyatt have extensive experience in designing job evaluation schemes for organisations which wish either to reinforce their own value system in the job grading process or to take account of a significant number of special job groups which would not be appropriately assessed using proprietary systems. In this regard they have designed a range of systems since the early 1980s, both in the UK and in North America. Due to their nature, each scheme is different both in terms of the factors used and the factor weighting. In all cases, Watson Wyatt takes a research-based approach, involving senior management and, where appropriate, trade union representatives in the initial design of the factorplan.

Methodology

Implementation of schemes such as these typically involves three stages:

☐ design phase
☐ modelling phase
☐ implementation.

Design phase

Watson Wyatt will work closely with organisations to design an appropriate factorplan and job information questionnaire. As described above, the questionnaire requires testing and refinement before collecting benchmark information. Using trained facilitators, Watson Wyatt will help organisations collect accurate job information. These questionnaires act as the source of information for benchmark evaluations. Evaluation panels are established to build the benchmark rank order, evaluating the job information against the designed factorplan.

Modelling phase

Once the benchmark factor evaluations are agreed, Watson Wyatt construct a mathematical model (similar to that described under EFPC) to replicate the panel's judgements. Using multiple regression routines, a 'predictive model' is built whereby future jobs are evaluated using questionnaire data and *not* evaluation panels. In addition to the scoring mechanism, error and logic checks and Watson Wyatt's 'Electronic Devil's Advocate' are built into the system. These checks provide companies with sophisticated tools to test the reasonableness of the job information as well as tests for factual errors.

Reporting facilities allow for comparisons to be made between jobs and functions, again providing detailed information to the end user.

Implementation phase

Once the modelling phase has been completed, the process for evaluating non-benchmark jobs is focused on collecting quality information using the structured questionnaire. In addition, Watson Wyatt will work with companies to finalise the factor weighting scheme and build this into the final software. The system provides not only predicted factor levels but also weighted point scores. These systems are audited over time and, if necessary, the factor weights can be amended (to reflect any changes in organisation values) without the recalibration of the whole system.

Features of the computerised scheme

In any of the approaches described previously, Watson Wyatt offer a choice in terms of computer operating environments.

Computerised job evaluation can be designed within a DOS-based system or in a Windows environment. Watson Wyatt will tailor the features of the systems – ie reporting requirements, network v standalone set-ups – depending on organisations' requirements. Both systems are designed to allow for easy data transfer between existing Human Resource Information Systems (HRIS), particularly where the salary management module is utilised.

In addition to job evaluation and salary management, these computerised job evaluation systems can form the platform to integrated human resource systems providing the link between job requirements (as described by questionnaires) and employee characteristics (skills profile). Watson Wyatt suggest that organisations can use these tools in a variety of ways:

- ☐ job design
- ☐ organisational structures
- ☐ career planning
- ☐ succession planning
- ☐ training needs analysis.

Once the core design has been completed and implemented, these modules can be designed and built into the system at a later date.

Competence-based job evaluation

Watson Wyatt also offer an alternative approach to job evaluation using a competence-based questionnaire rather than a generic-factor-based process. This approach is suitable either for homogeneous populations or for organisations who are graduating towards a more individually focused approach to managing employees.

The key differences between this approach and those described earlier are:

- ☐ the number of dimensions measured (competencies) is greater
- ☐ the terminology used is more individually (behaviour or skill) driven than organisationally based.

Point scores are generated by weighting both the individual competencies and the level descriptions.

Watson Wyatt say that the difficulty with this approach is the volume of data required to fully assess the role. It is more suitable for organisations that wish to move to flatter structures and broad bands. Watson Wyatt provide a software system, *Competency Manager*, which allows for data storage and reporting in a flexible way.

Jobs are profiled using structured questionnaires and scored by entering the information into the pre-weighted computerised system. In addition to a job grade, the outputs from this approach can be closely mapped onto the competences demonstrated by individual employees, thereby providing organisations with a powerful tool to manage development needs and career opportunities.

The Remuneration Database

The EPFC and the EFP are linked to the Remuneration Database, which holds pay data that has been matched against capsule descriptions. These capsule descriptions are re-evaluated using the EPFC methodology. This ensures that jobs are sized consistently across functions and industry sectors. In addition, the Watson Wyatt

European database is supported by the European Factorplan in much the same way. The intention is to provide an accurate size and match of jobs across different locations and industries.

KPMG EQUATE system

KPMG developed an approach to job evaluation using an expert shell system called EQUATE. This system is being used in both the private and public sectors and MEDEQUATE – a version designed specifically for the health sector – is used in a number of NHS Trusts. KPMG claim EQUATE is one of the most advanced and user-friendly systems on the market. Their methodology was designed with the requirements of equal-value legislation in mind, and in particular to reflect the diverse needs of organisations with a number of different job families. It has been used to provide a single integrated scheme covering all jobs up to the level of chief executive in many different sizes of organisation both in the UK and internationally.

Each EQUATE system is developed specifically for the individual organisation and is therefore able to reflect its unique culture and values. KPMG say that those organisations which choose to develop an EQUATE system do so because they require a job evaluation system which is

- designed to meet the needs of the organisation and is capable of reflecting organisational values
- able to provide a credible, effective, and accepted means of measuring job weight
- able to accommodate the range of jobs within the organisation
- flexible in the job factors used
- able to use job weights that reflect the organisational values and therefore does not impose an external set of values
- developed through consultation with staff and is thus understood and accepted
- is transparent and therefore felt to be fair.

Description of the system

Each scheme uses factors that describe the characteristics of the full range of jobs within an organisation. As such the titles of factors used and the type of information collected to determine these factors varies from scheme to scheme. KPMG's approach to selecting and developing factors is to start with a basic framework of main factor headings which are discrete but also accurately represent the sum total of demands that work places on jobholders. They do how-ever advise that the following job demands are captured by the fac-tors used:

- accountability
- job impact
- thinking demands
- communication demands
- knowledge skills and experience.

In addition, KPMG also recommend that organisations reflect some-thing of the environmental demands of jobs.

Data is collected by trained job analysts through a structured interview and summarised on a job analysis questionnaire. Each questionnaire varies according to the factor definitions used by the organisation, but KPMG's approach to its development aims to ensure that all relevant data is captured.

Application of the system

The scheme is developed through the following procedure:

- A factor workshop is set up with panel members and analysts to determine the factors to be used and the factor definitions.
- A number of benchmark jobs are selected for analysis. The benchmark jobs should reflect the range of job demands within the organisation.
- A questionnaire is developed to collect job data based on the fac-tors determined jointly with the client organisation.
- Analysts are then trained in interview techniques and the use of the questionnaire.
- Job information on the benchmark jobs is collected through structured interviews and summarised in the job analysis ques-tionnaire.
- The benchmark jobs are then evaluated by the panel. The panel comprises senior managers representing all functions within the organisation. The number and definition of job factors are not predetermined. The panel is asked to examine each job factor by factor and to develop a number of levels that reflect the differ-ences in job demand for each factor.
- The panel also undertakes an exercise to develop the appropriate job weights.
- The expert system is then configured. An input screen replicates

the job analysis questionnaire facilitating each input of job data. The expert system is then programmed with the scheme rules to replicate the decisions of the panel. New jobs can be evaluated because the rules are based on job demands rather than broad factor levels. They therefore focus on job characteristics rather than the whole job.

☐ Any subsequent jobs are evaluated by the computer system and, if necessary, ratified by the panel members.

Translating outcomes into job grades/pay scales

KPMG recommend that a pay and grading structure is developed as a result of the job evaluation exercise, taking into account the following factors:

☐ the organisation's objectives and reward management policies
☐ the relative size of jobs as determined by the job evaluation exercise
☐ the natural grade boundaries evident from the rank order
☐ the promotion breaks required
☐ career progression systems and structures
☐ existing pay expectations and ranges
☐ external pay market comparisons
☐ cost control requirements.

Link to pay database

KPMG can link the job evaluation results to a salary modelling facility to model the results of any pay or grading changes. There is a facility within this model to hold market data for benchmark positions. KPMG say this has been used by many of their clients to design revised pay ranges and to monitor their organisation's position against their relevant markets. KMPG also stress that an additional benefit of the software is that it gives an organisation the ability to model the impact of changes in basic salary, allowances, flexible pay elements, bonuses, etc.

Towers Perrin

Towers Perrin have recently developed a computer-aided scheme to enable clients to analyse job evaluation data, calculate a points score for jobs, manage certain job evaluation/employee data, and slot jobs into grades. It is aimed at all sectors and types of jobs.

In developing their software Towers Perrin have used an approach that has evolved from the structured 'Weighted Job Questionnaire' (WJQ) developed in the mid-1980s. This structured questionnaire had five predetermined factors:

☐ skills and knowledge
☐ problem-solving
☐ contacts
☐ scope of responsibility
☐ working conditions.

Towers Perrin say it became evident that more organisations were looking for a customised approach that enabled them to reflect their values (for example, those developed through a competence programme). Since the late 1980s Towers Perrin have found that most of their clients' plans have been customised. Towers Perrin describe their system as the latest generation of Windows-based software which will continue to offer a very high degree of flexibility in questionnaire design, factors, weights, and reporting capabilities.

Description of the scheme

Towers Perrin describe the scheme as a computer-aided job evaluation approach to points factor job evaluation. Towers Perrin guides the client through the process of selecting factors and weightings and designing the questionnaire. These processes vary, depending on individual clients' requirements and preferences. However, job and role data is generally collected via the questionnaire.

Each factor chosen is broken down into components or subfactors, and each of these subfactors is broken down into questions for the questionnaire. For each job being evaluated, the system uses the responses to each of these specific questions and determines the factor level required. The data is challenged by the system for accuracy of completion and internal consistency. For example, the system asks if the responses within a single question make sense both individually and in relation to each other. Once the internal consistency has been confirmed, the responses from several questionnaires for a single job can be compared with each other in an interrater comparator. Another check is made on how the responses for one job relate to that for others in the same job family. A profile comparison allows the responses for any two or more jobs to be compared.

Application of the scheme

Towers Perrin say that a typical approach to application has three phases:

1   Diagnosis: with a working group they define the factors to be used, develop the questionnaire, and put together all the processes for the testing of the questionnaire using benchmark jobs.

2   Scheme development: benchmark jobs are evaluated and reviewed for consistency of response and interpretation of the questionnaire. A series of standard tests and reports are run to review relativities between jobs. Factor weights are developed using a combination of statistical analysis and judgement of the working group.

3   The questionnaire is amended as necessary; a further pilot may then be conducted to test the final questionnaire and operating processes. These processes are client-specific but usually involve setting up a review body/panel to ensure consistent interpretation of evaluation.

Translating outcomes into pay

When job evaluation results are available Towers Perrin will help a client to develop a pay structure. Some initial modelling can be done using a PC, but this will be based on discussion with the client about the type of pay structure required and what is appropriate for the organisation (for example, narrow grades versus broad bands). The software allows an assessment of cost implications on different options.

As well as looking at the evaluation results, Towers Perrin will refer to their compensation database to assist with the design of pay structures.

PA basic job evaluation scheme

The factor based approach to job evaluation developed by PA Consulting Group gives, they argue, greater prominence to internal relativities than external comparisons. PA say their experiences have shown people at work place a relatively higher importance on pay comparisons with colleagues than with those doing similar work in other organisations. The PA basic scheme was developed for clients requiring a non-tailored system that can be implemented quickly and cost-effectively. It involves the use of fixed factor definitions, factor levels and factor weights. It has been developed from PA's experience of conducting job evaluation assignments for more than 30 years.

Alternatively, PA are able to provide a fully bespoke product that can be developed to meet the needs of clients who want systems fully tailored to their specific requirements. It involves customising factor definitions and factor levels, and includes the development of a set of factor weights that are unique to the organisation concerned.

Description of the scheme

The basic PA scheme consists of a maximum of eight factors:

- □ judgement
- □ planning and management
- □ communication
- □ job impact
- □ theoretical knowledge and application
- □ skills acquisition and practice
- □ effect of errors
- □ manual dexterity and effort.

Each factor consists of two interrelated dimensions, which enables the factors to be evaluated in depth. Each of the resultant 16 dimensions has its own comprehensive set of seven factor-level definitions. Clients can choose to use the standard factor definitions or to have the definitions tailored to their own unique requirements. Clients can use PA's standard factor weights or choose to have a special set developed specifically to reflect their own particular situation.

PA has also developed an advanced computerised system to simplify and improve the job evaluation process. Their *JE Manager* expert system, they claim, enables consistency and reliable evaluation of jobs through direct entry by jobholder and manager to a PC-based questionnaire eliminating all paperwork and panel meetings. Technical support for this system is provided by Pilat.

Application of the scheme

PA encourage their clients to set up a steering group to oversee the process. That group will select between 10 per cent and 20 per cent of the total number of jobs as benchmark jobs to be representative of both senior and junior levels in the organisation and of all functions. The steering group will appoint a panel that includes a wide cross-section of people in the company to evaluate the jobs.

Company job descriptions for benchmark roles are completed, either by the jobholder or by an analyst, depending on time and cost constraints. In addition to a traditional job description, a factor-based questionnaire is also completed. These are reviewed for consistency prior to the panel's meeting.

Jobs are evaluated by the panel, and weightings developed. The results are then carefully reviewed with the client to ensure that the scheme that has been produced is the optimum scheme for that client. The parameters of the system are tested and refined before proceeding to the application stage.

Following the validation of the tailored system by the evaluation panel, the computerised system will itself be tailored to reflect the clients' new system. This involves modifying and adding to the question library (the standard system has over 200 questions) the answer options and the 'evaluation rules' which the system will use to replicate the decision processes of the benchmark panel re-evaluating the jobs on the system.

Remaining jobs are then evaluated by the jobholder and manager following the questioning sequence presented to them on the PC without the need for job descriptions.

Translating outcomes into job grades/pay scales

PA stress that considerable care is taken to ensure that the grading structure designed meets the specific requirements of the organisation. For example, consideration is given to the need for flexibility, multiskilling, career paths and cost constraints.

A graph is plotted of job scores against current salaries to establish

☐ likely positions for grade barriers
☐ the salary line of best fit.

Detailed design considerations include any or all of the following:

☐ number of grades/ranges/paybands
☐ grade differentials
☐ size of ranges
☐ degree of overlap between ranges
☐ relationship to other elements of the pay package (bonuses, benefits, etc.)
☐ mechanisms for pay determination:
    general (market, pay-bargaining, cost-of-living)
    individual (merit)
☐ management control
☐ openness or secrecy
☐ dealing with changes:
    promotions
    new hires.

When the results are announced, employees are normally allowed to appeal against this grading, following a procedure recommended by the consultant. Once these appeals have been considered and settled, the scheme is in full operation. New and changed jobs are evaluated as necessary.

Computerisation of the scheme
PA say their computerised version of the scheme has been developed in response to the clearly articulated needs of their clients. The system offers the following options:

1   no preliminary job descriptions or questionnaires
2   no job evaluation specialists or panels
3   direct involvement of staff and line management
4   consistent and validated scoring for each job
5   a record of job content provided in a 'job overview'
6   restricted access to data to ensure security
7   overall audit control to remain with the human resources department.

The evaluation process leads the jobholder through a series of logically chosen and ordered questions, generating appropriate scores, weighted points, job grade, and a 'job overview' from the responses given. It produces a full rationale and audit trail for each score, cross-validating against previously evaluated jobs.

The system runs in Windows, and help screens are available throughout so that the ability to operate a mouse is all that is required from the operator. The evaluation of any one job typically triggers a route through about 50 relevant questions (selected by the system on the basis of a library of over 200 questions).

The system is paperless and user-friendly, being open to appeal by jobholders simply by re-evaluating their own job. The evaluation process is devolved to line management, the HR department retaining only the overall audit validation and control functions.

P-E Consulting, human resource practice: the Pay Points System
The Pay Points System was developed in the late 1970s using the then 20-year-old database provided by the P-E survey of executive salaries. The objective of the system was to provide a greater degree of precision in the pricing of executive jobs. The system was subsequently extended to cover all white-collar jobs, enabling a common

system to be applied to all such jobs in an organisation. A later adjustment increased the original five factors to six to allow for posts which include physical demands.

P-E claim that the system is currently aimed at all industries and any job defined as white-collar. They say that the Pay Points System is appropriate thus for jobs ranging from senior executive to junior clerical positions. The system is computerised and directly linked to the P-E Annual Survey of Executive Salaries and Benefits in the United Kingdom. P-E also have the facility to offer further pay database links on a bespoke basis for international companies through the P-E European and International databases.

Description of the scheme

Every job is evaluated according to the five factors: knowledge and experience; complexity and creativity (of problem-solving); judgement and decisions; operational responsibility; and contacts and communications. In addition there is a sixth factor – working conditions – which may be applied to some jobs.

This evaluation yields a basic score that is a measure of job size. The basic scores for management jobs can be related to assessed salaries by applying a series of multipliers which take account of organisational size, job premiums, industry, region, company policy, and salary implementation date.

Methodology

P-E claim that the system is highly flexible. For example, at one extreme it can be used by a consultant working directly with, say, a chief executive to assess the salaries of members of the board. In this kind of example job profiles would not be an essential requirement. At the other end of the spectrum, the scheme can be used by evaluation panels, initially working under the direction of a consultant, to assess a wide range of jobs. In this type of case it would be essential to use agreed job profiles prepared in a simple two-page format. This latter type of project would be suggested by P-E for an organisation that requires the development of staff grade structures.

Whatever type of project is undertaken, clients are free to use the system after the project provided that they have reached proficiency in its application.

Translating outcomes into job grades/pay scales

P-E stress that every project needs to be considered on its own merits. Their philosophy emphasises that there is no one right way to create a pay structure, and that the process is more art than science. However as a general rule they recommend the following:

1   Basic pay point scores are used to give a rank order.
2   The rank order is divided into an appropriate number of grades which seek to
    □   provide a logical progression of salaries such that good salary administration practice is established
    □   have break points which accommodate 'natural' groups of similarly evaluated scores
    □   have break points which do not cut across historical groupings of jobs
    (In practice these three criteria are usually never met and the result is a compromise of the ideal.)
3   Midpoint salaries are determined by the paypoint link.
4   Salary structure criteria (increments, band widths and band overlaps) are designed according to best practice.

Key features

P-E describe the key features of the Pay Points Scheme as:

□   It covers a full range of white-collar jobs.
□   It has a salary link to the largest survey of its type in the UK which is not a 'club' survey but has an annual turnover of approximately 35 per cent of its contributors.
□   It uses straightforward language that can be easily understood by non-personnel professionals.
□   It has a short learning period and can be used without consultant supervision when proficiency is reached.
□   It is particularly well suited to executive salary determination in group situations where there are a large number of different-sized companies.
□   It has a 15-year track record of use at all levels in a wide range of industries.

The Factor Plan Approach

P-E developed this approach in the early 1960s as a means of getting a greater degree of participation in the evaluation process. P-E claim that by simplifying the decision process and computerising the analysis work, employees were able to join evaluation panels without a crippling administrative burden. The 'paired-comparison' approach to decision-making was originally applied by INBUCON consultants to job evaluation but is now a method in the public domain.

To meet the demands of employment legislation in the late 1970s and early 1980s, this approach has been extended by P-E to accommodate evaluation factors that can be closely tailored to an organisation's needs.

Description of the scheme
The Factor Plan Approach starts by deriving a set of factors which are the most appropriate for the job population to be evaluated. Having defined the factors, an evaluation panel uses the paired-comparison ranking system on each of a set of benchmark jobs to determine rank lists under each factor, and finally for overall job demand. Using multiple regression analysis, a computer program calculates the relative weights of each factor. From these weights and the factor scores a final rank order is determined. To develop the Factor Plan, sets of factor guidelines are tested against the panel's decisions so that each level within a factor can be assigned a points value. All jobs are then evaluated using the Factor Plan.

Methodology
The following methodology is suggested by P-E:

1 Establish a steering group to oversee the project.
2 Working with the steering group, set up a benchmark sample of jobs in populations.
3 Working with the steering group, select and test a set of factors that are appropriate.
4 Draw up a factor definition for each factor.
5 Draw up job profiles for every job, taking the benchmark sample first.
6 Establish an evaluation panel representative of the employee population of the organisation.
7 Train the panel and carry out initial paired-comparison decisions.
8 Review inconsistent decisions with the panel and test out draft factor guidelines.
9 Calculate (by computer) factor weights and issue factored rank list.
10 Using the above results produce score charts which relate to the finally agreed factor guidelines.
11 Issue the factor guidelines and score charts to the original evaluation panel (and additional panels if they are deemed necessary) to enable the total job population to be evaluated using the factor plan.

Translating outcomes into job grades/pay scales

P-E stress there is no direct link between the Factor Plan Approach and market salaries. In most cases, they say, they would probably suggest the use of the Pay Points System to price some of the benchmark jobs in order to get the likely span of salaries. They also suggest that a pay or grade structure is designed in accordance with the steps described above under the description of the Pay Points System.

Key Features

The key features of the plan, as described by P-E, are that it is:

- [ ] ideal for organisations that specifically do not want to use proprietary brand (pre-scored) evaluation systems
- [ ] specifically tailored to the norms of an organisation: in view of the necessary involvement of staff in the process there should be a high degree of commitment to the results.

The Direct Consensus Method

The Direct Consensus Method is a shorter version of the Factor Plan Approach. It is recommended by P-E when there is no need for a benchmark sample and all the jobs can be evaluated by the panel in the first instance.

P-E stress that this approach is ideal when rapid analytical job evaluation is required, and particularly where the involvement of non-personnel professionals is considered important.

The Price Waterhouse Profile Method

Price Waterhouse describe their scheme as a framework for developing bespoke schemes rather than a single off-the-shelf product. They claim that the Profile Method has been applied successfully to both blue- and white-collar jobs, and all levels of management. The 350-plus applications currently in use span a wide range of private and public sector organisations.

The Profile Method is based on a system developed by the Urwick Orr consultancy, which merged with Price Waterhouse in 1985. It was originally devised in the 1960s with emphasis on employee participation. This proved particularly effective in helping implement schemes in highly unionised environments. Participation remains a strong feature of the method, although many applications have been developed by working with small groups of managers and, occasionally, in collaboration with the human resources function alone.

Description of the scheme

Price Waterhouse stress that the Profile Method results in a bespoke scheme. However, typical applications are based on an analysis of jobs in terms of the following six general job demands:

- responsibility
- knowledge
- mental skills
- physical skills
- environmental conditions.

These general job demands are developed into a series of characteristics – usually no fewer than 8 and rarely more than 12 – which provide the basic measurement tool. The nature of the client organisation strongly influences the extent to which each of the six general job demands is subdivided into specific job evaluation characteristics. This is in turn often strongly influenced by the technology of the organisation and the range and level of jobs to be covered by the scheme.

Relevant levels of demand are identified within each characteristic around which the scoring system is developed. Typically, between four and seven levels are identified within each characteristic.

Methodology

A Profile project typically involves working with two groups within the client organisation:

- a steering group to oversee the project, agree the benchmark sample, approve the factors and level definitions and, if applicable, the grading structure developed
- the assessment team, usually selected to represent key interest groups within the organisation; the members of the team are involved in developing the detailed design of the job evaluation scheme and applying it to the benchmark sample.

Membership of the steering group varies from organisation to organisation. A typical membership includes senior members of management and, where appropriate, trade union or other employee representatives. The group needs sufficient authority and experience within the organisation to act and take decisions on behalf of the management and employee groups.

The bulk of the work of designing and implementing the scheme is carried out jointly by PW consultants and the assessment team. The team's main tasks:

□ to gather job facts for the agreed benchmark sample of jobs

□ to define the range of characteristics required to reflect the demands of jobs in the target population

□ to identify and define the relevant levels that can be discerned within each characteristic

□ to establish a felt-fair rank order for the benchmark jobs

□ to produce profile scores for the benchmark jobs

□ to apply the scheme to the balance of jobs within the population covered.

Although the main work of the assessment team lies in developing and designing the scheme, the team members represent a trained, knowledgeable resource for the future operation and maintenance of the scheme.

Particular care is taken over the development of the felt-fair rank order. Tried and tested methods are used to ensure that this is an objective view of the benchmark jobs. Other aspects of the method enable the assessment team both to design the detail of the scheme and, at the same time, produce raw profile scores for each of the benchmark jobs.

The felt-fair rank order and raw profile scores are compared statistically, using specially designed software. The output of this analysis is used to calculate the weighting to be applied to each characteristic in the scheme.

Implementation of the scheme

Once the benchmark phase is complete, the scheme can be applied across the balance of the job population, usually by panels drawn from members of the assessment team who designed the scheme. Where appropriate, agreed forms for job descriptions and job analyses are developed for the client. Alternatively, tailored questionnaires may be used to gather job facts about the balance of the population.

Translating outcomes into job grades/pay scales

When translating job evaluation points into their pay and grading implications, either one of two situations is typical:

□ Where little formal structure exists, or the existing arrangements are discredited or out-of-date, the results from applying the scheme may be used to develop a fresh grading structure.

☐ Where an existing grading structure is formally established (sometimes, as in the public sector, through national bargaining) the results of applying the job evaluation scheme are 'mapped back' to the existing grading structure.

In the first case, natural clusters of jobs and obvious break points in the continuum of evaluation point scores are used to identify potential grades and grade breaks. Where necessary, statistical techniques are used to ensure that the progression of grade widths is sensible and appropriate. In the second case, statistical techniques are used to determine evaluation point boundaries for the existing grade structure.

Computerisation

A small number of applications of the Profile Method have been developed into computerised 'expert systems'. Given the bespoke nature of the schemes developed, this required specialised programming for each application. Typically, this has been appropriate in particularly large applications and/or where decentralisation or networked operation has been required. The functionality of these applications is also bespoke to each scheme.

Special features

Price Waterhouse claim that the particular strengths of the Profile Method include:

☐ The schemes are tailor-made and derive from the facts concerning the jobs in the client organisation. As such, Profile applications achieve a high level of fit with the client organisation, and a high level of acceptance.

☐ The design process can be highly participative, involving employees and managers. Typically the wider the range of people involved the higher is the quality of debate, the less likely that important facts are missed, and the better the scheme functions.

☐ The schemes are analytical, analysing jobs by virtue of the different factors/demands; the design methodology avoids the dangers of stereotyping and overlooking important features. Profile schemes are therefore robust in terms of equal-value legislation.

The Saville and Holdsworth Job Evaluation Method

This scheme is aimed at any job in any industry, and dates from 1986 when SHL took the decision to develop a new integrated job

analysis system in the UK. This was to become known as the Work
Profiling System (WPS). The development of the WPS was sponsored
by 21 major UK organisations. The key aim was to produce an integrated job analysis system that would profile a job both in terms of
the tasks and context concerned, and the relevant human attributes
necessary for effective performance. An approach focusing on job
content was necessary to meet the specified job description and job
evaluation applications.

The exploratory research took place between January and June
1987, mainly within sponsoring organisations. Overall the research
covered approximately 1,000 job positions including manual, technical, managerial and professional positions.

Trialing of the initial questionnaires took place between October
1987 and January 1988. More than 200 questionnaires were completed for analysis, mainly from the sponsoring organisations.

Description of the scheme

The SHL Job Evaluation method is described by SHL as a state-of-
the-art computerised system for producing standardised job descriptions and automatic points-rated job ranking that

☐ is set up and applied in a way that is fair and acceptable to the
people it affects

☐ is easy to operate and simple to understand

☐ is a rigorous, analytical and standardised method independent of
bias on the part of employees and employers alike

☐ provides consistent evaluation and comparison of jobs at all
levels within the organisation

☐ establishes a comprehensive database of job information for an
integrated employment strategy

☐ is tailored to the specific needs of user organisations

☐ uses SHL's sophisticated computer technology to collect and
process data quickly and accurately

☐ supports the recommendations of the Equal Opportunities
Commission on avoiding bias

☐ can deliver job-based and/or skill-based pay schemes.

SHL claim that the system is a practical, cost-effective and flexible
method that provides a fair basis for determining relative job values,
that meets organisation requirements and that satisfies employee
expectations.

Application of the system

There are two distinct steps: first a pilot study to set up and tailor the method; second the application of the method to all relevant jobs in the organisation.

Stage 1: pilot study

The organisation establishes a small panel/committee representative of the range of job roles and levels in the company.

A representative sample of jobs – benchmark jobs – is selected from the various levels by the committee.

The committee selects and weights 10–15 factors – dimensions of job worth – that are most relevant for determining relative job values within the organisation.

Job information is collected on the jobs using the SHL *Work Profiling System* Questionnaires which are usually completed by the benchmark jobholder and/or managers.

From the information obtained, two complementary reports are prepared:
- a full job description with job evaluation points scores on each benchmark job
- a comparative report on the points scores for all the benchmark jobs

A review and validation of the comparative results is carried out, including a comparison of the proposed points-based ranking of relative job values against an independent 'felt-fair' whole job ranking.

Stage 2: application

On successful completion of the review and validation, the SHL Job Evaluation Method can be applied to all other jobs in the organisation using the questionnaires and factor weights established in the pilot study.

Translating outcomes into job grades/pay scales

SHL has a multistage approach to pay and grades as follows:

1 policy – the organisation establishes its pay strategy/policy including
   - relevant external market(s) for pay comparison
   - target position in that market
   - number of grades required
   - extent of overlap in pay bands
2 job values
   - job evaluation scores on benchmark jobs are used to establish appropriate bands of job scores for each grade

- □ all jobs are positioned in one of the grade bands according to their overall job scores
- □ jobs of which the scores fall within a 'grey area' close to the dividing values between grades are reviewed for accuracy.
3   pay scales
- □ a survey of pay scales with appropriate competitive employers is carried out
- □ pay ranges for each grade are established in line with the policy agreed for the organisation
- □ individual pay rates are determined by means of these pay scales.

Special features

The following are special features for the system as claimed and described by SHL:

- □ The scheme gathers job data using the WPS questionnaire. This procedure does not require jobholders to write narrative job descriptions, thus saving the time of jobholders, managers and HR staff.
- □ The questionnaire gathers detailed data first on the tasks performed by the post-holder, and second on the job context that provides the data for evaluation of the post's relative weight.
- □ The WPS computer system analyses the data collected by the questionnaire and produces two complementary reports on each job:
    a job description setting out the main tasks carried out by the post, with an importance rating for each group of tasks
    a job evaluation report setting out the scores on each factor and total score for the job.
- □ The objective analysis of each job and scoring on the computer system provides a consistent approach. It does not require the individual assessment of jobs by a special committee or analysts.
- □ The questionnaire may be completed within an hour and a half using either a paper answer sheet or directly onto a PC screen with easy windows-style prompts.
- □ The structure of the SHL Job Evaluation method meets the EOC recommendations for avoiding bias.
- □ The SHL Job Evaluation method is extremely cost-effective in:
    collecting data swiftly and accurately using a questionnaire
    analysing the data by computer to produce job descriptions and job evaluation reports
    providing a valuable HR database for other applications.

□ The questionnaire approach enables a quick and cost-effective review of jobs which change rapidly in a changing environment.

□ The SHL Job Evaluation Method can be applied either to job tasks or to competences. It can be applied to a predefined job or to the contribution of an individual post to team objectives.

□ The data gathered in the WPS questionnaire provides a database which may be used to produce other reports on the jobs. These reports include:

> person specification to meet the job requirement
> job/person matching for selection and placement
> assessment methods report
> individual development planner
> performance review form.

The IAM computerised Job Evaluation Scheme

This scheme is aimed at all levels of job within any organisation. IAM say that its most effective use is probably in organisations that have between 100 and 5,000 employees. No job or industry is excluded.

The IAM scheme was originally introduced in 1942, since when IAM claim it has served many blue chip companies to great effect. The scheme was said to be the first off-the-shelf job evaluation scheme that evaluated jobs rather than people. The current scheme was totally revised and computerised in 1992 by HR Computing LogoSoft™. It now offers gradings for over 2,000 office and non-office elements that are added to daily by an active User Group using in-built algorithms that incorporate the original IAM job grading criteria. It also provides the facility to add and grade new posts on the same basis.

Other developments introduced during the review and computerisation were: the automatic generation of job evaluation questionnaires; procedural/scheme monitoring; the automatic generation of three types of job description; salary modelling; structure charting; and the direct import or export of data from other compatible computer systems.

It has now incorporated and superseded the IAM's original but very highly thought of Office Job Evaluation System, in the process becoming far wider in its application. IAM claim it also cuts down the costs of implementation and maintenance in terms of real time.

Description of the scheme

The new IAM Job Evaluation Scheme has been designed for both simplicity and ease of use. When installed, the scheme contains 2,000-plus graded job elements either created by the Institute or developed by users of the scheme. (These can be added to or deleted as required.) Further job elements are either downloaded from other users' disks or developed in-house using the algorithm and factor chart provided. In this way, say IAM, the system grows to exactly meet the user's purpose.

IAM also say the system is very user-friendly, incorporating switchable on/off help available at every stage. It is fully menu-driven, using drop-down menus with push-button controls, and integrates a full word-processing function as well as one of the best quick-reporting functions available.

The system is PC-based and can be networked across all platforms. It can be tailored to meet the user's needs, and although training is provided it can usually be learned in one day. There are seven different levels of read/write security for each field and screen, and an in-built audit trail operates from day one to show who has used the system when, what they have accessed, and what, if anything, has been changed. It has a very fast report generator that stores regular reports or produces custom reports which can be designed and run within minutes.

Jobs are selected for evaluation, and questionnaires are generated containing appropriate job elements (or they can be added should all elements not be covered). These are distributed for jobholders to mark on them which are applicable and to add the time spent on each (as a percentage of total time spent on the job). Managers/supervisors then agree this input with the employee, referring any disputes to the scheme administrator or other person acting as referee. The data is entered onto the computer and the appropriate grades for each job element appear. An inbuilt algorithm then compiles these grades on a basis of time spent, and an overall grade is produced for the job. This can then be accepted or rejected by the scheme supervisor or administrator. If it is rejected, the grade can be changed, but it needs an explanatory comment and the original grade remains permanently available through the audit trail.

Once all jobs have been evaluated, existing salaries/pay rates are put against each job so that current pay ranges can be established for each grade This data is then transferred automatically to the salary modelling tool so that it can be used to develop new grading structures using external as well as internal indicators. Finally, new wage/salary structures are generated and printed, as are letters to the employees concerned.

IAM stress that job evaluation panels are not usually needed.

They recommend that the whole exercise be carried out by two to three staff, and that data input is used for data entry, but without allowing access to any of the salaries or grades.

IAM's experience has shown that for an organisation of approximately 500 employees the complete exercise can be carried out in two to three months from installation of the system to sending details of new/revised salaries.

Translating outcomes into job grades/pay scales

Once all jobs have been graded within the system and any manual adjustments made, actual wages or salaries are downloaded from payroll to give ranges for each grade. These appear on the screen as Max/Min; Upper Quartile/Lower Quartile; Median, and so forth, for each grade. This obviously shows up anomalies in the existing structure and the extent of wages or salary drift that exists. The range is then compared with external salary data, interactively on the screen or from hard copy, and broad bandings established. From this, maxima, mid-points and minima for each band or grade are established and employees are slotted in, dependent upon the budget available. Once this has been done 'what-if' exercises and costings can be carried out until a new/revised structure has been established, savings made and employees informed.

Appendix B:

EXAMPLE OF A POINTS-FACTOR

JOB EVALUATION SCHEME

FACTOR LEVEL SCORES						
Factor Levels						
	1	2	3	4	5	6
1 Knowledge and skills	50	100	150	200	250	300
2 Responsibility	50	100	150	200	250	300
3 Decision-making	40	80	120	140	180	220
4 Complexity	25	50	75	100	125	150
5 Contacts	25	50	75	100	125	150

Factor 1: Knowledge and skills

Factor definition
The knowledge and skills gained through education, training and experience required to achieve the overall purpose of the job by attaining the outputs and standards relating to each key result area or main task.

Level definitions
1 Ability to carry out standardised work routines and/or use simple equipment. A satisfactory standard can be achieved after a few weeks' practical experience.

2   Straightforward administrative procedures are carried out such as maintaining records, dealing with routine queries, and correspondence and/or operating specialised but not necessarily complex machines – eg word processors. Up to six months' practical experience is required possibly coupled with concentrated training for a few weeks.

3   Advanced administrative work is carried out which may involve the use of complex equipment – eg desk-top computers. The work may involve maintaining complex records, dealing with non-routine queries, analysing data, or preparing standard reports. Up to two years' practical experience may be required probably backed up by intensive training for a few months.

4   Proficiency is required in a professional, administrative or specialist field involving the understanding and application of fairly advanced practices, procedures, concepts or principles. Five years' experience may be required, plus graduate level education or ability and professional/technical training of at least a year (additional years of high-level experience may, however, be substituted for this training).

5   Considerable competence in a managerial or professional field is required in order to understand and apply advanced policies, practices, procedures, concepts or principles. Broad experience over a number of years (five plus) is required, together with – usually – appropriate academic qualifications or professional training.

6   A very high level of competence is required in directing and controlling high-level activities; such competence can be acquired only by means of deep and comprehensive experience over many years (ten plus).

Factor 2: Responsibility

Factor definition
The particular obligations assumed by jobholders in terms of their accountability for results in each of the main areas of the job. The level of responsibility is related to the impact of the job on end results, the consequence of errors, and the size of the resources controlled (people, money and equipment, etc.).

Level definitions
1   The impact of the job and the effect of errors are limited to less important aspects of the work group, and errors can be detected

almost immediately. No resources of any significance are controlled.

2 The job impacts on the performance of the work group and errors can have a short-term detrimental effect although it is quite easy to detect them. The resources controlled are limited to those personally required by the jobholder to do the job.

3 The work can make a significant impact on the work of the section and although errors can be detected without too much difficulty, they can have considerable short-term detrimental effects on the department. Quite valuable equipment may be controlled and the jobholder may be responsible for the routine work of up to three staff.

4 A significant impact is made on the work of the department and this extends to other parts of the organisation. Errors are not always easy to detect and can do considerable damage to departmental results. A section of four to six or so people may be controlled, together with the section's budget.

5 The jobholder is expected to make a significant contribution to achieving objectives in an important aspect or area of the organisation's work. Errors may be very difficult to detect before they have a severe detrimental effect on the department's and, often, the organisation's performance. Control may be exercised over a medium-sized department and budget.

6 The jobholder is responsible for the formulation and implementation of major functional policies and plans that can have a considerable impact on the longer-term performance of the organisation. Errors of judgement may not be detected for some time and can be very costly. Control may be exercised over a major department or division and a considerable budget.

Factor 3: Decisions

Factor definition
The degree to which the job involves choice of action, covering the extent to which the work is routine or prescribed, the amount of supervision and guidance provided, and the degree to which judgement has to be exercised.

Level definitions
1 The work is entirely routine, tasks are clearly defined, choice of

action is within very narrow limits, and close and continuous supervision is exercised.

2   The work is fairly routine and repetitive. Choice of action is fairly limited but there is some scope for making day-to-day decisions within well-defined limits. Other matters are referred to higher authority. Supervision is fairly close, but not continuous.

3   A fair proportion of the work is standardised although there are a number of non-routine elements. Freedom of action exists to make independent decisions, but within well-established and clearly defined policy and procedural guidelines. Regular reference to higher authority is required. General supervision is exercised.

4   The work includes a large proportion of non-routine elements. To a degree it is self-directed and carried out under general guidance only, although work plans and objectives are spelled out in some detail. Judgement is fairly frequently exercised in deciding how to select the most appropriate course of action within explicit policy guidelines. Reference to higher authority on matters of other than short-term significance is required.

5   The work is largely non-routine. It is mainly self-directed within the framework of agreed work plans and objectives and policy guidelines. Judgement has frequently to be exercised without the benefit of clear policy rulings or precedents. Creative thinking is often required to reach decisions. Only occasional reference to higher authority is required.

6   The work is almost entirely non-routine. It continually requires the exercise of considerable judgement with relatively little guidance from defined policy guidelines. Creative thinking is a regular feature of the work. Only general policy direction is given.

Factor 4: Complexity

Factor definition
The variety and diversity of tasks carried out by the jobholder and the range of skills used.

Level definitions
1   Highly repetitive work in which the same task or group of tasks is carried out without any significant variation.

2   A fairly narrow range of tasks is carried out that tend to be closely related to one another and involve the use of a limited range of skills.

3   There is some diversity in the activities carried out although they are broadly related to one another. A fairly wide variety of skills have to be used.

4   A diverse range of broadly related tasks are carried out. A wide variety of administrative, technical or supervisory skills are used.

5   A highly diverse range of tasks are carried out, many of which are unrelated to one another. A wide variety of professional and/or managerial skills are used.

6   The work is multi-disciplinary and involves fulfilling a broad range of highly diverse responsibilities.

Factor 5: Contacts

Factor definition
The extent to which the work involves making contacts with people inside and outside the organisation. In evaluating this factor, consideration should be given to the extent to which the contact is concerned with routine or non-routine matters, the level and importance of the contact, and the impact of the results of the contact on the reputation and performance of the organisation.

Level definitions
1   Contacts are limited to routine matters of exchanging information, principally within the jobholder's own department.

2   Contacts of a mainly routine nature involve the exchange of information with people inside and outside the organisation, but not at a senior level.

3   Contacts, sometimes on non-routine matters, involve both the exchange and interpretation of information with people at a number of levels inside and outside the organisation. Failure to relate well to the contacts may have some detrimental affects on the jobholder's department, but not significant ones on the organisation.

4   Contacts are maintained with a wide range of people within and outside the organisation, but infrequently, if at all, at the highest level. Contacts involve making a favourable impression

and the exercise of a fairly high degree of negotiating or persuasive skills or joint problem solving (although the problems are likely to be of departmental or local significance and should not significantly affect the organisation as a whole). Mishandling of contacts can have some fairly short-term effects on the reputation of the organisation.

5   Contacts are maintained at a high level inside and outside the organisation which involve exercising a high degree of communicating, negotiating and persuading skills, and jointly solving important problems. The impact on the organisation's performance and reputation can be significant, at least in the short to medium term.

6   Contacts are maintained at the highest level, with a particular emphasis on external relations. These involve very considerable communicating, advocacy and negotiating skills which can make a major and long-term impact on the performance and reputation of the organisation.

Appendix C:

EXAMPLE OF FACTOR AND

LEVEL DEFINITIONS

Knowledge and skills

Functional and operational

The level of professional, technical, administrative or operational knowledge and skills required to be fully competent in the role.

1 The use of basic skills to carry out routine administrative or operational work.

2 The application of the administrative or operational knowledge and skills required to achieve a competent level of performance in carrying out or using specific systems, procedures or techniques within a particular area or section.

3 The application of specialised or technical knowledge and skills to achieve the level of competent performance required across a range of activities in a section or department.

4 The application of high levels of technical or professional expertise across a wide range of activities within a department.

5 The provision of technical or professional leadership within a department.

6 The provision of technical or professional leadership within a major function or across the whole organisation.

Planning and organising work

The requirement to plan and schedule work, and to allocate priorities.

1 Work is allocated on a continuous basis and is carried out in a pre-planned order with little or no variation.

2 Work priorities are planned on a daily basis within well defined section or departmental schedules and time-scales.

3 Work priorities are planned within departmental programme over the shorter term (within one week) but may have to be rescheduled or reprioritised frequently on a daily basis.

4 Work schedules and priorities for a section or department are planned over the short to medium term – weekly to monthly. Work has frequently to be reprioritised.

5 The work of a major function or department is planned, organised and prioritised over periods of up to a year. There is involvement in formulating functional or departmental strategies.

6 The work of a major sector of the organisation is planned and organised for a year or more ahead. There is involvement in formulating corporate strategies.

Leadership

The competences required to exercise leadership over people in groups, project teams, departments and functions: setting the direction, motivating team members, maintaining group cohesion, ensuring that team objectives are agreed and achieved, and exercising care and consideration for other people's needs.

1 Operation as a member of a work group or team, responding to leadership and working with the team leader to achieve team targets and standards.

2 Leadership of a compact operational, technical or professional group or project team responding effectively to normal leadership requirements.

3 Leadership of a diverse operational, technical or professional group which involves responding to challenges requiring the exercise of superior leadership skills.

4 Leadership of a major department, function or team in which acute leadership challenges may have to be met involving real issues of managing change and employee relations.

5 High profile leadership involving facing tough challenges in improving performance, getting results or dealing with employee relations issues.

Interpersonal skills

The skills required to achieve the expected level of competence in communicating and responding to people inside and outside the organisation, exercising influence over colleagues, customers, clients, suppliers and other contacts outside the organisation, negotiating and dealing with people generally.

1 Normal communication skills are used to keep others at

broadly the same level in the organisation informed of activities carried out by the jobholder, and accurately to pass on routine information to them. The work does not require the individual to exert influence over others.

2   The work requires the ability to communicate effectively with people in the organisation at the level of the jobholder on matters concerning sectional or departmental operations or performance. Some ability is required to influence others – eg encouraging colleagues or people in other departments to respond to own priorities. Routine contacts may be made with people outside the organisation – dealing with standard enquiries, placing orders, or providing information.

3   The work requires the ability regularly to contact and influence people in other departments at the same level, representing the department on complex issues. Frequent contacts with people outside the organisation may be necessary, exerting influence, dealing with complex enquiries and issues or handling complaints. It may also be necessary to conduct negotiations on day-to-day matters or assist with more important negotiations.

4   The work involves frequent contacts at senior level within the organisation, representing the department and influencing others in order to secure departmental objectives. Regular contacts with people from other organisations as the recognised representative of the company are required in order to achieve company objectives. It may be necessary to conduct negotiations on important issues affecting the organisation.

5   The work involves maintaining effective communication throughout the organisation and with external bodies, representing the company at the highest level on complex issues. It will be frequently necessary to become involved in conducting key negotiations with long-term implications for the organisation.

Teamworking

The competences required to work effectively in a team.

1   Effective contribution as a team member to the achievement of team objectives.

2   Participation as a team member in setting team goals and standards, and ensuring that quality, output and performance targets are met.

3   Retention of a key role as a team member in setting the direction

and ensuring that the members of the team work well together and deliver the results expected.

Role flexibility

The competences required to work flexibly in accordance with organisational requirements.

1   The requirements of the role are relatively stable and there is little scope or need for flexibility.
2   The role requires the individual to work flexibly within an operational or project team deploying varied techniques and skills as demanded by changes in the team's tasks or priorities and the need to make the best use of the collective skills of team members in meeting them.
3   The role requires the individual to take on different projects, responsibilities or tasks in other parts of the function or organisation, responding to new challenges in new contexts.

Manual dexterity

The level of manual dexterity required to perform the work effectively.

1   The work makes relatively little demand on individuals for manual dexterity or co-ordination.
2   Normal levels of dexterity or co-ordination are required in using a keyboard, equipment or hand tool, but specialised skills are not needed.
3   Considerable levels of dexterity or coordination are required; for example, the achievement of high standards of speed and accuracy in using keyboards or the use of specialised hand tools or delicate equipment.
4   Exceptional levels of dexterity are required involving rapid manual co-ordination in the use of highly specialised hand tools or delicate equipment.

Responsibility

Impact

The impact made by the individual in the role on the achievement of the objectives of the team, department, function or organisation.

1   Contribution as a team member to the achievement of team results within a department or function.

2   Contribution in a leadership or specialist role to team results within a department or function.

3   Significant contribution to the results achieved by the department or function.

4   Major impact on the achievement of objectives in a key area of the organisation's work.

5   Considerable impact on the longer term performance of the organisation.

Innovation and creativity

The degree to which the role demands original thinking to generate new ideas, concepts, products, markets, systems or processes, or to originate designs or other work requiring creative imagination.

1   The role is well-established, and there is relatively little scope for innovation or creativity.

2   Innovative thinking or creativity is required from time to time in the role.

3   Innovative thinking or creativity is a major component of the role.

Quality

The contribution made by the role to the achievement of the highest levels of quality in the goods or services provided by the organisation.

1   The role involves the effective provision of the continuous support required to achieve quality standards.

2   The role requires constant attention to the actual delivery of quality products or services.

3   The role requires the development and implementation of processes to achieve the continuous improvement of quality standards and the delivery of quality products or services.

Customer care

The contribution made by the role to the achievement of the highest levels of service and care to the customers or clients of the organisation.

1   The role requires the effective provision of the continuous support required to achieve high levels of customer care, but does not involve direct contact with customers or clients.

2   The role involves contact with customers or clients which directly impacts on their perceptions of the level of service provided by the organisation.

3   The role makes a significant and direct contribution to the creation of high levels of service or care for customers or clients, and therefore, on their perceptions of the organisation.

4   The role requires the development and implementation of processes to achieve the continuous improvement of levels of service and care and, therefore, the reputation of the organisation.

Decisions

Complexity

The variety and diversity of the work carried out, and the decisions to be made.

1   Work requirements are on the whole well-defined and the choice of action is fairly limited.

2   There is some diversity in the work, which involves a number of non-routine elements although they are quite closely related to one another.

3   The work is diverse, consisting of a number of different elements only broadly related to one another.

4   The work is highly diverse, involving many different elements which may not be closely related to one another.

5   The work is multidisciplinary and involves making a broad range of highly diverse decisions.

Freedom to act

The degree to which the role provides scope for the individual to act independently.

1   For most aspects of the work, specific and detailed instructions are given on both what has to be done and how it should be done. The work is fairly closely supervised.

2   Specific guidelines and procedures exist on what needs to be done, but there is some freedom to decide methods and priorities. Supervision is generally available to provide guidance.

3   Acton is taken within policy and procedural guidelines in accordance with accepted practice in the department or function, but only under general supervision.

4   Independent action is taken as required within broad policy frameworks and in accordance with generally accepted practice in the organisation.

5   Actions are constrained only by organisational strategies, policies and objectives.

Problem-solving

The level of competence required by the role in exercising judgement to solve problems.

1   The role involves recurrent work in which new problems seldom arise and, when they do, are usually dealt with at a higher level.

2   The role is clearly structured and well-defined. Problems are readily identified and standard solutions are available for solving them.

3   The role is carried out within a well-defined framework but problems can arise that require the exercise of some judgement in solving them by reference to established priorities and precedents.

4   The role requires the frequent exercise of independent judgement in solving problems with only general guidance available in the shape of established practices and precedents.

5   The role requires the exercise of constant judgement and strategic thinking to solve problems in circumstances where there is often little guidance available from established practices and precedents.

Effort and personal demands

Physical demands

The demands made by the job in terms of physical effort or exertion.

1   Normal physical effort is required in standing, walking, using equipment, carrying or lifting light articles.

2   Moderate physical effort is required because of prolonged standing, constant movement (manipulating objects or using equipment, walking, climbing stairs) or carrying or lifting fairly heavy articles.

3   Serious physical effort is required because of constant or prolonged lifting and carrying of heavy articles or high levels of physical exertion – eg handling equipment, digging.

Mental demands

The demands made by the job in terms of mental effort leading to pressure or stress.

1   Normal mental demands – the work is not particularly pressurised or stressful.

2   Moderate mental demands – the work involves some pressure or stress, arising, for example, from meeting deadlines, dealing with people, or frequent changes in priorities.

3   Considerable mental demands – the work is heavily pressurised or stressful because, for example, of the need to meet demanding deadlines, deal with difficult people, or cope with constantly changing priorities.

Appendix D:

QUESTIONNAIRES: ROLE

ANALYSIS/JOB ANALYSIS

Role analysis questionnaire

The purpose of this questionnaire is to obtain information that defines the main characteristics of your role as a basis for assessing its relative value in the organisation. You should complete the questionnaire yourself, but do consult your manager or team leader if you have any doubts about the most appropriate answer to any of the questions. When you have filled in the questionnaire it will be shown to your manager or team leader. If there are any points to raise, he or she will discuss them with you.

The questionnaire is divided into four parts providing:

1 Basic details – information on the purpose of your role and where it fits into the organisation, and the main activities you are expected to carry out to achieve that purpose.
2 Details of your organisation.
3 Further details about your role under the following headings:
    □ the knowledge, skills, education, training and experience required
    □ the equipment you use regularly
    □ the impact you make in your role to the performance of your team, department, function or the organisation as a whole
    □ the critical dimensions of your role
    □ working with other people
    □ the most challenging aspects of your work.
4 Information on the following main characteristics of your role:
    □ the knowledge and skills required
    □ the amount of responsibility involved
    □ the decisions you make
    □ the complexity of your work
    □ the contacts you make
    □ the physical and mental demands made by the role.

1: Basic details of the role

Job title:..

Purpose of role
Describe as concisely as possible (in not more than one or two sentences) the overall purpose of your role – what in general terms you are expected to achieve.

....

....

....

....

....

....

....

Key result areas
List the most important things you do in your role in terms of the results you are expected to achieve in each of its main areas. Please do not attempt to describe the tasks you carry out in detail or go into how you carry them out. Most roles can be described fewer than ten headings.

....

....

....

....

....

....

....

....

....

....

....

....

2: Organisation

Job title of your manager's or team leader's manager

....

Job title of your manager or team leader

....

Your job title...

Job titles of any other people reporting directly to your manager or team leader

....

....

....

....

....

....

....

....

....

Job titles of any people reporting directly to you (give numbers if more than one person in a job)

....

....

....

....

....

....

....

....

....

Job titles of people reporting to you direct, if any, and the total number of people for whom you are responsible

....

....

....

....

....

....

....

....

....

Please attach an organisation chart if one is available.

3: Other information about your role

The knowledge, skills and experience you require

Please describe the knowledge and skills you require to carry out your role effectively, and the education, training and/or experience you think is needed to acquire the necessary knowledge and skills. Knowledge could include such areas as professional, technical or scientific knowledge, knowledge of any other specialised areas of work with which you are concerned, and knowledge of relevant organisational and departmental policies and procedures. The skills could include those involved in planning and organising, leadership, working with other people (interpersonal and communicating skills), numerical and information technology skills, operating machines and equipment, and manual dexterity. Please indicate:

☐ what you believe to be the level of education and qualifications required and/or the type and amount of experience needed to reach the necessary level of knowledge, skill and expertise

☐ how long you think it would take for someone starting in this role with the required basic knowledge and skills to reach a fully competent level of performance.

....

....

....

Equipment used
Give details of any equipment, machines or tools you use or operate regularly. As appropriate, indicate the approximate proportion of your time you spend on operating this equipment.

....

....

....

....

....

....

....

....

....

Impact
Indicate the impact you believe you make in your role on the performance of your team, department, function or the organisation as a whole. To what extent does your role influence the results achieved by your team/section, department/function, division or the organisation, and in what ways?

....

....

....

....

....

....

....

....

....

Critical dimensions
Set out the 'critical dimensions' of your role – ie, any data which indicates its size or scope in such terms as the number of people for whom you are responsible, the size of the budget you control, the

sales you generate, the output for which you are responsible, directly or indirectly, the number of items you process in a typical day or week, the number of people you have to deal with daily or weekly, etc.

....

....

....

....

....

....

....

....

....

....

The people you work with
Give details of the people you are regularly in contact with either inside or outside your organisation (inside includes members of your team or department, and other people, including internal customers, elsewhere in the organisation; 'outside' includes customers, clients, suppliers, members of the public, etc.). Indicate the nature of these contacts – eg exchanging information, persuading people to take a course of action, negotiating, answering queries or dealing with complaints.

....

....

....

....

....

....

....

....

....

....

The most challenging aspects of your work
What do you regard as the most challenging aspects of your work?
In answering this question consider such aspects as:

☐ the need to make decisions on your own initiative without specific
guidance from your manager/team leader or established policies,
procedures or precedents
☐ the need to exercise independent judgement in solving problems
☐ the need to be creative in any aspect of your work
☐ the need to deal with other people – persuading, negotiating or
handling complaints
☐ the pressure to meet output targets, deadlines or quality standards, or arising from the need constantly to prioritise or re-prioritise work

....
....
....
....
....
....
....
....

Demands made on you by the role
What physical and mental demands does your role make on you in
such aspects as continuous and considerable exertion, lifting heavy
objects, using VDUs extensively, high levels of concentration, stress,
working unsocial hours or in uncomfortable or hazardous conditions?

....
....
....
....
....
....
....
....

4: Characteristics of the role

This section contains a number of statements about what your role requires of you under five different headings. For each heading please tick the statement that most closely fits what you believe to be involved in your job.

Knowledge and skills

Consider the level of professional, technical, administrative or operational knowledge and skills required to be fully competent in the role.

The role involves:

☐ the ability to carry out a number of well-defined tasks

☐ carrying out fairly well standardised administrative procedures such as maintaining records, answering straightforward queries or operating a word processor

☐ carrying out more advanced administrative work which may involve the use of complex equipment, maintaining complex records, dealing with non-routine queries, analysing data or preparing standard reports

☐ understanding and applying advanced practices, procedures, concepts or principles; professional training or some years of relevant professional level experience are required

☐ considerable competence in a managerial or professional field in order to understand and apply advanced policies, practices, concepts or principles

☐ a very high level of professional and managerial competence is required in directing and controlling activities.

Responsibility

Consider what the role requires in terms of its impact on end results, and the size of the resources controlled (people, money and equipment, etc.).

The role involves:

☐ the responsibility for carrying out specified tasks efficiently and well; no resources (ie people, equipment or money) are controlled

☐ the responsibility for carrying out a range of tasks important to the effective performance of the unit or work team; the resources controlled are limited to those personally required by the role-holder to fulfil the role

☐ work that can make a considerable impact on the performance of the unit or section; quite valuable equipment may be controlled and the role holder may control some staff carrying out the type of work described above and, possibly, a smallish budget

☐ work that makes a significant impact on the performance of a number of units or a major function or department; the role-holder may control a number of staff carrying out the type of work described above together with a sizable budget

☐ work that requires the role-holder to make a significant contribution to achieving objectives in an important aspect or area of the organisation's work; control may be exercised over a medium sized department and budget

☐ the formulation and implementation of major functional policies and plans that can make a considerable impact on the longer-term performance of the organisation; control may be exercise over a major department or division and a considerable budget.

Decisions
Consider the degree to which the role involves choice of action, covering the extent to which the work is well defined, the availability of clear policies, procedures and precedents, the amount of guidance available from your manager or team leader and the degree to which you have to exercise independent judgement in making decisions.

☐ The work is well defined, and for most aspects of the role specific instructions are given on both what has to be done and how it should be done.

☐ Explicit guidelines and procedures exist on what needs to be done but there is some freedom to decide methods and priorities; guidance on dealing with unusual situations or problems is readily available.

☐ Decisions are made and actions taken in accordance with defined policies and practices; guidance is available as required.

☐ Independent action involving the exercise of some judgement and initiative is taken from time to time as required within broad policy frameworks and in accordance with generally accepted practices in the function or department.

☐ The role frequently requires the exercise of judgement and initiative in dealing with situations and solving problems, which involves interpreting generalised guidelines and precedents.

☐ Decisions and actions are constrained only by organisational strategies and policies; judgement and initiative are continuously required in dealing with problems and handling situations where there are no clear guidelines or precedents.

Complexity
Consider the variety and diversity of tasks and activities you carry out, taking account of the extent to which they are conducted solely within your own area (your team or department) or extend into other areas of the organisation or outside. Consider also the range and variety of the skills you have to use.

☐ The work involves carrying out identical tasks or groups of tasks within a single precisely-defined area of activity.

☐ The work involves carrying out a range of similar tasks which are closely related to one another and require the continuous exercise of a particular type of skill within a clearly defined area of activity.

☐ There is some diversity in the work which involves a number of different elements; these are closely related to one another and require the exercise of a range of similar skills within a broadly defined area of activity.

☐ The work is diverse, consisting of a number of different elements; these are broadly related to one another and may require the use of a range of different skills (multiskilling); the work may take place within more than one closely linked but broadly defined area of activity.

☐ The work is highly diverse, involving many different elements which may not be closely related to one another and may extend to several areas of activity; a wide variety of managerial, professional or technical skills are used.

☐ The work is multidisciplinary and involves making a broad range of highly diverse decisions.

Contacts
Select the statement which best describes the usual way in which the role involves making contacts with others, inside and outside the organisation.

☐ Contacts are mainly concerned with passing on or exchanging information within the unit or team.

☐ Contacts are fairly frequently made with people at broadly the same level in other departments or units inside the organisation and/or clients, suppliers or other interested parties outside the organisation for the purposes of exchanging information or requesting a standard service.

☐ Contacts are regularly made with people at a number of levels inside and/or outside the organisation; the contacts are often on non-routine matters and include both the exchange and interpretation of information; the role-holder may sometimes have to influence others – eg encouraging colleagues or people in other departments to respond to own priorities, gaining acceptance of a decision.

☐ Frequent contacts are made at all but the highest level with people inside and outside the organisation; the contacts may mean persuading people to take a course of action, making a favourable impression or exercising a range of communicating skills.

☐ Contacts are made at all levels in the organisation and outside and involve the exercise of a high degree of communicating, negotiating and persuading skills and joint problem-solving.

☐ Contacts are made at the highest level with a particular emphasis on external relations and which require very considerable communicating, advocacy and persuading skills.

Physical demands
What demands are made by the role in terms of physical effort or exertion?

☐ Normal physical effort is required in standing, walking, using equipment, carrying or lifting light articles.

☐ Moderate physical effort is required because of prolonged standing, constant movement (manipulating objects or using equipment, walking, climbing stairs) or carrying or lifting fairly heavy articles.

☐ Serious physical effort is required because of the constant or prolonged lifting and carrying of heavy articles or high levels of physical exertion – eg handling equipment, digging.

Mental demands
What demands are made by the role in terms of mental effort leading to pressure or stress?

☐ Normal mental demands – the work is not particularly pressurised or stressful.

☐ Moderate mental demands – the work involves some pressure or stress arising, for example, from meeting deadlines, dealing with people or frequent changes in priorities.

☐ Considerable mental demands – the work is heavily pressurised or stressful because, for example, of the need to meet demanding deadlines, deal with difficult people, or cope with constantly changing priorities.

Appendix D1: Knowledge and Skills

Education, Qualification and Experience

For each of the two questions below, select the **single response** which best applies to your role, taking account of the guidance notes.

What is the **minimum** level of formal qualification required for the job?

- ☐ PhD or higher
- ☐ Master's degree. Bachelor's degree plus professional qualification, or equivalent, including MBA, all chartered professions and post-graduate professional qualification
- ☐ Bachelor's degree or equivalent professional qualification
- ☐ 2 'A'-levels, BTEC or equivalent, including ONC, and City and Guilds
- ☐ 5 GCSEs, BTEC(N) or equivalent, including NVQ/SVQ Business Administration Level 2 (Administrative), (Financial and Secretarial), and secretarial qualifications
- ☐ 2 GCSEs or equivalent, including typing and shorthand qualifications and NVQ/SVQ Business Administration Level 1
- ☐ No formal qualifications

Given the answer to the above, what period of work experience is required?

- ☐ More than 15 years
- ☐ Over 10 years–15 years
- ☐ Over 6 years–10 years
- ☐ Over 3 years–6 years
- ☐ 13 months–3 years
- ☐ 7 months–12 months
- ☐ 4–6 months
- ☐ 1–3 months
- ☐ Less than 1 month

Extract from Benefits Agency (JEGS) Questionnaire.

Appendix D2: Problem Solving

In this exercise you are asked to identify the types of problems you have to resolve, the degree of analysis required, and the extent to which your job operates within prescribed procedures and under supervision.

Level

1 The work is generally well defined, and solutions to problems are found through reference to the supervisor.

2 The work requires the resolution of problems which are **readily identified**. The solutions are **standard** and the required action is defined.

3 The work sometimes involves problems which are apparent, but precise identification requires further **inquiry** or search.

4 The work involves solutions to problems within a **specific** area which require **extensive** inquiry and interpretation and **some** independent judgement.

5 The work involves solutions to problems across a **number** of areas which require extensive enquiry and interpretation and a **high** degree of independent judgement.

6 The work involves solutions to problems which lack clear definition and may necessitate **strategic** thinking, development of new concepts and approaches or entrepreneurial action.

Extract from Cancer Research Campaign Questionnaire.

Appendix D3: Knowledge Dimensions

What types of knowledge are required to perform your job? Below is a list of types of knowledge that are relevant to Norwich Union's business.

Using the 1–5 scale defined below, indicate how much of each type of knowledge is needed by the job-holder (you may select any areas that are appropriate).

1 *General familiarity* – The job demands sufficient knowledge to understand in general terms the issues concerned but not enough to perform the work directly.

2 *Practical understanding* – The job demands sufficient knowledge to be involved with the type of work indicated but not to be able to cope with it fully.

3 *Full working knowledge* – The job demands sufficient knowledge for the jobholder to perform all the work of the type indicated at a competent level.

4 *Expert knowledge* – The job demands sufficient knowledge not only to enable the jobholder to perform the work of the type

indicated at a competent level but also at a level where the job holder is acknowledged as an expert for reference by other people, within the jobholder's work area or related work areas.

5   *Group expert* – The job demands sufficient knowledge not only to enable the jobholder to perform the work of the type indicated at a competent level but also at a level where the jobholder is acknowledged as an expert for reference by other people throughout the Norwich Union Group.

Extract from Norwich Union Questionnaire (copyright Norwich Union/Watson Wyatt).

Appendix D4: Essential Competences

List the essential competences for the job from your functional analysis including the defininite frequency of use, importance or criticality of the competence and the minimum duration of training required. Competencies should be grouped under major summary headings.

MAJOR COMPETENCE HEADING	COMPETENCE + DEFINITION (Including Frequency of use, criticality		
	1		
DEFINITION	Frequency of use	Criticality	Time to train
	2		
	Frequency of use	Criticality	Time to train
	3		
	Frequency of use	Criticality	Time to train
	4		
	Frequency of use	Criticality	Time to train
	5		
	Frequency of use	Criticality	Time to train
	6		
	Frequency of use	Criticality	Time to train
	7		
	Frequency of use	Criticality	Time to train

Extract from Pilkington Optronics Job Analysis Form.

Appendix D5: Job analysis questionnaire – manufacturing

1 What knowledge is essential to the adequate performance of this job? If this knowledge is gained by experience, how long would it take to acquire? How long does it take a suitably qual-ified/experienced person to become familiar with this particu-lar job?
   Educational knowledge: *Time to acquire:*
   Job knowledge or experience: *Time to acquire:*
   Time to become familiar with the job:

2 Describe the basic problem(s) which this jobholder deals with. Then note what difficulties and snags arise, and how often they occur.
   Job problems:
   Snags and difficulties:

3 What physical activities are involved in the performance of this job?

4 Discover the complexity of this job's tasks. Are they monoto-nous? routine? varied? complex? Is one task dealt with at a time? Do tasks run concurrently or overlap?

5 To what extent does this job demand fast or high-pressure work-ing, or the giving of constant attention to the work?

6 To what extent is a responsibility for costs etc. vested in this position? Can the holder spend money? order equipment? avoid or cause waste? bring in orders? cause damage? increase effi-ciency? etc. Note actual amounts where possible, and limita-tions of responsibility.

7 To what extent is the work of this position involved in the supervision of others and/or to what extent and how often is the work of this position subject to supervision?
   Supervision:
   Supervised:

8 What regular contacts are necessary between this position and others inside and outside the organisation?
   Inside:
   Outside:

9 What authority for making and implementing decisions about policy or practice is invested in this position? How often are such decisions made? What decisions are referred to superiors?

10 Does this position involve work with confidential information? Is any authority for disclosure given?

11   Describe the physical conditions in which the jobholder works; refer particularly to those that may be adverse to performance (noise, heat, dirt, space etc.). Note any hazards, unusual hours, excessive travelling, or overtime.

Appendix E:

ROLE AND JOB DESCRIPTIONS

Financial services company

Job Title: Client Services Clerk
Reporting To: Manager
Job Purpose: To administer life and pension policies in accordance with industry regulations, ensuring that the customer's expectation of quality service is exceeded.

Key result areas

Quality customer service

- To ensure customer's needs are met/exceeded by identifying and responding to service opportunities.
- To make reasoned decisions by assessing customer's individual circumstances when applying policy rules.
- To resolve complex cases by carrying out required investigations ensuring the customer is aware of progress at all times.
- To provide a courteous and efficient service to both internal and external customers by actioning all enquiries accurately and quickly.

Job knowledge

- To fully understand the company's life and pensions products, and administer them correctly within the specified guidelines.
- To accurately use the systems relating to the products, from inputting new application details through to processing claims.
- To continually develop existing skills and knowledge and to have the ability to be flexible within the department, responding to the changing demands of workloads.

Quality

- To action procedures accurately to ensure that best business practices are followed.
- To correctly action high volumes of work within predetermined time-scales, meeting the high standard of quality required.
- To prioritise individual and team workloads to ensure the through-put of the team is efficient and customer service-oriented.
- To constantly review procedures and working practices, and feed back recommendations for improvement to the manager, with an aim to enhancing the performance of the team.

Administration

- To assess and process policy claims accurately using the systems available.
- To interpret and respond to correspondence relating to new and existing policies, ensuring all aspects are answered in detail, in line with the customer's expectations.
- To monitor accounts on which claims are pending, ensuring that all follow-up procedures are actioned as quickly as possible.
- To complete general job-related paperwork in a comprehensive and accurate manner, including statistics as and when required.
- To be aware of the health and safety policy and regulations in the conditions of employment.

Preferred behaviours

Active listening
Tendency to identify key elements of others' communications. Tendency to gather further relevant information through effective questioning. Ability to reflect back the essence of what has been said.

Controlling
Tendency to establish and maintain monitoring systems and proce-dures to regulate the activities of self and others, and act on the results.

Detail handling
Tolerance for, and ability to handle, details and paperwork associ-ated with the job.

Initiative
Tendency to see opportunities and to originate action in pursuit of business goals.

Interpersonal sensitivity
Awareness of the impact of own behaviour on others and the tendency to respond appropriately to achieve results.

Spoken communication
Tendency to express information and ideas orally in a manner that is appropriate, concise and accurate.

Stress tolerance
Stability of performance and the ability to make controlled responses in situations normally found stressful, such as when faced with hostility or rejection or excess workload.

Work standards
Tendency to set high standards of performance for self and others. Tendency to be dissatisfied with average performance.

Written communication
Tendency to express information and ideas in writing in a manner that is appropriate, concise and accurate.

Skills

Customer care
Ability to handle customers effectively. It includes:

- listening to customers to identify needs
- innovating to meet those needs
- checking with the customer that the needs have been met.

Problem-solving
Ability to solve problems creatively. It includes:

- identifying the problem
- evaluating alternatives
- brainstorming to seek innovative solutions.

Report writing

Ability to produce written reports that are clear, logical and persuasive: It includes:

- ☐ defining the needs of the recipient
- ☐ setting clear objectives
- ☐ gathering and analysing data
- ☐ arriving at solutions, recommendations and actions
- ☐ formatting the report appropriately
- ☐ using style and language that most effectively meets the recipient's needs.

Appendix F:

COMPUTERISED JOB

EVALUATION

This appendix summarises some of the most popular job evaluation software available. It has been compiled from information supplied by the software suppliers and is not intended to be exhaustive of all the products currently on the market. Not all the software packages described actually carry out job evaluation; some provide support and record-keeping facilities, links to compensation software or market data.

Bryher Consultants & Associates

Bryher, 6 Cornflower Close, Simons Park, Wokingham, Berkshire
RG11 2UF
Tel: 01734 791002

EVALUATOR + is a computerised package suppled by Bryher consultants who claim that it can be used either in Standard mode to support the bespoke development of an analytical job evaluation approach or in one of two Audit modes, both designed to check on the efficacy of any existing approaches to job evaluation under the Equal Value Amendment (1984) to the Equal Pay Act.

The software is user-friendly, most processes being menu-led and with on-line help available. The software sets up job evaluation projects, each of which has the capacity for 99 benchmark jobs, up to a maximum of 14 factors and two groups. Benchmark jobs should be representative of the job population and of both sexes. Factors are usually determined by a panel chosen by the user, and the second group of decisions can help to test for bias in judges' decisions. The ideal number for the panel is around six.

Job descriptions are required for all jobs. Bryher Consultants recommend that these be written by the staff concerned to reflect the chosen factors, and then agreed with their managers. These can be entered and stored in the EVALUATOR + software.

EVALUATOR + then sets up the project according to the defined number of jobs, factors and judges, and Paired Comparison Decision forms are generated for the judges. Judges can work together to record their decisions on the forms provided by marking the winning job in each pair against each factor. They can input their decisions electronically if desired. Either way, the decisions are entered to EVALUATOR + and the computer performs consensus calculations to calculate the Multiple Regression Analysis (MRA) co-efficients; alternatively, consensus weightings can be entered into the system.

An initial rank order report for all or selected factors is generated, and a scores report is generated for all factors. Matrices are also available for all or selected factors indicating for each the percentage level of consensus achieved by the judges. All inconsistencies are identified and can be printed as reports, by factor, by factor/judge, by judge, or simply printed together in one report. A project report shows details of the current project and an audit trail enables the user to track back. A new rank order report is available from the MRA, as is a comparison report which compares the MRA rank order with the consensus rank order. A run facility processes all selected reports which may be date- and time-stamped if required.

The judges are invited collectively to review their results for consistency and fairness. If any of their decisions are changed by agreement, the factor weights are calculated anew and the reports printed again.

There is a modelling facility which allows the user to experiment with different scenarios – for example, by eliminating individual decisions from the paired-comparisons routine, reducing the number of groups if more than one was selected in the first place, eliminating individual judge's decisions, individual factors, or combinations of all these.

The judges agree the weightings of the factors used in designing a bespoke job evaluation factor plan. They can develop the word-definitions for each level in the plan which reflect the specific organisational language and culture, and can choose the number of levels within each factor. These are entered into the EVALUATOR + software, where they are stored and a points table created.

Before EVALUATOR + can generate a job-evaluated, graded salary structure it needs details of the people who occupy the jobs. It therefore incorporates a personnel management database in which information can be stored relating to job reference, title, job hold, sex, current salary, etc.

Example of an EVALUATOR + generated grade structure

The judges evaluate the selected benchmark jobs using their own factor plan. The results are input and, using a points table, EVALU-

ATOR + calculates the points value for each job and positions it in the rank order. This can be compared with the initial rank order and the new rank order; any agreed revisions can be re-input and the rank order changed. All non-benchmark jobs also have to be evaluated against the same factor plan, but not until the design of the graded salary structure has been concluded using the benchmark jobs and their current salaries. EVALUATOR + will identify any potential equal value issues in an equal-value report.

On-screen design features for designing the ideal natural grade structure are available. They include grade creation, deletion, salary data, identifying male and female jobholders, the line of best fit of the salary data, On/Off switch for grades, points salary levels parameters of individual grades, 'Who is that?', etc.

Bryher supply an optional piece of software – Performance-Related Increase Salary Modeller (PRISM) – for managing performance-related pay, and also an EVALUATOR + Report Generator Option (ERGO), which allows the user to design and produce his or her own personnel database records.

System requirements

- [ ] a 386SX 20 MHz PC or better (a 486DX 50 MHz or better is recommended, especially if there are a large number of records in the personnel database)
- [ ] a minimum of four megabytes of extended memory
- [ ] a Dot Matrix, Inkjet or Laser printer
- [ ] a colour EGA monitor or better
- [ ] a hard disk with at least two megabytes of free space
- [ ] a 3.5-inch high-density floppy-disk drive

Harwood Consultancy Ltd

73 Elm Bank Gardens, Barnes, London SW13 0NX
Tel: 0181 392 1172/1076

Harwood supply KeyValue Job Evaluator which, they claim, combines a systematic factor or questionnaire approach with the flexibility of evaluation based on individual assessment. According to Harwood, most evaluation models are typically snapshots of an organisation, and either become quickly outdated or need modification as business needs change. KeyValue allows the user to add or delete questions/factors to respond to changing priorities.

KeyValue recognises that each organisation has its own personality and characteristics, and so allows users to build templates to create models reflecting the culture, value system and priorities of their own organisations. These models can be modified as the evaluation process unfolds. Harwood consultants are on hand to assist in this development. However, Harwood claim that after the initial training and installation, users require only minimal external assistance and benefit from a high degree of independence and low on-going costs.

System features include:

storage of up to 100 benchmark evaluations
up to 30 questions per questionnaire
easy addition/deletion of questions/factors
unlimited levels for each question
standard ratings easily customised for precision weighting
user-definable confidence levels
scores and grades compared with benchmark jobs
job description processor
communicates key performance criteria to employees
grade structure defined
grade boundaries easily amended
common framework simplifies model maintenance
context-sensitive help messages
quick keys for common tasks

Harwood claim KeyValue is suitable for organisations with 500-plus employees looking to harmonise pay and benefits, ensure internal consistency of pay levels, boost employee motivation, and communicate key performance criteria to employees.

KeyValue is available in both Windows and DOS, and requires IBM or 100 per cent compatible PC with 80386 processor or higher.

Hewitt Associates

Romeland House, Romeland Hill, St Albans, Hertfordshire AL3 4EZ
Tel: 01727 866233

COMP+™ is a modular, PC-based compensation management system which Hewitt claim is designed to support the design, administration and management of all aspects of compensation. The system includes modules both for job evaluation and job description writing.

According to Hewitt the job evaluation module is designed to facilitate consistent evaluation of jobs across the organisation. The system can support a number of different evaluation approaches, such as point-factor, whole job ranking, rank-to-market, etc. For companies in which different evaluation schemes are used for different sites or job groups, COMP + can accommodate up to 99 job evaluation systems. There is complete flexibility to choose and weight factors on an individual organisation basis because the program automatically calculates the evaluation score for any job evaluated. It can also contain in-built checks to ensure that the balance of scores across factors is in line with the expected range.

In addition to job evaluation, COMP + has modules for producing job descriptions, either using information gathered from simple questionnaires completed by the user or by selecting from a wide range of generic job descriptions.

Additionally, Hewitt Associates claim that COMP + can help build grade and salary structures, giving the user the ability to create a number of different scenarios and test out the implications of these. There is also a Compensation Survey Manager module which facilitates the linkage with market data.

COMP + was developed more than 10 years ago and Hewitt Associates are concerned to continually update and improve the system. It is currently used by over 200 clients around the world. It is available both as a stand-alone PC version and a networked version.

System requirements

PC version: a typical fully-equipped 486 or Pentium IBM-compatible PC.

Multi-user version: most LANs are equipped to the necessary level to run COMP +.

GPC + is a spreadsheet-based job evaluation and record-keeping system. Unlike COMP + it does not perform a range of compensation support activities, but is aimed instead at organisations who need a computerised support system for carrying out evaluations and keeping evaluation records.

GPC + is designed to support a point-factor evaluation system, and was primarily developed to provide implementation support for organisations who have worked with Hewitt Associates during the job evaluation development stage. Nevertheless, Hewitt Associates claim the system has the flexibility to accommodate other approaches.

Users carry out evaluations by selecting the most appropriate level of demand for each factor and the system allows for reference against previous results to be made during the build-up of the evaluation. The program then automatically calculate scores, and if appropriate, gradings.

The system is written using Lotus 4 upwards for Windows with a link to Ami-Pro for its word-processing capabilities in working with job descriptions, commentary on evaluation results, etc.

System requirements:

The system will run on any system that runs Microsoft Windows version 3.1. Generally an IBM or compatible PC is needed with 4MB RAM, 4MB free hard-disk space, Microsoft Windows 3.1, DOS 5.0 or above, Microsoft-compatible mouse or other pointing device, VCA 9 (or better) display.

The Oakwood Partnership

15 Beaconhurst, Keymer, Hassocks, West Sussex BN6 8RE
Tel: 01273 842025

Oakwood is a job evaluation/pay consultancy which also provides a software solution called *Competency Manager*. This uses a competence-based approach to job evaluation. Oakwood claim it allows jobs and people to be profiled against the competences key to the business. The software does all the basics, such as job scoring, running different weighting scenarios, etc. However, according to Oakwood, it then uses the competences to match people to jobs, enabling the client to use the software to support a high range of HR activities such as:

☐ identifying the gap between what an individual has to offer and what the job requires (using competence language) – this is then used to build up a detailed training needs analysis

☐ identifying succession plans for jobs and identifying gaps in succession

☐ selecting employees with certain key characteristics for key projects/promotions

☐ reprofiling jobs on a 'what-if' basis to identify how the total HR picture would look if roles were changed – eg layers of management removed

☐ identifying the key competences required of a new recruit

☐ linking the achievement of competences into pay progression.

Critical success factors (CSFs) which define the key contributions required from staff are used to score jobs. These can be given a weighting and form cluster headings under which behavioural competencies are developed. Jobs are then scored according to the CSFs on the basis that the more a job contributes to the CSF, the more valuable it is to the business. A range of job score scenarios can be tested using different CSF weightings in order to reach the right solution for the business.

Competences are linked to the CSFs. For example, the CSF analytical skills will require behavioural competences such as 'collection and use of information', 'problem-solving', and 'written communication'. This enables the person to be compared with the job requirements and also produce a suggested competence profile directly from the evaluation, which can be edited by the line manager. On this basis Oakwood claim that *Competency Manager* can identify training needs for groups and individuals, plan succession, and be used to audit the strengths and weaknesses of departments, business units, or whole organisations.

The results of the job evaluation can be loaded into the Oakwood pay-modelling software, which allows modelling of new grade scenarios. These allow the client to identify winners and losers in any implementation and to cost the implications of any proposal.

The system requires Windows and any IBM-compatible PC 486.

Appendix G:

GOOD EQUAL OPPORTUNITIES PRACTICE IN ANALYTICAL JOB EVALUATION – A CHECKLIST

(Equal Opportunities Commission)

Scheme design

- ☐ Do the terms of reference recognise that avoiding sex bias means challenging existing relativities?
- ☐ Is the scheme appropriate to the jobs it covers?
- ☐ Are any job categories excluded from the scheme, and if so what is the rationale for this?
- ☐ Is there an unbiased use of generic/benchmark jobs?
- ☐ Is the steering committee representative of the jobs covered by the scheme and trained in job evaluation and avoiding sex bias?
- ☐ Is the chair likely to be impartial and aware of equality issues?
- ☐ Are there representatives of recognised trade unions on the steering committee?
- ☐ How might any equal opportunity specialists in the organisation contribute?
- ☐ If a proprietary scheme is used does the firm have equal opportunities guidelines?

Factors

- ☐ Are the factor definitions and levels precise and unambiguous?
- ☐ Do the factors omit any important job demands?
- ☐ Is there any double-counting?
- ☐ Does any knowledge and skill factor operate unfairly?
- ☐ Are the numbers of factor levels realistic?
- ☐ Do the points gaps reflect real steps in demand?

Weighting

- ☐ Do factor weights fairly reflect the importance of the job demands to the organisations as a whole?
- ☐ Is there a rationale for the weightings?
- ☐ Have the weightings been derived explicitly or implicitly to perpetuate the existing hierarchy?
- ☐ Do any high or low weights affect predominantly men or women?

Scheme implementation

Scheme awareness

- ☐ Are the people to be covered by the scheme aware of its purpose?
- ☐ Are they informed of the progress of the scheme?

Job descriptions

- ☐ Is there too much reliance on generic job descriptions?
- ☐ Are job descriptions consistent, realistic and objective?
- ☐ Does the format reflect the factor plan?
- ☐ Are trained job analysts involved?
- ☐ What guidance is provided on the completion of job descriptions?
- ☐ Are job titles gender based?
- ☐ Is the sex of jobholders identified?
- ☐ Is the jobholder involved in writing the description?

Appeals

- ☐ Is there equal access to any appeals procedure?
- ☐ Are appeal results monitored?

Maintenance

- ☐ Is future responsibility for the scheme clearly allocated?
- ☐ Has a review programme been decided?

Scheme impact

- ☐ Is the job-evaluated hierarchy the same as the existing one?
- ☐ Do 'men's jobs' and 'women's jobs' cluster at opposite ends of the hierarchy?

Pay and benefits

- ☐ Have the grade boundaries been drawn fairly?
- ☐ Do any special payments reward demands already built into the scheme?
- ☐ Is any red-circling free of sex bias?
- ☐ Are there objectively justifiable reasons for any inconsistency in the relation of pay and benefits to job evaluation results?

REFERENCES

ACAS (1988) *Job Evaluation: An introduction*, London, ACAS.

ARMSTRONG, M. (1974) *Principles and Practice of Salary Administration*, London, Kogan Page.

ARMSTRONG, M. (1993) *Managing Reward Systems*, Buckingham, Open University Press.

ARMSTRONG, M. and Long, P. (1994) *The Reality of Strategic HRM*, London, Institute of Personnel and Development.

ARMSTRONG, M. and Murlis, H. (1994) *Reward Management : A handbook of remuneration strategy and practice*, London, Kogan Page.

ARVEY, R. D. (1986) 'Sex bias in job evaluation procedures', *Personnel Psychology*, 39, pp. 315–335.

BENGE, E.J. (1944) *Job Evaluation and Merit Rating*, Washington DC, US National Foreman's Institute.

BENGE, E. J., BURK, S. L. and HAY, E. N. (1941) *Job Evaluation Manual*, New York, Harper.

BLUMMROSEN, R. G. (1979) 'Wage Discrimination, Job Segregation and Title VII of the Civil Rights Act of 1964', *University of Michigan Law Review*, Vol.12, pp. 397–502.

CANDRILLI, A. J. and ARMAGAST, R. D. (April, 1987) 'The case for effective point-factor job evaluation', *Compensation and Benefits Review*, pp. 49–54.

CBI (1989) *Equal Pay for Work of Equal Value: Report of the CBI Equal Value Group*, London, CBI.

CRAGGS, A. (February, 1990) 'Job evaluation and human resource management in France', *Benefits and Compensation International*, pp. 9–12.

CROSS, M (1992) *Skill-based Pay: A guide for practitioners*, London, Institute of Personnel Management.

CRYSTAL, G. (1970) *Financial Motivation for Executives*, New York, AMA.

DICKENS, C. (1846) *Dombey and Son*, London, Chapman & Hall.

EDWARDS, M. R., EWEN, A. J. and O'NEAL, S. (Summer 1995) 'Using multisource assessment to pay people not jobs', *ACA Journal*, pp. 4–17.

ELLIOTT, R. F. (1991) *Labour Economics*, London, McGraw Hill.

EMERSON, S. M. (January–February, 1991) 'Job evaluation: a barrier to excellence?' *Compensation and Benefits Review*, pp. 39–51.

Equal Opportunities Commission, (1985) *Job Evaluation Schemes Free of Sex Bias*, London.

FOURACRE, S. (1995) 'Women's pay: a tough issue for employers', *Croner's Human Relations Bulletin*, pp. 5–8

FOURACRE, S. and Wright, A. (May, 1986) 'New factors in job evaluation', *Personnel Management*, pp. 40–43.

FOWLER, A. (October, 1992) 'Choose a job evaluation system', *Personnel Management Plus*, pp. 33–34.

GERTH, H. H. and MILLS, C. W. eds, (1946) *From Max Weber*, Oxford.

GHOBANDIAN, A. and WHITE, M. (1987) *Job Evaluation and Equal Pay*: Research Paper No. 17, London, Department of Employment.

GHOSHAL, S. and BARTLETT, C. A. (January–February 1995) 'Changing the role of top management: beyond structure to process', *Harvard Business Review*, pp. 86–96.

GRAYSON, D. (1987) *Job Evaluation in Transition*, London, Work Research Unit, ACAS.

HASTINGS, S. (1989) *Identifying Discrimination in Job Evaluation Schemes: Trade Union Research Unit Technical Note No. 108*, Oxford.

HASTINGS, S. (1991) *Developing a Less Discriminatory Job Evaluation Scheme: Trade Union Research Unit Technical Note No. 109*, Oxford.

HASTINGS, S. (1992) *Virgin Territory: Job Evaluation in the Health Service and Other Recently Privatised Sectors: Trade Union Research Unit Technical Note No. 110*, Oxford.

HICKS, J. R. (1935) *The Theory of Wages*, Oxford, Oxford University Press.

HILLAGE, J. (1994) *The Role of Job Evaluation*, Brighton, The Institute of Manpower Studies.

IDS (September, 1991) 'Evaluation: jobs, people and skills', *IDS Focus No 60*, pp. 8–12.

IDS Study (February, 1992) *Skill-based Pay*.

IDS Top Pay Unit (March, 1992) *New Directions in Job Evaluation*, March, pp. 20–23.

Industrial Relations Services (March, 1987) 'Equal value in local authority job evaluation', *Pay and Benefits Bulletin*, pp. 8–12.

Industrial Relations Services (August, 1988) 'Job evaluation under review', *Pay and Benefits Bulletin*, pp. 2–7.

Industrial Relations Services (September, 1989) 'Job evaluation: the road to equality?', *Pay and Benefits Bulletin*, pp. 5–10.

Industrial Relations Services (October, 1993) 'Job evaluation in the 1990s', *Pay and Benefits Bulletin*, pp. 4–12.

Industrial Relations Services (January, 1994) 'Developments in job evaluation: shifting the emphasis', *Pay and Benefits Bulletin*, pp. 10–16.

International Labour Office, (1986) *Job Evaluation*, Geneva.

JAQUES, E. (1958) *Equitable Payment*, Harmondsworth, Penguin.

LAWLER, E. E. (March–April, 1986) 'What's wrong with point-factor job evaluation', *Compensation and Benefits Review*, pp. 20–28.

LAWLER, E. E. and LEDFORD, G. E. (September, 1985) 'Skill-based pay: a concept that's catching on', *Personnel*, pp. 30–37.

LIVY, B. (1975) *Job Evaluation: A critical review*, London, Allen & Unwin.

LOTT, M. R. (1924) *Wage Scales and Job Evaluation*, New York, Ronald Press.

MADIGAN, R. M. and HILLS, F. S. (1988) 'Job evaluation and pay equity', *Public Personnel Management*, Vol.17, No.3.

MCBEATH, G. and RAND, D. N. (1964) *Salary Administration*, London, Business Books.

MCHALE, P. (Summer, 1990) 'Putting competencies to work: competency-based job evaluation', *Competency*, pp. 39–40.

MCNALLY, J. and SHIMMIN, S. (1984) 'Job evaluation and equal pay for work of equal value', *Personnel Review*, Vol.13 No.1, pp. 27–31.

MCNALLY, J. and SHIMMIN, S. (1988) 'Job evaluation: equal work – equal pay?', *Management Decision*, Vol.26 No.5, pp. 22–27.

MILLWARD, N., STEVENS, M., SMART, D. and HAWES, W. R. (1992) *Workplace Industrial Relations in Transition*, Hampshire, Dartmouth Publishing.

MORONEY, M. J. (1953) *Facts From Figures*, Harmondsworth, Penguin.

MSF (1994) *Job Evaluation in the Health Service*, London, MSF.

MURLIS, H. and FITT, D. (May, 1991) 'Job evaluation in a changing world', *Personnel Management*, pp. 39–43.

NEATHEY, F. (1994), *Job Evaluation in the 1990s*, London, Industrial Relations Services.

O'NEAL, S. (July, 1994) 'Work and pay in the 21st century', *ACA News*, pp. 2, 21.

PATERSON, T. T. (1972) *Job Evaluation: A new method*, London, Business Books.

PHELPS BROWN, E. H. (1962) *The Economics of Labour*, Newhaven, CT, Yale University Press.

PLACHY, R. J. (March–April, 1987a) 'The case for effective point-factor job evaluation, viewpoint 1', *Compensation and Benefits Review*, pp. 45–48.

PLACHY, R. J. (July–August, 1987b) 'The point-factor job evaluation system: a step-by-step guide, part 1', *Compensation and Benefits Review*, pp. 12–27.

PLACHY, R. J. (September–October, 1987c) 'The point-factor job evaluation system: a step-by-step guide, part 2', *Compensation and Benefits Review*, pp. 9–24.

POTTINGER, J. (October, 1989) 'Engineering change through pay', *Personnel Management*, pp. 73–74.

PRITCHARD, D. (1995) 'What's new in job evaluation', *The Human Resource Management Yearbook*, London, AP Services.

PRITCHARD, D. and MURLIS, H. (1992) *Jobs, Roles and People: The New world of job evaluation*, London, Nicholas Brealey.

QUAID, M. (1993) *Job Evaluation: The myth of equitable assessment*, Toronto, University of Toronto Press.

RISHER, H. W. (January–February, 1989) 'Job evaluation: validity and reliability', *Compensation and Benefits Review*, pp. 22–36.

ROETHLISBERGER, F. and Dickson, W. (1939) *Management and the Worker*, Cambridge, Mass, Harvard University Press.

RUBERY, J. (1992) *The Economics of Equal Value*, London, Equal Opportunities Commission.

RUBINSTEIN, M. (September–October, 1992) As reported in 'Making the visible invisible: rewarding women's work', *Equal Opportunities Review*, pp. 23–32.

SUPEL, T. M. (March–April, 1990) 'Equivalence and redundance in the point-factor job evaluation system', *Compensation and Benefits Review*, pp. 48–55.

TIJOU, F. (Autumn, 1991) 'Just rewards: implementing competency-related pay', *Human Resources*, pp. 147–150.

TORRINGTON, D. and HALL, L. (1992) *Personnel Management: A New Approach*, London, Prentice Hall.

Trade Union Research Unit (1986) *Job Evaluation and Equal Value: Similarities and Differences*, Oxford.

TREIMAN, D. J. and HARTMANN, H. (1981) *Women, Work and Wages*, Washington DC, National Academy of Sciences.

Wyatt Company and Institute of Personnel Management (1989) *Survey of Job Evaluation Policies and Practices*, London, Institute of Personnel Management.

YEANDLE, D. and CLARK, J. (June, 1989) 'Personnel strategy for an automated plant', *Personnel Management*, pp. 51–55.

ZISKIN, I. V. (Fall, 1986) 'Knowledge-based pay: a strategic analysis', *ILR Report*, pp. 56–66.

INDEX